EMPLOYEE ENGAGEMENT

Through Effective Performance Management

—— *A PRACTICAL GUIDE FOR MANAGERS* ——

EMPLOYEE ENGAGEMENT

Through Effective Performance Management

— *A PRACTICAL GUIDE FOR MANAGERS* —

Edward M. Mone

CA, Inc.
Islandia, NY

Manuel London

State University of New York at Stony Brook
Stony Brook, NY

Routledge
Taylor & Francis Group
New York   London

Routledge
Taylor & Francis Group
270 Madison Avenue
New York, NY 10016

Routledge
Taylor & Francis Group
27 Church Road
Hove, East Sussex BN3 2FA

© 2010 by Taylor and Francis Group, LLC
Routledge is an imprint of Taylor & Francis Group, an Informa business

Printed in the United States of America on acid-free paper
10 9 8 7 6 5 4 3 2 1

International Standard Book Number: 978-1-84872-820-2 (Hardback) 978-1-84872-821-9 (Paperback)

Library of Congress Cataloging-in-Publication Data

Mone, Edward M.
    Employee engagement through effective performance management : a practical guide for managers / Edward M. Mone, Manuel London.
        p. cm.
    Includes bibliographical references and index.
    ISBN 978-1-84872-821-9 -- ISBN 978-1-84872-820-2
    1. Achievement motivation. 2. Employee motivation. 3. Career development. I. London, Manuel. II. Title.

    BF503.M66 2010
    658.3'14--dc22   2009025776

Visit the Taylor & Francis Web site at
http://www.taylorandfrancis.com

and the Psychology Press Web site at
http://www.psypress.com

Dedication

To Ceil and Marilyn for their warm and continuing support of our collaborative efforts, which span more than 20 years.

Contents

About the Authors

Edward M. Mone has more than 25 years of experience in career, leadership, and organization change and development. He is currently vice president for organization development at CA, Inc., where he is responsible for management and leadership training and development, succession planning, mentoring, the company-wide employee opinion survey and employee research, coaching and 360-degree feedback, and performance management. He was previously vice president for organization development at Cablevision and director of people processes and systems at Booz Allen Hamilton, Inc. He was HR division manager for strategic planning and development at AT&T, where he also held a variety of human resource and organization development positions. Before that, he was a partner in an outplacement and career management firm. He is an adjunct faculty member at the College of Business, State University of New York at Stony Brook, and at Hofstra University's I/O Psychology Program. He holds an MA in counseling psychology, and has completed doctoral coursework in organizational psychology, as well as in individual, team, and organization learning at Teachers College, Columbia University. He has coauthored and coedited books, book chapters, and articles in the areas of human resources and organization development, including *HR to the Rescue: Case Studies of HR Solutions to Business Challenges* (published by Gulf Publishing in 1998); and *Fundamentals of Performance Management* (Spiro Press, 2003). He also maintains a limited consulting practice specializing in organization, leadership, and career development.

Manuel London is associate dean of the College of Business at the State University of New York at Stony Brook. He is also professor and director of the Center for Human Resource Management at Stony Brook. He received his Ph.D. from the Ohio State University in industrial and organizational psychology and taught for 3 years at the business school at the University of Illinois in Champaign-Urbana. He then held a variety of research and human resource management positions at AT&T, moving to Stony Brook in 1989. His research interests are in employee and management development, including career motivation, performance evaluation, feedback, and training. His recent books include *Continuous Learning in Organizations* (coauthored with Valerie Sessa, 2006); *Leadership Development: Paths to Self-Insight and Professional Growth* (2002); and *How People Evaluate Others in Organizations* (2001), all published by Erlbaum/ Taylor & Francis.

Preface

You might ask the following questions:

- What is employee engagement?
- Why does employee engagement matter?
- And if it does matter, what can I do to drive employee engagement?

Whether you are a manager or a practitioner in the field of human resources, these are valid questions. Chances are you have heard something about employee engagement at a conference, at a seminar, or through consultant-sponsored web casts, or read something about it in the popular press, a management "how-to" book, or the more professional or academic literature. Chances are, as well, that you find the concept of employee engagement somewhat hard to define if not confusing. In fact, that is a major reason for writing this book. We were somewhat dismayed by our search for practical definitions of *employee engagement* and clear strategies and tactics that managers can use to create an engaged workforce. So based on our research and experience, we provide our definition of employee engagement and present the idea that an expanded view of performance management and its related processes, tools, and techniques are the keys to driving employee engagement. Although this book will be of value to managers, students, and a wide range of practitioners, we have written it in a "how-to" style for managers, and the remainder of the book will take that perspective and voice; we will show what managers can do to achieve the objective of fostering high levels of employee engagement in their organizations. Consultants and human resource practitioners can use this book as a practical and reliable resource for helping leaders and managers create an engaged workforce, whereas those instructing students in business, management, and human resource courses at the undergraduate or graduate levels can use the book as a primary or complementary text to help their students understand the main components of excellent performance management and ways to achieve an engaged workforce. Because this book is to be a practical guide, we have purposely limited our literature references to those that make sense for this style of book to give evidence, without being exhaustive, that our recommendations and the best practices we have developed and used with client organizations over time are grounded in solid theory and research.

So, let's begin with our definition of employee engagement: An *engaged employee* is someone who feels involved, committed, passionate, and empowered and demonstrates those feelings in work behavior. Employee engagement can be considered a trait (something that is characteristic of an employee's personality), a state (a condition that an employee may be in for some period of time), and a behavior that an employee demonstrates, for example, challenging the status quo, being innovative, or just being a good organization citizen (Macey & Schneider, 2008). As a test of our ideas about employee engagement, we used our definition as the basis for creating a set of questions that we incorporated into an employee opinion survey conducted at XINC (a pseudonym), a large, global company (we describe this study in more detail in Chapter 1). The result of this effort was the identification of a highly reliable set of 18 questions that, taken together, created an employee engagement index—another way of saying a measure of employee engagement. With an index in place, we were able to determine specific drivers of employee engagement, which then allowed us to identify the management actions necessary to create an engaged workforce. Although this study was limited to one organization, the results validate much of the research in the field and strengthen the credence of the recommendations we make throughout this book.

In general, our advice and direction for what managers can do to create a more engaged workforce are really about better performance management. In this book we expand upon the boundaries of the traditional notions of performance management to include building trust, creating conditions of empowerment, fostering team development, and maintaining ongoing, straightforward communications about performance, all of which we have found to be essential to employee engagement.

In some respects, employee engagement is similar to employee satisfaction. But there is a difference. Satisfaction describes a condition or state of satiation. When employees are satisfied, they feel good or happy. When employees are *engaged*, they also take action in support of the organization. Although employee satisfaction remains highly important and has been linked to customer satisfaction, employee engagement goes further. Engagement "is strongly correlated to a number of individual, group and corporate performance outcomes including recruiting, retention, turnover, individual productivity, customer service, customer loyalty, growth in operating margins, increased profit margins, and even revenue growth rates" (Gibbons, 2006, p. 10).

What can you do as a manager to drive employee engagement? As suggested by our own research, as well as the work of others (see for instance, Gibbons, 2006; Macey & Schneider, 2008), you can take the following actions to build an organization of engaged employees:

- Establish a foundation of trust and empowerment with your employees.
- Ensure your employees have challenging and meaningful work and that you clarify its importance to your organization.
- Establish clear performance goals for your employees that are challenging and aligned with overall workgroup and organization goals.
- Establish clear development goals for your employees and help them to understand the career growth opportunities available to them.
- Regularly communicate with your employees about their goals and the organization's goals to help ensure their work is aligned with corporate objectives and to help them recognize that their efforts are meaningful and valuable.
- Provide ongoing coaching and feedback to your employees to ensure performance and development are on track.
- Recognize and reward your employees for their achievements and successes.
- Encourage your employees to be innovative and creative.
- Conduct fair and effective performance appraisal discussions, and write effective appraisals.
- Foster team-level learning and development in support of group-level engagement and performance.
- Monitor the overall climate and efforts of your employees and teams, ensuring that organization demands do not lead to burnout.

Again, this book is a straightforward guide to driving employee engagement through an expanded view of performance management processes, strategies, and approaches. Our goal is to convey the essence of good management in helpful and clear terms. We hope to assist you, as managers, with the tough, interpersonal aspects of performance management, especially when it comes to creating the conditions for trust and empowerment and providing feedback.

Let us now describe *performance management* as we refer to it in this book. When most managers think of performance management, they tend to think of the annual performance appraisal, a once-a-year event. Or some might go further and state that as a process it includes goal setting, feedback, and appraisal. However, we view performance management as an ongoing process that requires constant attention. It includes goal setting, feedback, development, recognition, coaching, and performance appraisal, built on a foundation of trust and empowerment, with a constant focus on communication. We have found that in many companies, the more formal processes, such as goal setting and performance appraisal, are complex or given short shrift because of the daily press of business. The informal processes, such as giving feedback and coaching for learning and development, are functions that managers often don't feel comfortable doing. In this book we stress how important these formal and informal processes are and reinforce not only how they contribute to increased performance but also how they foster and sustain employee engagement. We cover these processes concisely so that managers can use this book as a reference guide throughout the performance management process.

Performance management involves a continuous cycle of activities, and it is most effective under conditions of high trust and empowerment. Goal setting and performance appraisal are the beginning and end points of performance management. They frame the daily performance management process such as providing feedback to employees and recognizing and rewarding their efforts.

In Chapter 1 we provide an overview of performance management and why it is important. We also discuss and present findings from our study at XINC that clearly show how you can use performance management to drive employee engagement in your organization. In subsequent chapters, we cover each aspect of our expanded view of performance management, highlighting how each element of the process impacts engagement.

The first element we discuss—performance appraisal—is the focus of Chapter 2. It is the most familiar part of performance management, and the appraisal is often the basis for making personnel-related decisions. We show you how to be more effective at performance appraisal, describe the two major types of appraisal you will likely encounter, and show you how to effectively discuss the link between appraisal and compensation with your employees.

What it will take for you to build, create, and sustain the conditions of trust and empowerment, central to both effective performance management and high levels of employee engagement, is the subject of Chapter 3. We invited our colleague, Jamie Moore, senior principal of organization development (OD) at CA, Inc., to cowrite this chapter. We present a variety of tools, checklists, and assessments throughout the book, and in this chapter, you will find a reliable and valid survey that you can use to gauge the extent to which you have created a climate of trust and empowerment with your team.

In Chapter 4, we focus on goal setting, the foundation of the traditional performance management process. Goals enable you to align individual and team performance with organizational-level performance. Goal setting helps you drive engagement as it clarifies expectations, often leading to more challenging work. It also helps you add meaning to your employees' jobs and work when you link their efforts to your department's and company's purpose and being. In addition, goals serve as the basis for communication about development and performance.

Goals also set the stage for the ongoing process of giving feedback. Giving feedback is often the hardest part of a manager's job. Managers shy away from giving feedback to their employees about their performance—perhaps because they fear they will be defensive or angry. After all, we want people to like us, and giving them feedback to help change behavior or improve performance may not endear them to us. But it should. We should all appreciate feedback because it helps us to grow and improve our performance. Let's also recognize that feedback is not necessarily negative. Giving positive feedback is important, too. It makes others feel good about themselves, and it lets them know they are on the right track. Feedback is important to sustaining engagement—helping employees to know that their contributions are aligned with and of value to the organization. So the question becomes how can you give feedback in a way that will help the other person listen? Chapter 5 describes the benefits of feedback and ways to provide constructive feedback, as well as techniques for how to have some of the more difficult manager–employee performance-related conversations.

On the other hand, there are many ways to recognize excellent performance and promote employee engagement, but these, like feedback, are often avoided or ignored. Managers just don't seem to feel comfortable telling employees that they appreciate how hard they are working and how important their work is to the department and the company. They may be afraid of offending others who are not being recognized or embarrassing those who are. In Chapter 6 we cover ways of recognizing employees' accomplishments and encourage you to use recognition, along with feedback and coaching, to reinforce and drive expected levels of performance.

In Chapter 7, we describe the increasingly popular topic of 360-degree feedback surveys. Today, these surveys are used in many organizations to formalize the collection of feedback from multiple sources and to guide a manager's development and performance improvement. We try to demystify the process so you can understand more clearly what it is, how it is typically used, and the benefits that it offers your management employees as part of their continuous development and learning. In fact, 360-degree feedback is the most frequently used tool in conjunction with more formal coaching efforts—and we discuss coaching in Chapter 8.

Although feedback is key to enhancing performance, coaching can significantly increase the value of feedback, further improving your employees' chances of success. In Chapter 8 we explain the purpose and value of coaching, describe how the coaching process works, answer key questions, show you what it takes to coach effectively, and discuss the pros and cons of working with a professional coach. By the way, not only does the act of coaching in and of itself tend to increase engagement, but also you can use coaching to focus directly on increasing your managers' capacity to drive engagement in their own organizations.

After the coaching chapter, we turn, in Chapter 9, to managing employee and team learning and development. Here we emphasize the importance of fostering self-development and learning from experience. In addition, we present several constructs, such as career motivation and expansiveness, to help you better assess and understand the extent to which your employees are self-developers. We also show you how to promote and guide informal learning and how to help your employees capitalize on that learning through reflection. As our research will show, helping your employees to develop their skills is important for employee engagement. In Chapter 9 we also define team learning, discuss how to assess team-learning needs, and show you how to facilitate team learning to improve your team's performance and create a more engaged team.

In Chapter 10, we approach employee engagement from the opposite end of the spectrum—burnout (Maslach & Leiter, 1997). Although in previous chapters we describe the processes, techniques, and tools that can drive engagement, in this chapter we focus on helping you to prevent and cope with employee burnout. In fact, if your employees or teams are close to or suffering from burnout, they will need focused attention to bring them back to a normal level of effectiveness before they can be reengaged. We invited two other colleagues, Kathryn Acritani and Christina Eisinger, each in the role of principal of organization development at CA, Inc., to cowrite this chapter with us.

So you might be asking, "What does it look like when all the elements of performance management come together, and how does that impact employee engagement?" Our last chapter answers this question through a short case in which we illustrate the everyday realities of performance management, its holistic nature, and how it affects engagement. You will recognize the importance of trust and empowerment, how a manager's actions can create the conditions for burnout, and how personality factors can affect a manager's expectations and behavior. You will also recognize the value of having clear goals; providing, seeking, and using feedback constructively; how 360-degree surveys and coaching can support performance and development efforts; and how the end-of-year performance appraisal and discussion provide understanding and closure to the end of one performance year, while setting the stage for the beginning of a new one.

Finally, we leave you with a short set of expectations for how to use performance management to drive engagement. We hope you will exceed these expectations!

Acknowledgments

A portion of this book was originally published in Great Britain by Spiro Business Guides in 2002 under the title *Fundamentals of Performance Management*. When Spiro exited the business and relinquished the copyright, we proposed to Taylor & Francis that we revise the text to incorporate a focus on driving employee engagement. We updated and expanded the original chapters, added chapters on building trust and on burnout, and included new research on the connection between employee engagement and performance management strategies and techniques. We thank Anne Duffy, our editor, and Taylor & Francis for their support.

We would also like to formally thank Kathryn Acritani, Christina Eisinger, and Jamie Moore—all excellent OD practitioners—for their contributions to this book, and specifically for their cowriting of Chapter 3 (Jamie) and Chapter 10 (Kate and Chris).

Chapter 1

The Performance Management Process and Employee Engagement

An Introduction

This book addresses how you, as a manager, can create an engaged workforce through effective performance management. We explain how to use state-of-the-art goal setting, feedback, coaching, development, appraisal and recognition processes, strategies, and techniques and how to build a climate of trust and empowerment. You will learn about 360-degree survey feedback, professional coaching, and self-assessment. Overall, *Employee Engagement Through Effective Performance Management* will help you to create a culture that encourages feedback and development, promotes self-direction for continuous learning, and fosters employee engagement.

You may work in a large multinational company; a smaller, perhaps culturally diverse domestic firm; or a corporate start-up such as an e-commerce business. Your company may have a traditional multilevel bureaucratic structure or a small, flexible structure. Your company may be stable or, more likely in today's world, be undergoing transformational change. Regardless of your organizational context, the fundamentals of performance management are the same. Setting goals, giving feedback, coaching for performance effectiveness, evaluating performance, and recognizing accomplishments are the cornerstones for maintaining an engaged workforce.

Although your company may have a human resources department that designs programs to support these elements (for instance, the corporate performance appraisal program), the principal responsibility for performance management rests with you and your company's management team. Performance management, though driven by human resources, is a process that is really "owned" by line managers, and will be most effective when it has strong executive-level sponsorship (Bersin, 2006).

In this chapter we define the performance management process, consider managers' attitudes about performance management, and highlight the importance of feedback as a central element of the process. We then describe our model of employee engagement and present our study of employee engagement conducted at XINC. This study examines relationships between perceptions of job conditions and feelings of engagement. Throughout the book, we use these results together with research and ideas from other sources to make our recommendations for supporting and improving employee engagement through performance management. We conclude the chapter with an overview of the book.

The Performance Management Process

Performance management is not a fixed sequence of events but a *continuous process* that is constantly renewing itself as performance unfolds, especially as key events create opportunities to demonstrate expertise and contribute to organizational goals.

In fact, the elements of the performance management process are not standalone human resource programs. They are part of an integrated system and actions that should be aligned with organizational objectives; under these conditions of integration and alignment, the entire process moves away from being event driven and becomes more strategic in perspective (London & Mone, 2009).

To reinforce the notion of integration, consider, for example, the following relationships between goal setting, feedback, coaching, and appraisal:

- Goals provide the standard for feedback and performance appraisal.
- Feedback leads to setting goals for development and performance improvement.

- Coaching helps to process feedback, set meaningful goals, practice new behaviors, and track changes in performance.
- Performance appraisal evaluates goal attainment and is a basis for feedback and development planning.

Managers' Attitudes About Performance Management

Performance management, done well, makes employees more competitive and engaged, enhances leadership development, supports transformational change, and, in general, contributes to higher levels of organization performance (Bersin, 2006). However, in research we have recently conducted at XINC (discussed later in the chapter), we found that little more than half (53%) of employees surveyed believed the performance management process was valued in the firm. Laff (2007) also reported that 56% of line managers believe their performance management programs are not valuable. Bersin has helped us understand why managers might hold these views, noting that only 32% of organizations surveyed have a consistent, enterprise-wide performance management process, and that organizations vary significantly in the extent to which they have adopted key performance management practices, such as cascading goals, self-appraisals, 360-degree feedback, development planning, and coaching. It is no wonder that human resource professionals are concerned about making performance management a viable strategic process (London & Mone, 2009).

A Focus on Feedback

Although this book covers each of the major elements of performance management, we emphasize feedback because it is the common thread stitching together all the elements of the process and it often causes the most difficulty for managers. Many managers simply don't know how to give feedback and don't feel comfortable doing it. For instance, managers may fear employees' defensive reactions and losing their loyalty and friendship if they give negative feedback. These managers avoid spending time talking to employees about their performance. Other managers don't value giving positive feedback, claiming that employees know when they are doing a good job.

Despite these difficulties, our research shows that the feedback element of the performance management process is a key driver of engagement. Feedback helps managers build a learning culture that is able to adapt to meet changing business needs. In this kind of culture, feedback and development are linked as employees take responsibility for their own performance improvement in order to meet new corporate expectations. As a result, employees value learning and development, and this strengthens the organization's ability to succeed in turbulent times.

In addition, employees generally feel that feedback and coaching will enhance their professionalism and help them to maximize their performance potential and outcomes. Your feedback positions your employees to be ready to meet future, unanticipated challenges and to remain competitive for key positions and advancement within the company.

Employee Engagement

Engagement, as a construct, is relatively complex. Remember we said that an engaged employee is someone who feels involved, committed, passionate, and empowered and demonstrates those feelings in work behavior. So when we set out to measure engagement and create an engagement index, we realized that we had to try to capture this complexity in the facets we chose and the questions we would use to measure the level of engagement in our survey research.

Our model of engagement, therefore, contains the following six facets presented with the associated behaviors and attitudes that, in totality, represent both our model *and* measure of engagement:

1. *Involvement* (for example, by feeling engaged, challenged by the work, energized to perform at your best, and feeling good about the future)
2. *Commitment* (for example, to a long-term career at the company, to the company's success, and to consistently working with a high level of focus and energy)
3. *Meaningfulness* (for example, by finding your work meaningful and understanding how you contribute to the success of your company)
4. *Empowerment* (for example, by feeling empowered to do your job, having the necessary resources to do your job effectively, and holding a well-structured job)
5. *Manager Support* (for example, for your career development efforts, for job-related training and recognition for a good job, and for feeling valued for your contributions)
6. *Loyalty* (for example, by intending to remain with your company, being proud to work for your company, and recommending your company as a place to work)

In the next section, we turn to our employee engagement study. It was in this study that we identified in statistically valid ways predictors of employee engagement, or, in other words, the most important actions that you can take to drive high levels of employee engagement; as you will see, the majority of those actions fall in the realm of performance management as presented in this book. If you don't want to read about this study, or find our description of this study a bit too technical, you can safely move on to the final section of this chapter— "Overview of the Book."

Measuring Employee Engagement: A Study at a Global Company

To test our ideas about employee engagement, we conducted a study using an annual employee opinion survey at XINC. The survey was conducted in early 2008. At the time of the survey, this global organization had more than 5,000 employees worldwide. The response rate for this Web-based survey exceeded 80%.

The survey contained more than 100 questions, answered on a 5-point (1–5) Likert-type scale, with a neutral midpoint and responses ranging from *strongly disagree* to *strongly agree*. Based on our ideas and on research by Kahn (1990), Macey and Schneider (2008), and others (e.g., Maslach & Leiter, 1997, 2008), a number of the company's standard benchmark survey questions had to be revised and some new ones were added to address employee engagement.

We decided on 18 questions that would be used to reflect and be a single measure of employee engagement—questions that possessed conceptual soundness and the ability to capture the many facets embedded in a construct as layered and complex as that of employee engagement. From a statistical perspective, this set of questions had a very high degree of internal consistency (Cronbach's alpha is 0.93), or, in other words, was a very reliable measure.

To measure the level of employee engagement, we created an index by computing the mean of the 18 questions, and then multiplied the mean (calculated on a 1–5 scale) by a factor of 20 to create an index that ranges from 20% to 100%. This simple average index resulted in a 78% level of employee engagement.

Next, to identify the drivers of engagement and to help XINC senior leadership focus their efforts, a path analysis was conducted. Very simply speaking, path analysis is a complex form of regression analysis. To better understand these drivers and to determine which specific organizational facets had an effect on engagement, we worked with the senior human resources executive to identify the key questions in the index of interest to senior leadership. So although the full index was reliable, we used a reduced number of questions (10 of the 18 questions used to create the index) for the outcome variable (the variable or construct we are trying to understand—in this case, engagement) in the path model for practical purposes and to conduct a more micro level of analysis. These 10 questions included:

1. I feel empowered to do my job.
2. My job is structured so that I can get work done effectively.
3. My job is challenging.
4. I understand how my work contributes to the overall success of XINC.
5. Overall, I find the work I do meaningful.
6. At XINC, I am energized to perform at my best.
7. Overall, I feel engaged at XINC company.
8. I consistently work with a very high level of focus, enthusiasm, energy, and effort to get my job done.
9. I am committed to XINC's success.
10. I feel valued as an employee of XINC company.

Results of the path analysis showed eight direct predictors (each predictor is a single survey question, and predictors are those actions or sets of actions that impact or drive the outcome variable) of employee engagement accounting for 61% of the variance (or being able to explain 61% of the reason for the level achieved) in the outcome variable, *employee engagement*. These eight predictors, along with their beta coefficients (or regression coefficients, which indicate by their size how much change a predictor can produce in the outcome variable for each unit of change in the predictor), include:

1. I am encouraged to look for ways to improve my work processes and productivity ($b = 0.19$).
2. The company communications I receive help me to understand XINC's strategy, vision and direction ($b = 0.13$).
3. Overall, I have the resources I need to do my job effectively ($b = 0.12$).
4. XINC's leadership acts with the best interest of employees in mind ($b = 0.11$).
5. I am satisfied with my opportunities for career progression and promotion ($b = 0.09$).
6. I consider the total value of my compensation, benefits, and work experience when I think about what XINC offers in exchange for my employment ($b = 0.08$).
7. My manager is someone I can trust ($b = 0.08$).
8. My manager provides me with ongoing feedback that helps me improve my performance ($b = 0.02$).

What is the practical implication for you? Although this study was conducted in one large, global organization, these predictors or actions serve to provide a roadmap for how you can improve employee engagement. When you take the specific actions or create the conditions indicated, you will more than likely drive employee engagement in your own organization.

Next, for each of these direct predictors of employee engagement, between three and five associated survey questions were found to be indirect predictors of employee engagement; a total of 28 survey questions fell into this category of indirect predictor. The 19 of the 28 questions most closely related to performance management as discussed in this book are listed by predictor in Table 1.1.

Table 1.1   Path Model Direct and Indirect Predictors of Employee Engagement Related to Performance Management

Path Model Direct Predictor	Path Model Indirect Predictor
My manager provides me with ongoing feedback that helps me improve my performance.	• I had the opportunity to set goals with my manager. • I am satisfied with the recognition I receive from my manager. • I had a career-planning discussion with my manager. • I am satisfied with the quality of my year-end performance appraisal discussion.
I am satisfied with my opportunities for career progression and promotion.	• I have sufficient opportunities for training. • My manager supports my career development efforts. • The organization's policies for career progression are fair.
I consider the total value of my compensation, benefits, and work experience when I think about what XINC offers in exchange for my employment.	• I am paid fairly for the work I do. • At XINC, raises and promotions are based on merit, not favoritism.
My manager is someone I can trust.	• My manager encourages me to be innovative and creative in my work. • My manager values my ideas and opinions. • My manager treats me fairly and with respect. • My manager listens to, and acts on, my needs and concerns.

(continued)

Table 1.1   Path Model Direct and Indirect Predictors of Employee Engagement Related to Performance Management (continued)

Path Model Direct Predictor	Path Model Indirect Predictor
I am encouraged to look for ways to improve my work processes and productivity.	• I can speak my mind without fear of reprisal. • People who challenge the way we do things around here are valued.
The company communications I receive help me to understand XINC's strategy, vision, and direction.	• My manager helps me understand how my work supports XINC.
Overall, I have the resources I need to do my job effectively.	• I can get the information I need to do my job. • I have the decision-making authority to do my job effectively. • I have control over the quality of my work.

Again, the practical implication for you is that in this table you will find a range of behaviors that you can demonstrate and conditions that you can create that should further increase your ability to create a fully engaged workforce.

In conclusion, for XINC, this study provided valuable direction for how to understand, address, and raise the level of employee engagement. The results are also consistent with what other researchers are saying regarding employee engagement, and more importantly, the study suggests very specific actions for managers. Therefore, as mentioned earlier, we will from time to time reference this study, although this book is largely a result of our knowledge of the field and accumulated experience in helping organizations to achieve success through strategic and effective organization-wide performance management.

Overview of the Book

In each of the chapters we address one specific element of performance management. In Chapter 2 we begin with the familiar performance appraisal. We describe the differences between formal and informal appraisals, and detail the major steps in the appraisal process. We show you how to prepare for the appraisal review meeting, and provide you with an easy-to-follow structure for conducting it. We suggest how you can be a more effective evaluator of performance and offer you a short assessment to determine if you are making any critical evaluation errors. We also share our thoughts on the popular *20–70–10* forced distribution.

In Chapter 3 we discuss the importance of building a climate of trust between you and your employees, and present a model to guide you in your efforts. Trust is not only important to driving employee engagement but also a necessary foundation for empowerment and crucial to successfully working with your employees through all the phases of your company's performance management process.

In Chapter 4 we stress the importance of setting goals, and we define the differences between *goals, strategies,* and *tactics,* which are often confusing terms to managers. We present a comprehensive goal-setting framework to help you ensure that your department's goals are meaningful, challenging, and aligned with your company's strategic direction. We then provide a step-by-step process for setting goals with your employees. Finally, we show you how to solve the "goal-setting and performance evaluation" conundrum.

Giving feedback is the focus of Chapter 5, and as mentioned earlier in this chapter, managers often have trouble with this part of performance management. Recognizing this fact, we include tips for delivering effective feedback, as well as a short feedback self-assessment. This assessment will provide you with insight into your own skill level and thinking about feedback. Drawing on research in the areas of self-monitoring and self-esteem, we suggest ways for you to assess your employees' receptivity to feedback. We then present a short case and two examples of feedback discussions to illustrate how to deliver feedback effectively and successfully. We believe that this chapter will convince you that feedback is indeed a valuable component of performance management, and that it will help you learn how to provide constructive feedback that your employees will seek, welcome, and accept. Your goal should be to create a culture in your department or organization in which your employees feel comfortable talking about how to improve their own and others' performance.

We presume you believe that your employees deserve recognition for their accomplishments, but chances are you also believe that salary increases and promotions are all they need to feel recognized for their efforts. In Chapter 6, we discuss what is probably the most often overlooked and underutilized element of performance management—recognition, another form of feedback. We will help you determine which behaviors and performance to recognize, how to choose the most appropriate forms of recognition, and how to make your efforts at recognizing your employees as effective as possible. When done well, your recognition will focus performance improvement and development actions and foster higher levels of engagement.

In Chapter 7 we address a method used to enhance the likelihood that your employees will receive and use feedback. Called *360-degree feedback,* this method involves using a survey to systematically collect performance feedback from direct reports, peers, supervisors, and sometimes customers. We discuss the advantages and disadvantages of using 360-degree feedback survey results for making administrative decisions about your employees or using the results solely for their development. We also answer many of the questions that you and your employees might have about the implementation and use of 360-degree feedback in your department. We close the chapter with a sample survey, a sample report, and a discussion of how to interpret the report. In terms of performance management, you will see that the results from a 360-degree survey can be used to prompt discussions about feedback, and can be a basis for establishing development goals and targeting performance improvement.

We address coaching from two perspectives in Chapter 8. First, we show you how you can improve your own capability as a coach, and then we describe the pros and cons of professional coaching. We define coaching, clarify your role as a coach, offer coaching tips, and show you how to use a five-step process we call *power coaching.* We then discuss in detail what is involved with professional coaching, including how to get a coach, what to expect, and the value a professional coach can offer.

Within the context of performance management, your employee's goals and performance appraisal, as well as your ongoing feedback and coaching, set the direction and focus for development actions. In Chapter 9, we show you how to manage your employees' development and how to help them become continuous learners and self-developers and capitalize on formal and informal learning opportunities. We include assessments for evaluating your employees' learning needs and strategies to manage your employees' ongoing learning. In fact, we show you how to help your employees "learn how to learn." We also specifically address how to manage and facilitate your team's learning.

No doubt your employees face considerable challenges for the use of their time and energy. Performance management helps you to focus their efforts. But sometimes your employees, even your currently highly engaged employees, can experience burnout. Chapter 10 focuses on burnout, the opposite end of the spectrum from engagement. We define burnout and its causes, show you how to identify the warning signs and symptoms of burnout in your employees, and discuss how you can address and prevent burnout in your organization. You will see that there is much you can do in your role as a manager to alleviate burnout and help your employees get back on track to feeling productive and engaged.

In the final chapter, we use a case to illustrate performance management in action and to show you how all the elements of the process work together to drive performance and engagement. You will discover the value of midyear reviews and coaching, of working with a professional coach, and of the use of 360-degree feedback. We hope the case, as well as this book in general, are affirming and motivational, encouraging you to devote time to performance management in spite of all the demands you face. The payoff for you is that your employees will be more involved in continuous learning, more focused on performance excellence, and more engaged.

Chapter 2

Understanding Performance Appraisal

Our guess is that when you, as a manager, have typically thought about managing performance, you more often than not thought about writing a "performance appraisal" and not about the ongoing, comprehensive process of performance management. Indeed, your company's appraisal process defines what is important—what should be appraised. Although the appraisal itself comes at the end of the performance management cycle, the focus of the appraisal—or what you will actually appraise at the end of the cycle—provides the direction for the other components of the performance management process. For example, it specifies the kind of goals you will set and how you will set them and defines critical behavioral expectations. These goals and expectations then serve as the basis for the feedback and coaching you will provide, target the direction for development actions, and set the stage for the achievements and results you will ultimately recognize and reward. So, because of its familiarity to most managers and its overall role in the process, we decided to begin our detailed discussion of the components of the performance management process with performance appraisal.

Appraising performance has often been referred to as a dilemma for managers. On the one hand, as a manager, you are asked to coach and develop your employees, but on the other hand, you are required to evaluate your employees' performance. You are expected to develop trusting relationships and coach performance at one point in time, and to be a final arbiter of performance at another. Your decisions about performance drive your employees' overall performance rating, their base compensation and bonus, and their future career moves and promotions.

Throughout this book, we will emphasize that performance management is a collaborative process. Yes, as a manager, you are accountable for your organization's success. It is also true, however, that your employees are accountable for their own performance and career success. We will show you how to engage in a collaborative goal setting process with your employees, how to help them to create their development plans for current or future job performance, and how to provide them with effective performance feedback, coaching, and recognition on a regular basis. In doing so, you empower them to be accountable and to succeed while modeling managerial behaviors that drive engagement.

You will have numerous performance-oriented feedback conversations with your employees throughout the performance management cycle. You will be letting them know where they stand in your view. As a result, the final end-of-year performance conversation and performance appraisal should come as no surprise to your employees. Helping your employees to understand their roles and accountabilities throughout the performance management process will also help them to enter the performance appraisal discussion with more realistic expectations. This will lead to increased satisfaction with the discussion—a predictor of employee engagement—and increased feelings of involvement in the process.

Performance Appraisals

The term *performance appraisal* normally refers to the formal evaluation conducted at the end of a performance period, usually annually. Appraisals, however, can and should be conducted more often, whether formally or informally.

An appraisal is typically considered formal when it is documented on company forms and is used to determine a performance rating that drives human resources decisions. In other words, it officially "counts" and can be used to determine pay, promotion, termination, or other human resources decisions.

Informal appraisals may or not be documented on official company forms and typically do not significantly impact other human resources processes or decisions. In general, we advise our clients to have quarterly informal performance reviews with their employees, with the option of making the second quarter or midyear review more formal. Think of the quarterly and midyear reviews as ways to help you focus attention on performance management and development in your otherwise hectic schedule.

The purpose of both the quarterly and midyear informal performance appraisal is to provide you with the opportunity to "sit down" with each of your employees to

- Check progress toward the achievement of their performance goals;
- Determine if their goals are still valid and modify the goals, as necessary;

- Provide feedback on their development efforts; and
- Given where all this stands, offer a summary evaluation of performance.

This summary evaluation can be as simple as "Given what we have just discussed, if we had to do your formal appraisal today, I see your overall performance as meeting expectations."

The informal appraisal session is not just a check-up. Use this time to work with your employees to identify any potential obstacles to achieving their goals and to determine ways to overcome them. Verify that they have the necessary resources to perform successfully, which is another key driver of employee engagement. Ensure that your employees leave their informal review sessions with clear feedback about their performance to date and with the feeling that, with your ongoing support, they can be successful in achieving their goals.

Document the outcome of these sessions, describing what was discussed, including whether or not changes were made to your employee's goals and what the changes were, the strategies discussed to ensure that performance will stay on track, the progress made in development areas, and the summary evaluation of performance. If your company has official forms for this documentation, use them; otherwise, you can write a memo-to-file. In either case, you should give a copy of this documentation to your employee. Because this is an informal appraisal, there is typically no need to have your employee "sign off" on the documentation.

If you are doing a formal midyear review, follow the same process as outlined above. The only difference is that your company would certainly have official forms for documenting this session. There may also be a requirement to have these forms signed by both you and your employee and to provide a copy of the signed forms to your human resources department. The employee is signing not to indicate agreement but to verify he or she read the review. There may also be a place on the form for employees to write their opinions or comments about the written review or the performance conversation.

Formal Performance Appraisals

In this section, we focus on the end-of-year formal performance appraisal by outlining the major steps typically involved in the formal appraisal process.

Your company probably has a human resources–driven process that notifies or reminds you that formal performance appraisals are due. The specific process often depends on whether or not formal reviews are conducted on a common anniversary date, or on the anniversary of the employee's hire date, job change, or promotion.

The major steps involved in the process include

1. Being notified by the human resources department that an appraisal is due and what forms to use;
2. Telling your employee that his or her appraisal is due, and providing a timeline for completing the process;
3. Asking your employee to complete a self-appraisal;
4. Meeting with your employee to discuss the self-appraisal (this is your opportunity to understand how your employee would rate him or herself and why; it becomes the last in a series of discussions before you complete the appraisal);
5. Making requests for performance feedback from your employee's colleagues, teammates, customers, and so on who are familiar with the employee's performance;
6. Reviewing all the performance-related information you have for your employee;
7. Using your company's official forms to complete the employee's performance appraisal;
8. Ensuring your own fairness and consistency by reviewing the appraisal with your supervisor, and making changes to the appraisal as the situation requires;
9. Signing the appraisal and forwarding a copy of it to your employee to review before you have the formal appraisal meeting a day or two later;
10. Conducting the formal appraisal meeting;
11. Asking your employee to sign the official form; and
12. Providing a copy of the appraisal to your employee, keeping a copy in your file, and forwarding the original, if necessary, to your human resources department.

If your formal appraisal drives a merit increase or bonus process, discuss performance and pay separately, not in Step 10 above. Most employees are generally more interested in their pay information, and most managers have difficulty addressing the performance feedback. As a result, most of the appraisal discussion winds up focusing on pay. Therefore, hold two meetings: one to focus on the end-of-year feedback, and the other to focus on the compensation associated with your employee's level of performance. At the end of this chapter, we provide our advice for productive conversations with your employees about how their performance may impact their pay.

Approaches to Performance Appraisal Rating Systems

Broadly speaking, there are two main ways to categorize the kind of ratings you will find in a performance appraisal: *relative* and *absolute*. If you are required to compare one employee against another in order to provide your employees with formal appraisal ratings, you are using a *relative* rating system. You may be asked to compare employees on key traits, such as creativity, quality of work, or teamwork, as well as on their overall performance—which may include both behaviors and results achieved.

Today, the most publicized example of a relative rating system is the forced distribution method, also know as *forced ranking*, and its most ardent proponent is Jack Welch (Welch & Welch, 2005). Using this method, you position or place predetermined percentages of your employees into performance categories (at GE, under Jack Welch, the categorization was the top 20%, middle 70%, and bottom 10%). Welch advocated this approach as a way to apply his views on the importance of *differentiation* to people. However, an effective appraisal process neither demands nor requires a forced-ranking method in order to appropriately differentiate performance among and between your employees (more on this later when we discuss absolute rating systems). In fact, the position we hold is similar to that voiced by Lawler and Worley (2006) in their book *Built to Change*, in which they argue that organizations today cannot sustain performance excellence unless they not only embrace change but also are ready to change and change frequently: "B2 [built to] change organizations reject the notion of ranking subordinates and using rating scales that require the rater to place a fixed percent in each category.... One rating practice that B2change organizations should never use is forced distributions" (Lawler & Worley, pp. 132–133).

If you are using a forced distribution in your company, you might already be aware of the various problems with this method. For example, it

1. Makes an *a priori* assumption about the distribution of performance among employees—in other words, there will be 20–70–10 distribution, for example, in all groups of performers, all of the time, in your organization.
2. Causes difficulty when setting performance goals—it will be almost impossible for you to provide a clear definition or description of excellent performance to your employees at the beginning of the performance management cycle because performance evaluation is relative, regardless of what level of results each of your employees achieves; so your employees will never be sure what level of performance versus the goals set will lead to a top rating until the end of the cycle.

3. Creates a challenge when providing feedback—it will be difficult for you to clearly say and your employees to truly know what your positive feedback means when given throughout the performance year, that is, it will be hard to say that he or she is performing like the top 20% or the middle 70%, because you won't know for sure until the end of the cycle.
4. May force you to rate one of your employees in the bottom 10%—even though the employee could actually be fully meeting performance expectations.
5. Is disempowering to you as the manager—your freedom to rate your employees based on their own contributions toward set goals is restricted, if not eliminated.
6. Is demotivating to your employees—even if their results go above and beyond expectations based on set goals, they might not get a top rating because they know the appraisal process has a built-in governor for how many employees can earn that rating.

The question, then, is, why is this method being used by so many companies? Unfortunately, the answer seems to be that it is a way to control a problem caused by factors that truly have nothing to do with a well-designed and executed appraisal process: managers giving inflated performance appraisal ratings, or what is technically called a *leniency error* (we address this and other errors in the upcoming section, "Avoiding Common Rating Errors"). This situation can be attributed to a problem at the top of the organization, as senior leaders fail to hold managers accountable for effective and ongoing performance management and writing fair and accurate performance appraisals.

What specifically can you do, then, to capitalize on performance management to drive employee engagement if you are required to use a forced distribution method? Although the strategies, principles, processes, techniques, and tools we present throughout this book still apply, you may also want to consider the following:

■ Be sure your employees understand how the forced distribution method works in your organization.
■ When setting goals and discussing what success looks like, be sure to clarify that the final evaluation of performance is against one's peers, although performance against one's goals is obviously critical to the employee's overall evaluation.
■ When providing feedback and recognition to one of your employees, be clear about what specific results or behaviors you are recognizing and why, and if possible, indicate how that performance compares to the performance of his or her peers.

- The development goals you set for an employee not only should be targeted at general improvement and preparation to achieve his or her current performance goals, but also should focus on helping the employee reach the top distribution category.
- Pay attention to everyone's performance—show no favoritism toward top-tier performers.

In its simplest sense, an *absolute* rating system allows you to evaluate, describe, and appraise an employee's performance based on the extent to which he or she has achieved expected results—regardless of the performance of other employees in your organization. It involves measurement against a standard established during the goal-setting phase of performance management. We encourage the use of the absolute rating system, and strongly recommend an appraisal that focuses on both the assessment and evaluation of (a) the demonstration of key or critical behaviors, and (b) the achievement of performance goals that are outcome based. Table 2.1 shows an actual sample of the set of behaviors used by one of our clients in the company's annual performance appraisal. In Chapter 4, we more fully address performance goal setting and show a page of another client's appraisal used for documenting performance goal achievement.

So, for those of you who are not yet convinced of the value of an absolute rating system, or for those of you who currently use such a system and want to know what you can do to make it more effective, consider the following organization-level strategies for enhancing the system's capacity to effectively differentiate among and between performers:

- After collaboratively setting goals with your employees and clarifying expectations, review your employees' goals and expectations with your manager to ensure alignment with department and corporate goals, as well as to gain buy-in for how you will evaluate expected results.
- Have a joint meeting with your colleagues to validate the kinds of goals and expected results each of you have set for your employees; this will help each of you to gauge the relative difficulty of the goals and expected results, and provides the opportunity to make adjustments as needed to ensure a sense of fairness when it comes to appraising performance.
- At the end of the performance year, meet again with your colleagues to discuss employee goals and results, and to drive to a consensus decision on each employee's overall rating.
- Ensure that your manager reviews each of your performance appraisals as a final check for fairness and consistency in your ratings.

Table 2.1.   Effectiveness Evaluation

Rate each Behavior and Key Effectiveness Area using the scale below. Then provide an Overall Effectiveness Rating using the scale at the end of the evaluation.

>   1 = Does not meet expectations
>   2 = Partially meets expectations
>   3 = Meets expectations
>   4 = Exceeds expectations
>   5 = Far exceeds expectations

Key Effectiveness Areas and Behaviors	Rating
1. Communicates effectively	
a. Listens well and understands the needs of customers	
b. Expresses ideas clearly and directly	
c. Conveys confidence when communicating	
d. Persuasively communicates in a way that produces positive results	
2. Develops relationships	
a. Builds and sustains customer relationships to achieve goals	
b. Collaborates effectively within and across departments	
c. Acknowledges the contributions of others	
d. Is an effective team leader and member	
3. Plans Effectively	
a. Ensures work plans support department goals	
b. Creates efficient processes and work plans	
c. Anticipates problems and takes corrective action	
d. Effectively balances long-term and short-term priorities	
4. Makes Results Happen	
a. Stays focused on satisfying customer needs	
b. Keeps focused on results by clarifying processes, roles, and responsibilities with others	

Table 2.1. Effectiveness Evaluation (continued)

Key Effectiveness Areas and Behaviors	Rating
c. Makes sound, timely decisions that lead to results	
d. Takes personal responsibility for achieving results	
5. Demonstrates Resilience and Flexibility	
a. Deals effectively with multiple demands and shifting priorities	
b. Shows resilience when faced with setbacks or criticism	
c. Is receptive to new ideas	
d. Actively supports organization change efforts	
6. Manages and Develops People (applies only to those with supervisory responsibility)	
a. Conducts and completes performance appraisal reviews on time	
b. Actively supports employee career planning and development	
c. Provides coaching and performance feedback where appropriate	
d. Works to discuss and resolve employee work issues and concerns	
7. Supports Company Values and Policies	
a. Practices and promotes the company's values	
b. Consistently follows the company's policies	
c. Acts honestly and ethically in the workplace	
d. Treats others in a fair and respectful manner	
8. Develops Self	
a. Knows own strengths and weaknesses	
b. Learns from experience	
c. Actively seeks feedback for improvement	
d. Takes responsibility for completing development plan	
Overall Effectiveness Rating	

Of course, there is more help to come as each of the chapters in this book is targeted to improve your capability in all aspects of performance management and to use performance management as the primary vehicle for fostering employee engagement in your organization. However, let's now finish our discussion about performance appraisal.

Rating Behaviors and Competencies

The approach we are taking in this book regarding goal setting and appraisal is to focus on setting and evaluating performance and development goals and assessing key behaviors or competencies. In this section, we address the process for assessing or rating behaviors and competencies, recommend measurement scales, and identify the typical errors managers make when evaluating performance. Note that Chapter 4 has a detailed discussion of setting and evaluating goals.

Evaluations of behavior are built into many performance appraisal processes. Although some of these evaluations can be based on formal 360-degree feedback data (discussed in Chapter 7), most of the time these evaluations are determined by you, the employee's manager. If your performance appraisal evaluation includes a behavioral component, try to communicate during the goal-setting process how much "weight" this evaluation will have toward the overall performance rating. For example, one of our current clients uses a manager-driven behavioral evaluation in the business unit's new appraisal process. An example of this section of the client's management performance appraisal appears in Table 2.1. It requires managers to evaluate their employees in eight different categories, called *effectiveness areas*. Each effectiveness area contains four behaviors that help to define its domain. In practice, managers are asked to (a) rate each of the behaviors and each effectiveness area, and (b) determine an overall rating of effectiveness.

In most appraisal processes, if there is an evaluation of behavior, it typically will count for no more than 50% of the overall rating. However, we have had clients whose appraisal processes were solely behavior based (Mone & London, 1998). You may have the opportunity to decide what behaviors are important to evaluate. If so, our advice to you is to be sure the behaviors link to your employee's job description and performance goals as well as to the strategic direction of the business. In this way, your choice of relevant behaviors and competencies will be very well grounded in the reality of your day-to-day business and have greater meaning to you and your employee.

Measurement

Although your company's appraisal may have somewhere between 3 and 10 scale points, in most instances, we advise our clients to use a 5-point scale in the performance appraisal process. A 5-point scale typically is defined as having the following variables:

1. *Does not meet expectations*
2. *Partially meets expectations*
3. *Meets expectations*
4. *Exceeds expectations*
5. *Far exceeds expectations*

The 5-point scale offers you a good balance, with two possible evaluations of performance above and below the level of meeting expectations. This enables you to make clear distinctions between performance levels or, in other words, to differentiate performance more effectively than with a 3-point, forced-distribution rating. Five-point scales are also quite effective when the appraisal process is used to make pay or promotion decisions, helping both to determine the degree of rewards a given employee deserves based on his or her own merits, and to determine how rewards should be distributed based on a comparison of performance among a group of employees.

We have worked with managers who preferred a 3-point scale. A 3-point scale typically has the following categories:

1. *Does not meet expectations*: 1
2. *Meets expectations*: 2
3. *Exceeds expectations*: 3

These managers prefer the ease of fewer categories and have difficulty determining differences in performance between an *exceeds expectations* and a *far exceeds expectations*.

Somehow, regardless of the number of points on the scale, the complaint we always hear is that not all the points on the scale are used. It seems that most managers, for example, rate their employees as *exceeds expectations* or better if a 5-point scale is used—back to the idea of leniency and inflated ratings. We already described this result as a failure of leadership, which creates a culture of collusion that encourages managers to inflate their ratings. And because so many managers are uncomfortable dealing with poor performance, they further avoid confrontation and rate poor performers as *meets expectations*. Again, these concerns have less to do with the structure of the rating scale—tempting as it might be to conclude—than with the way the scale is used. We encourage you to understand the meaning of the different scale points of your organization's appraisal, to rate your employees fairly and accurately, and to coach your problem performers.

Avoiding Common Rating Errors

Honestly think about whether you would agree or disagree with each of the following:

1. I tend to be generous and give high ratings to most employees.
2. I tend to be tough and give low ratings to most employees.
3. If I can evaluate and rate an employee on one or two key areas, I tend to use that rating as the overall rating.
4. I tend to rate most people right down the middle of the scale.
5. I tend to rate people who are similar to me higher than others.
6. I base most of my ratings on my most important impression of an employee's performance, my first impression.
7. I judge employees by what they have done most recently, and put less emphasis on whatever they did early on in the performance cycle.

Each statement basically defines a type of rating error. The definitions below explain these errors and correspond to the above statements.

1. *Leniency*: You provide mostly favorable ratings on all aspects of performance, but they are not usually deserved. Your standards, compared to others, are probably too low.
2. *Severity*: You provide mostly unfavorable ratings on all aspects of performance, but they are not usually deserved. Your standards, compared to others, are probably too high.
3. *Halo*: You let one area of performance affect your overall rating of performance in all other areas. You tend to value one area and then rate an employee's overall performance based on your assessment of that one valued area. By the way, if it is a positive rating, it is called a *halo effect*; if it is a negative rating, it is called a *horns effect*.
4. *Central tendency*: When you tend to rate all performance areas as average, but this is not the real case. You find yourself rating most people close to the middle of the performance scale, and you rarely, if at all, use the lower or upper ends of the scale. Don't be afraid to branch out!

5. *Similarity*: Just because an employee is similar to you, maybe in terms of age, sex, education, experience, and the like, you rate that employee favorably, even when it is not deserved.

6. *First impression*: When you determine your employee's end-of-year performance evaluation based largely on how well your employee did early on in the cycle. You tend to ignore later performance data, whether positive or negative.

7. *Recency effect*: When you determine your employee's end-of-year performance evaluation based largely on how well your employee did at the end of the cycle. You tend to ignore earlier performance data, whether positive or negative.

One of the earliest approaches to correct these kinds of rating errors was focused on increasing rating accuracy (Hedge & Kavanagh, 1988), essentially making managers aware of these errors and showing them how to avoid them. Of course, the errors or effects described above may not necessarily be errors. For example, the employees who report to you may indeed be all excellent performers, and this would not be evidence of leniency on your part. Don't be shy about asking your HR or training manager about frame of reference (FOR) training, which can provide you with examples of good, average, and poor performance for each behavioral dimension in your appraisal process. This kind of training is a good way to improve your ability to identify and classify observed performance correctly, increasing your rating accuracy (London, Mone, & Scott, 2004). As a result, you would develop an enhanced schema or perspective for processing employee performance information, and this schema would help you to increase your recall of this information to produce more accurate ratings. Frame of reference training typically involves having the chance to evaluate actors presented on videotape, receiving feedback on your rating accuracy, and practice rating varying degrees of performance effectiveness (Latham, Almost, Mann, & Moore, 2005).

Another way to improve your rating and evaluation accuracy is to keep a record of performance during the performance year—a process referred to as "structured diary-keeping" (Latham et al., 2005). In this approach, you keep an ongoing record for each of your employees, capturing performance information by goal or by behavior. This record of performance data not only will be useful for determining an accurate overall rating, but also can serve as the basis for feedback discussions about specific goals or demonstrations of behavior.

In general, if you follow the strategies presented throughout this book, your likelihood of making any of the above errors will be minimized. We also encourage you to return to this section of the book when it is time to appraise your employees' performance and to use the above list to check that you are being as fair and honest as you can with yourself and the employees you are evaluating.

Preparing for the Appraisal Meeting

As the manager conducting the appraisal meeting, your responsibility is to ensure you are prepared to make the meeting as effective and productive as possible. Be ready to provide specific feedback about both the strengths that you have seen and how your employee can improve his or her performance. In addition, consider possible areas for development that can be built into next year's goal-setting process.

Mastering the facts and knowing the points you want to make will allow you to focus on the interaction, listen more attentively to what your employee has to say, and, in general, better manage and enhance the quality of this performance conversation.

Ideally, both you and your employee should be open-minded and focused on listening to each other and exploring any performance-related issues that may arise. Neither of you should be defensive. If you feel that you are being so, ask yourself why and try to do something about it immediately. As a manager, you should be committed to your employee's improvement and continued success, so you should be demonstrating an attitude of support and reassurance, as well as satisfaction (we hope) with your employee's performance. Review Chapter 5 on feedback strategies and techniques before you conduct this appraisal session.

What You Would Typically Cover in the Meeting

Presuming you have followed our recommendation, your employee will come to the meeting having read your final appraisal. Some authors suggest having the meeting in a conference room rather than your own office. Here's a suggested structure for the meeting and what you would typically cover:

1. Welcome your employee, make sure that he or she is comfortable, and check to see that the appraisal was read.
2. Explain the intent of the meeting and how long the meeting will last.
3. Begin by thanking your employee for his or her performance contributions and the success achieved. Offer an overall statement regarding performance, such as "Sally, you had a strong year" or "Bill, your performance this year shows significant improvement over last year."

4. Ask your employee if he or she has any major concerns about the appraisal or disagreements with your ratings, identify them, and then address them as you review the appraisal in detail.

5. Review and discuss each performance (individual and/or team) goal, strategy, tactic, and so on. Provide feedback about how you feel each was accomplished, and explain why you have rated each goal as such. Ask your employee for comments along the way. Be open to questions and possible discussion to be sure that your employee understands your evaluation correctly.

6. Review and discuss each behavioral area or competency rated, providing examples, as appropriate, of how the behavior or competency was demonstrated. Again, ask your employee for comments along the way, and be open to questions and possible discussion.

7. Review and discuss each development goal, commenting on the progress you have seen. Ask for feedback. Try to determine if continued development in the same areas is warranted.

8. Explain and discuss how you have arrived at your employee's overall performance rating. This should be an obvious outcome based on the evaluation of each goal and your behavioral or competency assessment.

9. Ask about and discuss any additional comments, concerns, or questions your employee might have about his or her performance or the appraisal.

10. Ask your employee to sign the appraisal.

11. If compensation is a related process, explain how and when this will be handled.

12. Determine and agree to a time when you can have a goal-setting meeting for the next performance year.

These steps will help you to conduct an effective appraisal meeting, but feel free to modify them to fit your particular management style or to satisfy your company's human resources policies and processes.

Performance Appraisal and Compensation

Our research at XINC shows that employees' satisfaction with their total rewards, including company benefits, and feeling that they are paid fairly are predictors of employee engagement. Although satisfaction with compensation is not a measure of engagement per se, it can affect the level of engagement in your organization, particularly if your employees also feel that they are not paid fairly. If employees feel that their pay does not seem fair in comparison to that of others—or, stated differently, that their efforts and what they receive in return do not compare fairly to what they perceive the efforts of others are and what they get in return—they will be dissatisfied, and their motivation will decrease. For you, as a manager, the implications are that you should not think of pay in and of itself as *the* motivator and that the perceived *fairness* of how you distribute pay is more important than the amount of pay any one employee receives. We end this chapter with our advice for moving to productive conversations with your employees about how their performance may impact their pay.

First, explain to your employees your company's compensation philosophy, policy, practices, and components; you would be surprised how many of your employees don't understand how all this fits together. Once your employees know, you replace their sense of mistrust or suspicion with the truth, and help them to see that the compensation program in your company is designed to be fair and equitable.

Next, be sure your employees understand the fact that their compensation range is first and foremost determined by the positions they hold, and that your company's overall ability to fund merit and bonus pools depends on its financial health and performance in any given year. So, although your company may have a pay for performance philosophy, in some years the pools may be larger than others; and frankly, some positions on your team may demand higher levels of pay due to the fundamental nature of the work involved, as well as prevailing market conditions. In essence, you need to clearly establish the fact that performance is an input to compensation decisions, but that it is not the only factor used to determine merit increases and discretionary bonuses.

Of course, you will always be working within a limited compensation budget, but in principle, you should be making the hard decision to allocate more of your budget for your higher-rated performers. This becomes challenging—and we recognize that you may feel bad or guilty about making this decision—when the typical merit increase budget ranges between 3% and 4%. Why? In order to adequately reward your highest-rated performers, some others on your team may receive little to no raises. And you have to explain your decision to them. But if your employees understand the company's compensation program and believe that they were fairly appraised, they will understand your decision, whether or not they are 100% happy with it—because they know you treated them fairly and equitably.

Probably the most difficult decision you will face is what to do when one of your employees is at or near the top of his or her pay range. If that is the case, depending on his or her performance, explain to your employee your rationale for providing

- A small increase (so you can bring your employee to the top or slightly over the top of the pay range)

- A small increase, and a discretionary bonus (so you can adequately reward your employee without going over, or too far over, the top of the range)
- A discretionary bonus (because you want to reward your employee but you could not go over the top of the range)
- No increase at all (because your employee is at, or already over, the top of the range and his or her performance did not warrant any further compensation treatment)

In addition, you could also provide your employee with more responsibility, or promote your employee to a higher paying job—which would help to justify a raise or bonus.

Well, that is not quite the end of the story. Two other predictors of engagement will go a long way toward making your employees feel appreciated for their efforts regardless of their compensation levels or the increases in pay or bonuses you provide: feedback and recognition. Chapters 5 and 6 provide best practices, resources, and tools to help you increase your skills in providing feedback and recognition, and as result, your effectiveness in ongoing performance management and your ability to drive higher levels of employee engagement.

Conclusion

We started this chapter by noting that, on the one hand, performance appraisal is a formal process involving you, the manager, evaluating your employees' performance and often using your judgment to make administrative decisions about them. On the other hand, it is the basis for your ongoing feedback and coaching to help them do better. We argued that these are not necessarily contradictory processes if you engage in collaborative goal setting and help your employees to create their own development plans and take responsibility for their own performance management and improvement. Formal performance appraisal, then, is a component of a collaborative, performance management process. We also outlined the steps in the typical annual appraisal process. In addition, we described the rating process and the appraisal discussion, including how to avoid rating errors and how to make the most of the performance appraisal discussion. Finally, we addressed how you can have more productive conversations with your employees about the connection between their performance and their pay.

The next chapter lays the foundation for effective performance management and fostering employee engagement—how to build a climate of trust. After that, we will address each phase of the performance management process, moving from goal setting through recognition.

Chapter 3

Building a Climate of Trust

In Chapter 1 we reported that one of the key predictors or drivers of employee engagement was being able to trust your manager. Trust, of course, is also a necessary ingredient for effective performance management. In this chapter, we discuss the concept of trust, present a model that can guide you in building a climate of trust, and provide you with tools and tips you can use to initiate and maintain a high level of trust and empowerment within your organization. We also show you how your company's norms can affect the climate of trust and what you can do to ensure a fair and equitable performance management process for your organization.

Trust: An Overview

Trust is the "willingness of an individual or group to be vulnerable to the actions of others based on the expectation that they will perform a particular important action, irrespective of the ability to monitor or control performance" (Mayer, Davis, & Schoorman, 1995, p. 712). Trust helps you develop effective individual, intragroup, and cross-group relationships and provides the foundation for a mind-set that can lead to greater levels of performance, as well as collaboration, within your organization (Jones & George, 1998; Poon, 2006). This mind-set includes:

- A sense of obligation to cooperate with others
- A high degree of self-confidence and confidence in one's colleagues

■ A willingness to support one's colleagues
■ A willingness to subjugate one's personal needs for the greater good
■ A willingness to engage in a free exchange of knowledge and information

We describe a *climate of trust* as the everyday feeling or level of trust in your organization. The climate of trust is largely driven by you, as a manager, but it is also influenced by the combination of all the individual relationships within your organization. Your more local climate of trust can also be affected by organizational factors outside your control. In addition, trust in management is at an all-time low as a consequence of "rapid technological change and evolving organizational structures, downsizing, rightsizing, streamlining, working smarter and the other now passé buzzwords that mean companies are trying to do more with fewer long-term employees" (Moore, 2000, p. 3). The result is that although today's flatter organizations demand higher levels of trust, you may have more trouble being seen by your employees as trustworthy. So you may have a more difficult time creating an overall climate of high trust and empowerment in your organization.

In general, a low-trust climate is the result of your employees feeling angry and betrayed because their expectations of the organization's obligations toward them are not met (Morrison & Robinson, 1997). You can recognize a low-trust climate by the results it produces—results no manager would want to have:

■ Lost productivity due to time spent being defensive
■ Missed goals
■ Upset customers due to poor communication
■ Stagnant growth due to a reduced ability to see and accept new ideas
■ Delayed decisions as each potential backlash is assessed
■ Employee turnover, particularly the exit of people the organization needs to retain

Therefore, although a challenge, you do want to invest in building a climate of trust, as the benefits are certainly worth the effort. These benefits include:

■ Open communications about expectations and performance
■ More effective coaching and mentoring, resulting in improved performance
■ Faster decision making due to greater openness and less defensive and protective behavior
■ Overall increased levels of loyalty, retention, collaboration, performance, satisfaction, and engagement

Trust and Performance Management

The Relationship Between the Climate of Trust, Performance Management, and Employee Engagement

From our study with XINC, we not only found that being able to trust your manager was important to feeling engaged, but also found that trust led to greater satisfaction with a manager's performance feedback. In addition, *trust in your manager* was also an indirect predictor of satisfaction with the resources available to do one's job, development and career progression opportunities, and total rewards. This leads us to conclude that trust not only is important to engagement, but also plays a critical role in how key aspects of performance management are viewed by employees.

How Do You Create a Climate of Trust to Drive Effective Performance Management?

You, your employees, and your company's senior leadership all affect the climate of trust in your organization. Although senior leadership defines the overall parameters of trust—expectations, accountability, and consequences—you can be a "climate engineer" (Salamon & Robinson, 2008), creating and sustaining your own local climate of trust by providing your employees autonomy, empowerment, flexibility, rewards, and recognition. Your employees can also be viewed as "climate engineers" in terms of how they respond to the larger organizational conditions and your efforts toward building your local climate of trust.

Although you may not fully control the climate of trust for your employees, you are the main climate engineer. When it comes to performance management, although you may have no control over corporately mandated aspects of the process (e.g., the time frame, rating scale, etc.), by your actions you determine how performance management is executed in your organization and how it influences each of your employees. Your actions, therefore, will lead to either diminishing or building the level of trust in your organization. To exercise your influence to create a more trusting climate, you will need to understand the drivers of trust, evaluate your current climate, address areas of need, and actively manage the climate of trust for your employees. These four factors are interrelated, as depicted in Figure 3.1.

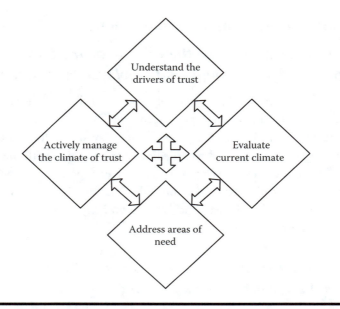

Figure 3.1 Creating a climate of trust.

Understanding the Drivers of Trust

Each of the following drivers is important to promoting (or inhibiting) a climate of trust. In this section, we will describe each of these drivers. Later, we will show how you can use these drivers to make your performance management efforts as successful as possible. The drivers include:

- Power difference
- Propensity to trust
- Perception
- Reciprocity
- Managerial trustworthy behavior

Power Difference

As a manager, keep in mind the inherent inequality in your manager–employee relationships. You have the ability to directly impact an employee's workload, career, salary, and the like. This is "legitimate" or "position" power in that it is granted to you by the position you hold in your organization. If you abuse this power and use it on behalf of yourself and not on behalf of your employees, you will exacerbate the power difference and diminish the climate of trust in your organization. You need to use your power, for example, to get your employees the resources they need to do their jobs.

Propensity to Trust

Your employees bring their history of personal experiences with trust to their relationships with you. As you probably realized by now, some people are more trusting than others. Leading researchers have labeled this concept the "propensity to trust" (McKnight & Chervany, 2006). The propensity to trust directly affects behavior at the beginning of a new relationship, and these early actions, whether trusting or nontrusting, influence how the relationship unfolds. A relationship in which you and one of your employees have very different propensities to trust has the potential to start off with difficulty. For example, what would your response likely be if you started working with a new employee on your team who immediately shows that he or she doesn't trust you? You need to understand your own basic propensity to trust, as well as that of your employees, your colleagues, and even your own manager. To foster engagement and to build the foundation for effective performance management, it will be incumbent upon you, the manager, to demonstrate your trust first.

Perception

Try to position yourself as worthy of trust. Your knowing that you are trustworthy is not enough. The reality of how your employees perceive your trustworthiness is a key factor to building a climate of trust.

Your employees' perceptions are based on their propensity to trust as well as their experiences with you and other managers, not to mention hearsay from colleagues. As a result, your behavior may even be viewed somewhat differently by each of your employees. So pay extra attention to your behavior and the management practices you use. Be fair and foster the impression of fairness among your employees (Brockner, 2006).

Also, consider the fundamental attribution error. This is the tendency to attribute the cause of a perceived negative outcome to other people or situations, not to oneself (Werner & DeSimone, 2006). So, if your employees experience a negative outcome, they may attribute it to you, personally. How does this affect you? Being in a position of power and authority, you may be asked or required to withhold information, assign employees to undesirable projects, make personnel cuts, or take any number of other actions that may be perceived negatively by your employees. Employees are likely to mistakenly attribute the causes of these actions to you (that is, blame you) rather than realize that their own behavior or factors beyond your control determined your decision. Of course, this would affect their perception of your trustworthiness. Your best tool to avoid the fundamental attribution error is open and honest communication, explaining as much as you are able. Provide your employees with the context for any negative action on your part whenever appropriate.

Reciprocity

Reciprocity builds trust. As a manager, this means your first action with any employee should show that you trust him or her, and in response, your employee is more likely to trust you. Trust is built in the relationship over time through a series of transactions that demonstrate you trust one another. Acting this way with each of your employees will ultimately help create a climate of trust in your organization. See Table 3.1 to learn more about how reciprocity can impact employee performance.

Consistent behavior is the key to using reciprocity as a driver for creating a climate of trust. Any behavior on your part that is perceived as negative or inconsistent can break an established trust chain. Even if you violate the expectations of your employees only once, "that incident can create a significant drop in the level of trust and make followers more sensitive to future actions that may be interpreted as a violation" (Dirks, 2006, p. 24). Dirks also reminded us—and this is worth noting—that building a climate of trust takes longer and is harder than generating a climate of distrust.

Table 3.1   Impact of Reciprocity on Employee Performance

Manager's Choice	Employee's Choice	Impact on the Relationship and Employee Performance
High trust	High trust	• Continued high trust in the relationship. • Employee performance will be high.
High trust	Low trust	• Potential for improved trust in the relationship. • Employee performance can improve over time.
Low trust	High trust	• Employee's trust lowered. • Employee performance will decrease over time.
Low trust	Low trust	• Continued low trust in the relationship. • Employee performance will be low.

Managerial Trustworthy Behavior

Each of the drivers discussed so far depends heavily on your behavior—how you minimize power differences, adapt to different propensities to trust, manage perceptions, and reciprocate trust. Your choices and actions are critical to defining the climate between you and your employees. With this in mind, consider the following seven behaviors (Brower, Schoorman, & Tan, 2000; Mayer, Davis, & Schoorman, 2007; Pastoriza, Ariño, & Ricart, 2008; Weber, Kopelman, & Messick, 2004) that will further demonstrate your trustworthiness to your employees.

Behaviors That Build Trust

Act as an advocate for your employees. Stand up for the rights of your employees by providing them with achievable goals, negotiating for resources to help them do their jobs and develop their skills, and protecting them when their performance is unfairly questioned. Treat conversations with each of your employees as confidential, as a seemingly innocent breach of confidentiality may be perceived as a serious breach of trust. In addition, treat your employees fairly and equitably by, for example, striving to provide them with equivalent amounts of coaching and feedback. Overall, your approach should be to place the interests of each of your employees on par with your own.

Show confidence in your employees. Demonstrate that you are comfortable relying on your employees to accomplish their goals. Refrain from micromanagement, and try to overcome your feelings of vulnerability. You can do this by clearly empowering your employees with accountability and responsibility for key projects, even high-profile projects where you are likely to believe that you can do it best.

Act with integrity. This means doing what you say you will do. When your employees see predictable patterns of behavior, they will become more comfortable and more trusting. Taking responsibility for your actions and maintaining your principles under pressure will show that you can be trusted. Finally, be consistent in what you say to your employees. They talk to each other, after all. If you tell one version of a story to one employee and a different version to another, when the two employees share the story (which they will), they will doubt your integrity and trustworthiness.

Display an interest in your employees. You may spend more time with your employees than you do with your family. And, much like with your family, it is important to show an interest in your employees' opinions and desires, and what they like to do. Again this behavior should be equitable, not equal. Certain people are going to be more forthcoming than others, but you should present each person with the opportunity to share and then respond according to his or her comfort level. You may find that you are more comfortable with some employees; in these cases, you should make a conscious effort not to show favoritism.

Demonstrate openness. Have more than just an "open door" policy. Although it is important to make yourself available and listen to your employees, you need to go further. Open yourself up to influence from your employees. Your employees may have more knowledge, insight, or experience than you do in particular areas, and you should take advantage of this rather than be intimidated or dismissive. Share, as appropriate, all relevant information with your employees so they can better achieve their goals and support you in achieving yours. Withholding needed information without a strong reason is a serious breach of trust. You will find that unintentional breaches of trust are more easily diffused if you consistently open up to your employees in a genuine way, sharing your feelings, expectations, and concerns. Your openness with your employees will allow them to feel more comfortable and open with you.

Manage the performance of your employees. Performance management is at the center of your relationships with your employees. To ensure that they are on the right track, provide fair and reasonable goals and consistently share your expectations. Encourage, support, and reward successful performance. Provide development opportunities that support your employees' current responsibilities, as well as support their career development goals.

Act as a trusted coach. Coaching is central to building trust. Given that the most emotionally fragile moments are when you deliver feedback, your ability to be constructive and make your employees comfortable is important for not only behavior change but also building trust. Although you should not minimize poor performance by your employees, refrain from criticism. Focus instead on being open about your concerns and working together to develop an approach that will lead to better results. Let your employees know they can discuss their performance concerns with you frankly. (See Chapter 5 for a discussion of giving feedback and Chapter 8 for effective coaching strategies.)

In summary, you are responsible for managing your employees' performance and making administrative decisions that affect their jobs and careers. There is a visible power difference, and you are the one with the power. Although some employees will instinctively trust you, others are less likely to have this propensity to trust. Your ability to reciprocate trust and influence your employees to do the same is critical to building a climate of trust. Each of your employees will also have a general outlook based on his or her preferences, prior experiences with management and senior leadership, and "street knowledge" gained from colleagues. This general outlook, combined with the employee's propensity to trust, shapes his or her perception of your trustworthiness. This perception is further informed by your trustworthy behavior toward the employee and the employee's perception of that behavior; and the two may not be the same. In the end, you have to manage not only your employees' performance but also their perceptions of power, reciprocity, and your behavior.

Evaluating Your Current Climate, Addressing Areas of Need, and Actively Managing the Climate of Trust

In this section, we address the remaining three components of our model for building a climate of trust (see Figure 3.1). We accomplish this using three levels of analysis in the context of performance management—the organization, your core team, and your colleagues—each of which contributes to the climate of trust you can create.

At the *organization* level, you and your team necessarily need to follow the company's performance management process. You and your team also live within the greater organizational environment and are subject to the organization's norms (the typical behaviors in an organization) regarding performance management. In your *core team*—composed of you and your employees—you influence the level of trust your employees experience by the kinds of performance management interactions you have with them. Both you and your employees, when interacting with *colleagues*, make observations and comparisons about performance management in their organizations that can be validation points or challenges to the level and climate of trust between you and your employees.

Organization-Level Analysis

Within the context of performance management, the organizational drivers of trust consist of the organization's performance management process and organization norms for goal setting, feedback and coaching, performance appraisal, and development opportunities for current and potential future jobs.

Although it is unlikely that you can greatly influence the organization-level process and norms, you can manage your employees' expectations and perceptions. For now, let's first examine how you can assess the organization-level process and its associated norms. Ask these key questions:

- What are the organization-level expectations with regard to the performance management process?
- Are there resources available to adequately support this process?
- Will all employees go through the same process?
- Is the process fair and equitable for everyone?
- Is there accountability for using the performance management process?
- Are there consequences aligned with that accountability to drive appropriate compliance?
- Are there protections for any unwarranted repercussions that arise due to engagement in the performance management process?
- Are the performance management–related norms effectively supporting each component of the process, as well as the overall process?

You will probably have trouble maintaining a climate of trust with your employees if you cannot answer any of these organization-level questions in a way that demonstrates fairness and justice. However, because you are probably not in a position to change these processes or procedures, what can you do to address performance management at the organization level? Table 3.2 describes a number of responses you can choose to drive an equitable and fair process for your own department and the organization overall. As you will see, some of the responses may require assistance from your human resource partner or your legal department representative.

Table 3.2   Responding at the Organization Level

Your Finding	Impact	Your Response
• Few to no organization-level expectations regarding performance management.	• Lacking a clearly defined process makes it hard to build trust and demonstrate fairness with your employees.	• Request that HR define and clarify organization-wide expectations, and/or • Define department-level expectations for each aspect of the performance management process.

Table 3.2   Responding at the Organization Level (continued)

Your Finding	Impact	Your Response
• Employees across the company do not follow the same process, and/or the process is not fair and equitable for all employees.	• Employees perceive that they may not be treated fairly in comparison to their peers. • Harder to conduct an effective performance management process.	• Determine if there are valid reasons for the differences; if not, raise the issue with your HR or legal representative. • At the department level, be open and honest about expectations and maintain a fair and equitable approach.
• There is little to no accountability for using an effective performance management process.	• Lack of accountability perceived by employees diminishes the value of the performance management process. • Unclear managerial expectations.	• Address your concern with your manager and HR. • Hold yourself accountable for effective performance management. • Hold your employees accountable for active involvement in ongoing performance management.
• There is little protection against unwarranted repercussions.	• Threatens integrity of the process and willingness to be open and honest.	• Raise these issues with your HR and legal representatives, and determine what level of protection is available so that you can conduct a fair and equitable process.
• Organization-level norms are not supportive of effective performance management.	• Threatens integrity and value of the overall process. • May lead to lack of commitment to performance management, in general.	• Address the issue with your manager and HR. • Create your own timelines and norms for how you will approach performance management in your organization.

Core Team-Level Analysis

The organization-level performance management process and norms set the overall parameters, but you and your employees ultimately determine how the process will unfold in your own organization. Your goal is to get your employees actively engaged in the performance management process. Consider the following drivers of trust that will influence your employees' engagement:

■ Perceptions of power differences that influence performance
■ Perceptions of reciprocated trusting behavior
■ Individual propensities to trust
■ Perceptions of the process, procedures, or expectations for performance
■ Perceptions of managerial trustworthy behaviors

Note the importance of *perception*. Perceptions may or may not match reality. Therefore, you have to manage not only what you actually do but also how your employees perceive your actions. Fortunately, you can have a direct influence on shaping these perceptions. Begin by asking the following questions:

■ How can I reduce the impact of perceived power differences between me and my employees that influence performance?
■ Am I reciprocating behavior in a way that builds trust with my employees?
■ What is my propensity to trust, and how do my employees perceive me and my engagement in the performance management process?
■ What perceptions exist that would influence my ability to effectively manage my employees' performance? What misperceptions exist?
■ Am I demonstrating trustworthy behavior when managing performance?

Addressing the Power Difference

To help you minimize the impact of your power difference, we suggest the following:

■ Use the performance management process and the performance appraisal as means of communication and motivation, not punishment.
■ Recognize and reward your employees fairly and equitably.
■ Explain to your employees any changes in your performance expectations rather than just announcing them.
■ Collaborate with your employees on major decisions.
■ Provide more opportunities for your employees to be empowered to act on their own.

Addressing Reciprocating Behavior

- Use coaching and feedback to discourage untrustworthy employee behavior.
- Avoid micromanagement.

Addressing Perceptions: Your Propensity to Trust and Managerial Trustworthy Behavior

You cannot build a climate of trust if your employees perceive that your approach to managing their performance is based on a lack of trust in them, or if your behavior is not perceived as trustworthy. So, to help you better understand the climate of trust between you and your employees, we recommend using the assessment described below.

The Trust and Empowerment Climate Assessment

We designed a 2-day management development program for one of our clients, and developed assessment surveys for use in the module on Trust and Empowerment. These surveys and a sample report are presented in Appendixes 3.1, 3.2, and 3.3. We have also successfully used these assessments for stand-alone interventions with managers and organization leaders. You can feel very confident when using these surveys, as they have been shown to be very reliable measures (based on an analysis of more than 2,800 completed surveys by managers and employees, we found high scale reliability: For the employee version, Cronbach's alpha is 0.95; for the manager version, 0.88; and for both groups combined, 0.94).

The assessment surveys ask you and your employees about your propensity to trust, your managerial trustworthy behavior, and the level of empowerment within your team. Based on the results of the assessment, you would complete a trust action plan (see Table 3.3) to implement with your direct report team, as well as an empowerment action plan that you would implement with each of your direct reports (see Table 3.4). We urge you to take these steps as a way to identify and address issues regarding your propensity to trust, managerial trustworthy behaviors, and your ability to empower your employees. We are introducing the concept of an empowerment plan at this point in the book because you need to address the inherent power difference between you and your employees, and empowering your employees is an excellent way to reduce the power distance. However, you have to balance your level of control and the level of empowerment you provide your employees.

How can you launch this survey with your direct report team? First, explain the goals of the survey, and that you are committed to sharing the results of the

Table 3.3   Trust Action Plan

Purpose	To identify actions you can take to strengthen the climate of trust with your employees
Instructions	**Step 1** Review the results of your Climate Assessment. **Step 2** Select the behavior dimension(s) you feel would be most important for you to improve. Answer the following questions.

Action Plan	**My most important behavior dimension to develop is**
	
	_____.
	
	• **The 3–5 actions I can take to positively demonstrate the trust behaviors in this dimension are**
	    1.
	    2.
	    3.
	    4.
	    5.
	
	• **The 3–5 key skills I need to develop in order to demonstrate the behaviors noted above include**
	    1.
	    2.
	    3.
	    4.
	    5.
	
	To impact the inhibitors of trust between you and your employees:
	• Identify how you will minimize the adverse effects of the power difference between you and your employees.
	• Determine how you can minimize the adverse impacts of both your own and your employees' propensity to trust.
	
	Consistently demonstrate trustworthy behavior
	Identify one important action for each of the following behavior dimensions that you will demonstrate more regularly:
	• Being an advocate for your employees
	• Showing confidence in your employees
	• Acting with integrity
	• Displaying an interest in your employees
	• Demonstrating openness
	• Managing your employees' performance
	• Acting as a trusted coach

Table 3.4   Empowerment Plan

Purpose	To identify actions you can take to empower your employees
Instructions	**Step 1** Identify an assignment where it is appropriate for you to give up your direct involvement and control. Select an employee with the skills to accomplish this assignment. **Step 2** Evaluate both the assignment and your employee to answer the following questions.
Action Plan	**Employee Name:** _____ *Identify the assignment this employee will be empowered to accomplish and your expectations.* • Goal of the assignment: • Expectations: • What knowledge, skills, and abilities are required for this employee to be successfully empowered for this assignment? • Of these knowledge, skills, and abilities, which need(s) to be further developed in order for this employee to be successfully empowered? • What are the risks and rewards of empowering this employee on this assignment? Risks: Rewards: • What barriers need to be removed? What additional access or control of resources is needed? • What is the extent of this employee's discretion on this assignment?

survey with them and to creating and implementing an action plan based on the results. Then, to ensure your employees' anonymity and confidentiality, enlist the support of your HR partner to distribute and collect the surveys, and to populate the results for your direct reports. Next, in order to calculate the averages as described in the report in Appendix 3.3, you will also need to provide your HR partner with your self-assessment results. Finally, share the results with your employees, ask for their input on areas for improvement, and design and launch your trust action and empowerment plans.

When examining the results of your own survey, you might want to keep in mind the key findings from our analysis of the 2,800-plus surveys. These findings may help you to better understand and interpret your own assessment results.

- Employees hold more distinct, binary perceptions of their managers' style than managers do of themselves. That is, employees tended to categorize their managers as either promoting a climate of trust or displaying a controlling attitude.
- There appear to be systematic differences between managers and employees with respect to the evaluation of climate dimensions such as a manager's ability to treat employees fairly, delegate, or take responsibility for mistakes. In such domains, however, managers typically express more positive views of themselves than their employees express of them.

In summary, there are a number of things you can do to maintain a climate of trust within your core team. First of all, your main focus should be on managing perceptions. You can accomplish this by establishing an environment of open communications and periodically assessing the overall climate of trust in your core team and making the necessary changes to keep it strong. Additionally, keep in mind what can disrupt the balance you've created (e.g., new employees in the group, new projects, or new levels of responsibility), and compensate accordingly.

Colleague-Level Analysis

From the perspective of performance management, trust-related concerns about others in the organization will focus on perceptions of whether the performance management process appears fair and equitable. So in this section, we consider how you can evaluate the impact that others outside of your core team can have on your climate of trust. Specifically, we focus on the following questions, and once again, the answers to these questions should point to a fair and just process for performance management.

- Does senior management support a fair and equitable process?
- Does senior management ensure that all employees have the resources necessary for successfully meeting or exceeding goals?
- Are managers in other parts of the organization held similarly accountable for implementing a fair and equitable performance management process?
- Will my colleagues and their teams in other organizations support my team's performance?

Addressing Senior Management's Role

If senior management does not support a fair and equitable performance management process, how likely are your employees to trust that you will appraise them accurately? How engaged will they be if they are certain that their work will not be accurately appraised or rewarded?

Your employees are likely to lose trust in the performance management process and in you if they see the process as unfair and are expected to meet goals without having the necessary resources. In this situation, you should first ensure that you have all the relevant information and resources available. If support is severely lacking, raise the issue with your manager and human resources partner. Also, let your employees know that you will support them as best you can. Share the steps you are taking to make sure they receive fair and equitable treatment.

Addressing Differences in How Managers Approach the Process

If other managers in the organization are not held accountable for a similar performance management process, what is the effect on your employees? Each of your employees has a network that they use to gauge their relative position and treatment in the organization. If they perceive that your managerial colleagues are treating their employees more fairly, their level of engagement and their trust in you will suffer.

There are two separate issues here: the difference in the process used and the perceived difference in the process. You will need to respond accordingly. If there is an actual difference in how other managers are treating employees in the organization, escalate the issue to your manager, your human resource partner, and/or the organization's legal department. If there is a perceived difference by your employees in how others are treated, handle it directly by uncovering the reality of the situation. Your approach should be in collaboration with your employees, not in conflict. Work with your employees to discover if there is unfair treatment. Try to find out what led to false perceptions. Perhaps you are contending with the idea that "the grass is always greener on the other side." However, it is also possible that your colleagues may be managing the perceptions of how they treat employees better than you, that is, intentionally trying to give that impression.

Addressing Organization Support and Collaboration for Your Team's Performance

The willingness of your colleagues and their teams to provide support and work collaboratively can affect the performance of your core team and the ability for your team members to achieve their goals. Again, there could be two issues, actual and perceived collaboration.

In the case of an actual lack of collaboration, approach your colleague who manages the team that isn't supporting your employees. If this does not solve the problem, then escalate the issue to your management. Although it might be easier and even necessary to find a work-around, stay with the issue until it is resolved satisfactorily. If you avoid or abandon the issue, you are not showing your employees that you are willing to support them in accomplishing their goals. Without your support, how likely are they to feel engaged?

If there is a perceived lack of collaboration, take a similar approach to the one outlined above for addressing perceived managerial differences. Work with your employees to delve into the issue so you can both discover that it was merely a perception, not reality.

To summarize, your focus should be on driving equitable and fair treatment for your team when it comes to performance management, as well as managing your team members' perceptions. If there seems to be a lack of senior management support and appreciation for a sound and just process, raise this with your manager and your HR and legal representatives. To prevent or mitigate possible issues, maintain a dialogue with your managerial colleagues on their approaches and styles. When you can ensure that there are no actual differences in treatment, focus on your employees' perceptions. This may be achieved by simply asking them if they see any differences or have any concerns.

Conclusion

In this chapter, we have discussed how building a climate of trust is critical for you to manage your employees' performance and increase their levels of engagement. Furthermore, we presented and discussed five key drivers of trust and described how the organization, the core team, and colleagues can impact the climate of trust in your organization from the perspective of their influence, views, and actions regarding performance management.

As you engage your employees in building a climate of trust, remember that open communication and consistency in your behavior are the key elements to your success. Recognize, as well, that you are not immune to stereotypes, preferences, and perceptions of your own. Finally, the drivers of trust are not static; they change based on the situation and the people involved. Any change in the makeup, support, or expectations of your core team necessitates a new analysis and renewed effort on your part to sustain or improve the climate of trust in your organization.

Appendix 3.1: Trust and Empowerment Climate Assessment Survey, Manager Version

Human Resources Department, OTCX1000, Inc.

Introduction

The Climate Assessment was designed to help managers analyze the current climate of trust and empowerment between themselves and their direct reports. Research on organization performance shows that higher levels of trust and empowerment increase employee satisfaction, improve performance, and create stronger levels of engagement.

The behaviors in this survey will be used to determine differences between your Self-Assessment scores, the scores of your Direct Reports, and the Company Norm. Any areas of significant difference can be used as a foundation for future development.

General Instructions for Self-Assessment

This survey is designed to collect information on your personal perceptions of the behaviors listed in this survey. The results of this survey will be used to help you understand how your managerial behaviors directly affect the trust and empowerment of your employees.

Please take the time to rate each behavior carefully and honestly. Your rating should be based on the extent to which you perform the listed behavior or thought processes using the scale definitions given in the table below. You can also provide comments, using the section at the end of the self-assessment.

Scale Definitions

Scale	Extent Rating	Definition
1	Little extent	Never or very rarely demonstrates this behavior. It would be out of character for this behavior to occur.
2	Some extent	Demonstrates this behavior occasionally, but by no means on a regular basis.
3	Moderate extent	Demonstrates this behavior a fair amount, but not consistently.
4	Considerable extent	Demonstrates this behavior fairly consistently.
5	Great extent	Demonstrates this behavior often, if not always, and considers it normal practice.

Please refer to the definitions and use the full range of ratings as you complete this survey.

Manager Climate Assessment

Instructions

Use the scale given in the Scale Definitions table to rate the items listed below. For each item, rate how characteristic that item is of your thoughts or behaviors.

Manager Climate Assessment—Trust and Empowerment Behaviors

No.	To What Extent Do You:	
	1 Little extent 2 Some extent 3 Moderate extent 4 Considerable extent 5 Great extent	
Act as Your Advocate		
1	Stand up for the rights of your employees?	1 2 3 4 5
2	Keep conversations with your employees confidential when appropriate?	1 2 3 4 5
3	Treat your employees fairly and equitably?	1 2 3 4 5
4	Put your employees' interests on par with your own?	1 2 3 4 5
Show Confidence in Employees		
5	Feel comfortable relying on your employees to accomplish their goals?	1 2 3 4 5
6	Delegate tasks to your employees that you can do better?	1 2 3 4 5
7	Keep tasks where mistakes would be highly visible?	1 2 3 4 5
8	Feel vulnerable when your employees take on highly visible tasks?	1 2 3 4 5
Act With Integrity		
9	Admit and take responsibility for your mistakes?	1 2 3 4 5
10	Keep the promises that you make?	1 2 3 4 5
11	Behave in a predictable and consistent fashion?	1 2 3 4 5

Manager Climate Assessment—Trust and Empowerment Behaviors (continued)

No.	To What Extent Do You:					
12	Maintain your standards and principles under pressure?	1	2	3	4	5
13	Make promises to buy yourself time or keep people from pressuring you?	1	2	3	4	5
Display Interest in Your Employees						
14	Seek out the opinions of your employees?	1	2	3	4	5
15	Ask what your employees want to work on?	1	2	3	4	5
16	Show concern by asking your employees about their lives outside of work?	1	2	3	4	5
17	Feel you are "too close" to one employee over another?	1	2	3	4	5
Demonstrate Openness						
18	Feel you are open to influence by your employees?	1	2	3	4	5
19	Open yourself up to your employees in a genuine way?	1	2	3	4	5
20	Withhold information from your employees?	1	2	3	4	5
21	Keep an open door?	1	2	3	4	5
22	Believe your employees can be open in providing you feedback about your work style and performance?	1	2	3	4	5
Manage Employees' Performance						
23	Share your expectations for performance with your employees?	1	2	3	4	5
24	Provide your employees with fair performance goals and appraisals?	1	2	3	4	5
25	Encourage, support, and reward appropriate behavior?	1	2	3	4	5

(Continued)

Manager Climate Assessment—Trust and Empowerment Behaviors (continued)

No.	To What Extent Do You:	
26	Work with your employees on their development and career plans?	1 2 3 4 5
Act as a Trusted Coach		
27	Provide your employees with constructive coaching and feedback?	1 2 3 4 5
28	Make your employees as comfortable as possible when giving feedback?	1 2 3 4 5
29	Criticize poor performance?	1 2 3 4 5
30	Think you can be open in discussing performance concerns with your employees?	1 2 3 4 5
31	Think your employees can be open in discussing their performance concerns with you?	1 2 3 4 5
Show a Propensity to Trust		
32	Demonstrate trust in others before they demonstrate trust in you?	1 2 3 4 5
33	Think that in general your employees are fundamentally trustworthy?	1 2 3 4 5
34	Feel your relationships with your employees are based on trust?	1 2 3 4 5
35	Think that your employees trust you?	1 2 3 4 5
Empowerment		
36	Provide adequate resources for your employees to achieve their goals?	1 2 3 4 5
37	Encourage your employees to solve their own problems?	1 2 3 4 5
38	Give your employees the authority to act on their own?	1 2 3 4 5
39	Provide support for and encourage your employees to take risks?	1 2 3 4 5

Manager Climate Assessment—Trust and Empowerment Behaviors (continued)

No.	To What Extent Do You:	
40	Step in and take over a task when things go wrong?	1 2 3 4 5
41	Have the authority from your manager to empower your employees?	1 2 3 4 5
42	Recognize and reward your employees for going above and beyond their goals?	1 2 3 4 5
43	Tell your employees how to do their jobs?	1 2 3 4 5
44	Encourage your employees to take the initiative to establish their own performance goals?	1 2 3 4 5
45	Monitor your employees' daily performance?	1 2 3 4 5
46	Feel comfortable delegating control to your employees over major projects?	1 2 3 4 5
47	Feel results would be better if you "did it"?	1 2 3 4 5
48	Enable your employees and hold them fully accountable for achievement of expected results?	1 2 3 4 5
49	Feel comfortable in supporting your employees' efforts when their approaches may differ from yours?	1 2 3 4 5
Comments:		

Appendix 3.2: Trust and Empowerment Climate Assessment Survey, Employee Version

Human Resources Department, OTCX1000, Inc.

Introduction

The Climate Assessment was designed to help managers analyze the current climate of trust and empowerment between themselves and their direct reports. Research on organization performance shows that higher levels of trust and empowerment increase employee satisfaction, improve performance, and create stronger levels of engagement.

The behaviors in this survey will be used to determine differences between your manager's Self-Assessment scores, your scores combined with all of your manager's other Direct Reports, and the Company Norm. Any areas of significant difference can be used as a foundation for future development.

General Instructions for Manager Assessment

This survey is designed to collect information on your personal perceptions of your manager's behaviors listed in this survey. The results of this survey will be used to help your manager understand how his or her managerial behaviors directly affect the trust and empowerment of his or her employees.

Please take the time to rate each behavior carefully and honestly. Your rating should be based on the extent to which your manager performs the listed behavior or thought processes using the scale definitions below. Any comments you provide will be reported anonymously with all other comments.

Please refer to the definitions and use the full range of ratings as you complete this survey.

Assessment of Your Manager

Instructions

Use the scale below to rate the items in this assessment. For each item, rate how characteristic that item is of your manager's thoughts or behavior.

Scale Definitions

Scale	Extent Rating	Definition
1	Little extent	Never or very rarely demonstrates this behavior. It would be out of character for this behavior to occur.
2	Some extent	Demonstrates this behavior occasionally, but by no means on a regular basis.
3	Moderate extent	Demonstrates this behavior a fair amount, but not consistently.
4	Considerable extent	Demonstrates this behavior fairly consistently.
5	Great extent	Demonstrates this behavior often, if not always, and considers it normal practice.

Assessment of Your Manager—Trust and Empowerment Behaviors

	1 Little extent 2 Some extent 3 Moderate extent 4 Considerable extent 5 Great extent					
No.	*To What Extent Does Your Manager:*					
Act as Your Advocate						
1	Stand up for your rights?	1	2	3	4	5
2	Keep conversations with you confidential when appropriate?	1	2	3	4	5
3	Treat you fairly and equitably?	1	2	3	4	5
4	Put your interests on par with his or her own?	1	2	3	4	5
Show Confidence in You						
5	Seem to feel comfortable relying on you to accomplish your goals?	1	2	3	4	5
6	Delegate tasks to you that he or she can probably do better?	1	2	3	4	5
7	Keep tasks to him- or herself where mistakes would be highly visible?	1	2	3	4	5
8	Seem to feel vulnerable when you take on highly visible tasks?	1	2	3	4	5
Act With Integrity						
9	Admit and take responsibility for his or her mistakes?	1	2	3	4	5
10	Keep the promises that he or she makes?	1	2	3	4	5
11	Behave in a predictable and consistent fashion?	1	2	3	4	5
12	Maintain his or her standards and principles under pressure?	1	2	3	4	5
13	Make promises to buy time or keep people from pressuring him or her?	1	2	3	4	5

(continued)

Assessment of Your Manager—Trust and Empowerment Behaviors (continued)

No.	To What Extent Does Your Manager:					
Display Interest in You						
14	Seek out your opinions?	1	2	3	4	5
15	Ask what you want to work on?	1	2	3	4	5
16	Show concern by asking you about your life outside of work?	1	2	3	4	5
17	Act "too close" to one employee over another?	1	2	3	4	5
Demonstrate Openness						
18	Seem open to influence by you?	1	2	3	4	5
19	Open up to you in a genuine way?	1	2	3	4	5
20	Withhold information from you?	1	2	3	4	5
21	Keep an open door?	1	2	3	4	5
22	Seem to believe you can be open in providing him or her feedback about his or her work style and performance?	1	2	3	4	5
Manage Your Performance						
23	Share expectations for performance with you?	1	2	3	4	5
24	Provide you with fair performance goals and appraisals?	1	2	3	4	5
25	Encourage, support, and reward appropriate behavior?	1	2	3	4	5
26	Work with you on your development and career plan?	1	2	3	4	5
Act as a Trusted Coach						
27	Provide you with constructive coaching and feedback?	1	2	3	4	5
28	Try to make you as comfortable as possible when giving you feedback?	1	2	3	4	5

Assessment of Your Manager—Trust and Empowerment Behaviors (continued)

No.	To What Extent Does Your Manager:					
29	Criticize poor performance?	1	2	3	4	5
30	Seem to think he or she can be open in discussing performance concerns with you?	1	2	3	4	5
31	Seem to think you can be open in discussing your performance concerns with him or her?	1	2	3	4	5
Show a Propensity to Trust						
32	Demonstrate trust in you before you demonstrate trust in him or her?	1	2	3	4	5
33	Seem to think that in general, his or her employees are fundamentally trustworthy?	1	2	3	4	5
34	Seem to feel his or her relationships with employees are based on trust?	1	2	3	4	5
35	Seem to think that employees trust him or her?	1	2	3	4	5
Empowerment						
36	Provide adequate resources for you to achieve your goals?	1	2	3	4	5
37	Encourage you to solve your own problems?	1	2	3	4	5
38	Give your employees the authority to act on their own?	1	2	3	4	5
39	Provide support for and encourage you to take risks?	1	2	3	4	5
40	Step in and take over a task when things go wrong?	1	2	3	4	5
41	Have the authority from his or her manager to empower his or her employees?	1	2	3	4	5
42	Recognize and reward you for going above and beyond your goals?	1	2	3	4	5
43	Tell you how to do your job?	1	2	3	4	5
44	Encourage you to take the initiative to establish your own performance goals?	1	2	3	4	5

(continued)

Assessment of Your Manager—Trust and Empowerment Behaviors (continued)

No.	To What Extent Does Your Manager:					
45	Monitor your daily performance?	1	2	3	4	5
46	Seem to feel comfortable delegating control over major projects to you?	1	2	3	4	5
47	Seem to feel results would be better if he or she "did it"?	1	2	3	4	5
48	Enable you and hold you fully accountable for achievement of expected results?	1	2	3	4	5
49	Seem comfortable in supporting your efforts when your approaches may differ from his or hers?	1	2	3	4	5
Comments:						

Appendix 3.3: Trust and Empowerment Climate Assessment Results Summary—Sample Report

The Trust and Empowerment Climate Assessment was designed to help you analyze the current climate of trust and empowerment between you and your direct reports. Research on organization performance shows that higher levels of trust and empowerment create more employee satisfaction, stronger performance, and higher degrees of engagement. Identify any significant differences between your Self-Assessment scores, the scores of your Direct Reports, and the Company Norm. This analysis will help you determine areas of development on which to focus.

The scores in this summary report are based on the rating scale used in the assessment, which asked the extent to which you act in accordance with each behavior. (The summary and detail reports follow.)

Summary Report

Trust and Empowerment Behavior Dimensions	Direct Reports			Self-Score Average	Self+Directs Average	Self+Directs Company Norm
	Low	High	Average			
Act as an employee advocate.	2	5	4.19	3.25	4.08	4.18
Show confidence in employees.	1	5	3.94	3.25	3.86	3.82
Act with integrity.	2	5	4.10	3.20	4.00	4.08
Display interest in your employees.	1	5	3.72	3.00	3.64	3.78
Demonstrate openness.	2	5	3.90	3.20	3.82	3.91
Manage employees' performance.	1	5	3.69	2.75	3.58	3.82
Act as a trusted coach.	1	5	3.63	2.80	3.53	3.75
Overall trustworthy behavior (average of the seven dimensions above).	**1**	**5**	**3.88**	**3.06**	**3.79**	**3.91**
Propensity to trust.	**2**	**5**	**4.13**	**3.00**	**4.00**	**4.05**
Empowerment.	**1**	**5**	**3.86**	**3.00**	**3.76**	**3.79**
Number of direct reports responding: 8						

Note: 1: Little extent; 2: some extent; 3: moderate extent; 4: considerate extent; and 5: great extent.

Detail Report

The Detail Report provides you scores for the behaviors in each trust and empowerment behavior dimension. You should analyze the scores for each item to determine your strengths and development areas within each behavior dimension.

Trust and Empowerment Behaviors	Direct Reports			Self-Score Average	Self+Directs Average	Self+Directs Company Norm
	Low	High	Average			
Act as an Employee Advocate	2	5	4.19	3.25	4.08	4.18
Stand up for the rights of your employees.	3	5	4.38	4.00	4.33	4.12
Keep conversations with employees confidential when appropriate.	3	5	4.38	3.00	4.22	4.47
Treat your employees fairly and equitably.	2	5	4.63	3.00	4.44	4.44
Put the interests of your employees on par with your own.	2	5	3.38	3.00	3.33	3.69
Show Confidence in Employees	1	5	3.94	3.25	3.86	3.82
Feel comfortable relying on employees to accomplish their goals.	3	5	4.50	3.00	4.33	4.27
Delegate tasks to your employees that you can do better.	1	5	3.00	3.00	3.00	3.20

Keep tasks where mistakes would be highly visible.	*	2	5	4.00	4.00	4.00	3.80
Feel vulnerable when your employees take on highly visible tasks.	*	3	5	4.25	3.00	4.11	4.00
Act With Integrity		2	5	4.10	3.20	4.00	4.08
Admit and take responsibility for your mistakes.		3	5	4.13	4.00	4.11	4.15
Keep the promises that you make.		3	5	4.13	3.00	4.00	4.10
Behave in a predictable and consistent fashion.		2	5	3.88	3.00	3.78	4.00
Maintain your standards and principles under pressure.		2	5	4.00	3.00	3.89	4.07
Make promises to buy time or keep people from pressuring you.	*	3	5	4.38	3.00	4.22	4.10
Display Interest in Your Employees		1	5	3.72	3.00	3.64	3.78
Seek out the opinions of your employees.		2	5	3.75	3.00	3.67	4.05
Ask what your employees want to work on.		1	5	3.25	2.00	3.11	3.54

(continued)

* Item is reverse scored when calculating averages.

Detail Report (continued)

Trust and Empowerment Behaviors		Direct Reports			Self-Score Average	Self+Directs Average	Self+Directs Company Norm
		Low	High	Average			
Show concern by asking employees about their lives outside of work.		2	5	3.25	3.00	3.22	3.20
Be "too close" to one employee over another.	*	4	5	4.63	4.00	4.56	4.34
Demonstrate Openness		2	5	3.90	3.20	3.82	3.91
Be open to influence by your employees.		2	5	3.13	2.00	3.00	3.20
Open yourself up to your employees in a genuine way.		3	5	4.38	3.00	4.22	4.19
Withhold information from your employees.	*	3	5	4.13	4.00	4.11	3.95
Keep an open door.		3	5	3.75	4.00	3.78	4.31
Employees can openly provide feedback about your work style and performance.		2	5	4.13	3.00	4.00	3.92

Manage Employees' Performance	1	5	3.69	2.75	3.58	3.82
Share your expectations for performance with your employees.	2	5	3.75	2.00	3.56	3.93
Provide your employees with fair performance goals and appraisals.	4	5	4.25	4.00	4.22	4.15
Encourage, support, and reward appropriate behavior.	3	4	3.75	3.00	3.67	3.97
Work with your employees on their development and career plan.	1	4	3.00	2.00	2.89	3.24
Act as a Trusted Coach	1	5	3.63	2.80	3.53	3.75
Provide your employees with constructive coaching and feedback.	2	4	3.00	2.00	2.89	3.64
Make employees as comfortable as possible when giving feedback.	2	5	3.75	3.00	3.67	4.05
Criticize poor performance. *	1	4	2.88	4.00	3.00	2.85
Think you can be open in discussing performance concerns with your employees.	3	5	4.25	2.00	4.00	4.02

* Item is reverse scored when calculating averages.

(continued)

Detail Report (Continued)

Trust and Empowerment Behaviors	Direct Reports			Self-Score Average	Self+Directs Average	Self+Directs Company Norm
	Low	High	Average			
Think your employees can be open in discussing performance concerns with you.	2	5	4.25	3.00	4.11	4.19
Show a Propensity to Trust	2	5	4.13	3.00	4.00	4.05
Demonstrate trust in others before they demonstrate trust in you.	2	5	4.13	2.00	3.89	3.98
Think that in general, your employees are fundamentally trustworthy.	3	5	4.13	4.00	4.11	4.17
Feel your relationships with your employees are based on trust.	3	5	4.00	3.00	3.89	3.97
Think that your employees trust you.	3	5	4.25	3.00	4.11	4.07
Empowerment	1	5	3.86	3.00	3.76	3.79
Provide adequate resources for employees to achieve their goals.	2	5	3.88	2.00	3.67	3.86
Encourage your employees to solve their own problems.	3	5	4.00	3.00	3.89	4.07
Give your employees the authority to act on their own.	3	5	4.50	4.00	4.44	4.37

Building a Climate of Trust ■ 65

Provide support for and encourage your employees to take risks.		3	5	4.13	3.00	4.00	3.88
Step in and take over a task when things go wrong.	*	1	4	2.25	3.00	2.33	2.37
Have the authority from your manager to empower your employees.		2	5	3.25	3.00	3.22	3.95
Recognize and reward employees for going above and beyond their goals.		3	5	3.88	4.00	3.89	3.86
Tell your employees how to do their jobs.	*	3	5	4.00	4.00	4.00	3.73
Encourage employees to take the initiative to establish performance goals.		3	5	3.88	3.00	3.78	3.81
Monitor your employees' daily performance.	*	3	5	4.00	4.00	4.00	3.68
Feel comfortable delegating control to employees over major projects.		3	5	4.25	2.00	4.00	3.95
Feel results would be better if you did it.	*	3	5	4.63	2.00	4.33	4.14
Enable employees and hold them fully accountable to achieve expected results.		3	5	3.88	2.00	3.67	3.85
Support employees' efforts when their approaches differ from yours.		2	5	3.50	3.00	3.44	3.56

(continued)

* Item is reverse scored when calculating averages.

Detail Report (Continued)

Self-Assessment
Please add any comments you have on the overall climate between you and your direct reports.
(No comments added.)

Direct Reports Assessment
Please add any comments you have on the overall climate between your team and your manager.

- My manager is a great resource who has too many hats. Management has to decide what role they want my manager to fill and delegate the rest.

- Overall, my manager does a very good job. My only gripe is with scheduling when things are done last minute, but I realize that this is also most likely out of his hands.

- No complaints. Great manager.

- He's a good friend and supporter, but needs to improve on being an active manager. Hands-off managing is nice (and important) in our line of work, but we could benefit from a stronger feedback loop.

Chapter 4

Setting Meaningful and Effective Goals

Goal setting is a lever that helps you foster employee engagement in a number of ways; for example, it can

- Make your employees' jobs more challenging;
- Provide greater meaning to the work your employees do; and
- Energize your employees to perform at their best.

In general, research shows that you drive engagement when you take the time to set goals with your employees and establish development goals and plans that support their career success. We also found this to be true at XINC. Consider, as well, that when you set goals effectively with your employees, you empower them to act. How? By establishing clear performance expectations, creating challenging or stretch goals, and showing each of your employees how their goals are aligned with the overall direction of your organization and the company. Goal setting, in essence, lays the groundwork for participative management: "In order for participative management to succeed, employees must first know what they are attempting to achieve" (Rynes, Brown, & Colbert, 2002).

Goal setting and defining and establishing goals are the first steps in the overall performance management process.

Goal Setting

When you set goals, you establish a working contract between you, as a manager, and each of your employees. Goals define performance expectations: The clearer the goals, the clearer the expectations. Unfortunately, many managers spend less time on goal setting than they should. This often leads to one of the most common performance management problems you may encounter: a discrepancy between what you, as a manager, want and what your employees will deliver.

In this chapter we discuss the importance of goals, a goal-setting framework, where goals come from, types of goals, and a step-by-step goal-setting process you can use with your employees.

Why Are Goals Important?

Goals provide purpose, direction, alignment, and motivation.

- **Purpose**: Goals give reason to why each employee's job exists and what is fundamentally expected in each employee's role in the organization.
- **Direction**: In any job or role, there are many opportunities to pursue, but resources are always limited. Goals focus your employees on what you expect them to do and, consequently, on what they should not be doing. Goals help your employees maximize their time and energy, and help you to maximize the use of scarce company resources.
- **Alignment**: When clearly defined and consistent with the overall direction of the business, goals help ensure your employees' performance and results support the achievement of organization- and company-wide goals. Goal alignment is critical to overall organization success.
- **Motivation**: Your employees deliver higher levels of performance when their goals are challenging. Setting clear and challenging goals is one of the easiest ways for you to energize employee performance.

In addition, the ongoing pursuit of goals will always serve as the basis for communication (feedback) in the overall performance management process. Here's how:

- Goals drive performance, and as such, your feedback to your employees will largely focus on how, or the extent to which, your employees are achieving their goals.

- Formal or informal feedback processes (discussed more fully in Chapter 5) are designed to help your employees learn more about themselves in the context of achieving their goals and improving their overall performance.
- The expectations you create for employee development will be driven by an assessment of your employee's ability to achieve his or her goals and will focus your employee on acquiring the skills or knowledge needed to be successful.
- Informal performance reviews, as well as the end-of-period performance appraisal, will focus on evaluating goal achievement.

Again, goal setting is the first step in the performance management process, and goals can be considered the fundamental drivers of the process. But what is a goal?

A Goal-Setting Framework

Various authors define goals differently and offer any number of goal-setting frameworks (for example, see Kaplan & Norton, 1996). Our purpose here is to provide you with definitions and a framework that have, over the years, served our clients well.

A goal-setting framework is a way of looking at how goals are defined and organized. As an organizing structure, the framework guides your thinking about the goal-setting process and how to define all aspects of the performance you expect from your employees.

Some initial definitions to consider in our goal-setting framework are *goal*, *strategy*, and *tactics*.

Goal: The output or end result that you expect from an employee's effort. A goal helps answer the following kinds of questions:
  - "What are you trying to accomplish, fundamentally, with this effort?"
  - "What will change as a result of this effort?"
  - "What will be different?"

We tend to define or set goals at a high level. Goals may be increased customer satisfaction, maximization of profit, building a customer-focused culture, and creating a high-performing culture. Some of these are objective (a profit increase). Others are subjective and require agreed-to measures as evidence of results (e.g., customer satisfaction reflected in a customer survey, a customer-focused culture reflected in employee and customer surveys, and a high-performing culture reflected in operational indicators, such as product development time, cost reductions, and product or service quality improvement).

Strategy: Defines *how* a goal will be achieved. It is the manner in which your employee will approach a goal. Goals can have one or more strategies attached to them. The following examples correspond to the above goals:
- You can increase customer satisfaction by
  - Improving customer service response time
  - Developing product line variations
- You can maximize profit by
  - Developing a multitiered product-pricing strategy
  - Reducing the cost of sales
- You can build a customer-focused culture by
  - Training employees company-wide in customer relations skills
  - Redesigning the sales compensation program
- You can create a high-performing organization by
  - Implementing a new performance management process
  - Instituting a performance-based bonus plan

Tactics: The major steps supporting a strategy that will lead to achieving the goal. Tactics bring some definition to the strategy and reveal how your employee will go about implementing the strategy. Tactics fall between the broad strategies and the very detailed day-to-day activities necessary to achieve a goal. The following are examples of tactics:
- For the strategy "Improving customer service response time" you might find the following tactics useful:
  - Analyze current customer service effectiveness across all geographic regions.
  - Survey and interview customer service employees and management.
  - Survey and conduct focus groups with customers regarding overall service and service responsiveness.
  - Formulate recommendations, and plan for improving customer service response time.
  - Gain senior management approval for plan.
  - Implement plan.
  - Monitor plan effectiveness.
- For "Developing a multitiered product pricing strategy," you could
  - Establish a cross-departmental advisory committee.
  - Identify and determine appropriate product mix.
  - Formulate pricing models.
  - Pilot new strategy with select major- and middle-market customers.

- Evaluate and modify strategy.
- Implement strategy for all customers.
- Evaluate bottom-line impact.

Having read through these examples, we are quite sure that you are thinking of other ways you could act on the strategies. You might also have identified tactics you would consider important that are missing in the examples. We expect that. Identifying the key tactics is a way of looking at the significant steps that your employee will take to achieve the strategy and the goal. Essentially, the choice of specific tactics always depends on your employee's situation. We suggest, however, that you add monitoring and evaluative components to the list of tactics to help ensure and determine success. We highlight this fact because over the years, we have found that managers often leave these important components undefined, or to chance, and we think this is an error.

Activities: The next level of logical steps an employee would take to support a tactic, strategy, and goal. We normally don't recommend or see the need to specify the activities as part of the goal-setting process, but we always encourage you, the manager, as the situation warrants, to help your employees think through the activities necessary to achieve their goals. However, we do provide the following as an example of activities associated with tactics.

  – Below are some of the activities your employee may take to "Improve customer service response time," and these activities are primarily related to the tactic "Survey and interview customer service employees and management."

  - Arrange meetings with each customer service area director.
  - Discuss with the directors the best approach for collecting the data.
  - Contact each area's data analyst, and request historical response rate data for the past 6 months.
  - Develop a data analysis plan to analyze the data by region, as well as for the overall organization.

Measures of Success: The level of performance that describes the results you expect. Measures will help you to evaluate whether or not, or at least the extent to which, an employee achieves his or her goal. Goals may or may not have more than one associated measure. The measures of success bring further definition to the actual intent of the goal, just as the strategies further define how the goal will be achieved. As you can probably guess, the strategies, tactics, and activities should be designed to produce the expected measure(s) of success.

The following are examples of measures for two of the example goal statements discussed earlier:

- Measures of success for the goal "Maximization of profit" might include
  - Gross revenue increases 5–7%.
  - Overall manufacturing costs are reduced by 8.5%.
  - Cost of sales is reduced by 15%.
- Measures that might indicate "a high-performing culture" is in place may include
  - Employee productivity increases by 4.5%.
  - Employee morale improves (80% of employees indicate satisfaction with morale compared with 70% on the last employee opinion survey).
  - The new performance management process is implemented according to plan.

Goal Measurements: The processes or tools that you and your employee will use to provide the evidence or collect the data necessary to show whether or not success was achieved. Although not a difficult step, it is important that you and your employee determine how to collect the data; otherwise, your employee may have a set of mutually agreed-to goals, but neither of you will have a clear way of knowing if you can actually show evidence of his or her attainment.

For example, what would you use to measure employee morale? An easy answer is year-over-year changes in morale as measured by your company's employee opinion survey. Other measurements related to improvements in morale could be reductions in absenteeism and turnover. These two measurements may be viewed by some as less directly related to morale, but they may still be the best measurements—maybe the only measurements—available. What would you use to measure productivity? One possible measurement could be changes in the ratio of revenue in dollars to number of employees. And, if your employee was asked to reduce the cost of sales 15%, you could compare the direct cost of sales year over year, the measurement being the "percent reduction in the cost of sales."

In general, these are the primary components of the goal-setting framework that managers have found most helpful. You can choose to use this framework as it is or modify it to fit your particular business situation. There are three other, higher-level components to the framework that we will address in the following section: the company's mission and vision, its overarching goals, and your organization's mission and vision.

Where Do Goals Come From?

Three factors will help you determine the general direction for goal setting with your employees:

1. The company's overall mission and vision, as well as your department's mission and vision
2. "Overarching" company-wide goals
3. The employee's job description

The company's "mission" statement defines the fundamental purpose of the organization; it answers "why" the company exists. A "vision" statement is more aspirational in nature and answers the question "what" the company is striving to become, or to be seen as, at some point in the future, typically 3–5 years out. The examples below are typical of company mission and vision statements.

The first example is the mission and vision statement for a top-10 sales promotion and marketing firm in the United States; the second, for a major U.S. entertainment and communications company (Tables 4.1 and 4.2).

Although mission and vision statements almost universally exist at the company level, we have often found that managers have not created them for their own organizations. We believe that it is important for you, as a manager, to spend the time necessary to develop mission and vision statements with your team. These statements will provide guideposts for your goal setting. In essence,

Table 4.1   Example 1

Mission: Promotions, Inc., is a forward-thinking, full-service marketing communications agency dedicated to creating superior, results-oriented solutions that motivate actions consistent with client goals.
Vision: Promotions, Inc., will be recognized by marketing professionals as the premier full-service marketing agency in the United States.

Table 4.2   Example 2

Mission: At Media, Inc., we will utilize our unique resources—our broadband telecommunications network, our new and comprehensive suite of digital services, our live and televised entertainment properties, and our retail presence—to offer customers superior choice and unparalleled value in entertainment and communications.
Vision: Media, Inc., will be the premier full-service, customer-focused entertainment and communications company in the world's #1 market.

the goals that you set for your employees should be consistent with your organization's mission and vision. Your mission and vision will serve as your immediate overarching framework.

The company-wide mission and vision will serve as a higher level, overarching framework for your own organization. Your mission and vision, as well as your employees' goals, should comfortably fall within this larger framework; they should also fall within the framework of what we call *company-wide overarching goals*. These are typically broad goals set by the company's leadership that drive goal setting throughout the organization.

Overarching goals, such as "Grow profits" or "Maximize shareholder value," serve to be both guiding and provocative. Overarching goals basically provide you with direction, but they also challenge you to ensure that your mission, vision, and employees' goals are in alignment with the expectations set by the company's leadership. In this context, you should be asking yourself at least two questions when goal setting. First, "How can we support the company overall?" and second, "How will our specific goals contribute to the achievement of the company's overarching goals?"

Job descriptions may be another source of goals. Most good job descriptions identify broad areas of responsibility; some will also include more specific areas of accountability, as well expected programs or initiatives that may need to be designed, developed, or implemented. In principle, your employees' goals, strategies, and tactics should directly relate to their job descriptions. Said another way, a job description provides a framework for goal setting. As a result, don't overlook an employee's job description when it comes time to setting goals. Using the job description can not only help you identify relevant goal areas but also help you to customize an employee's goals that are driven by the broader mission, vision, and overarching goals.

Putting the Elements Together

In summary, the following are the components of our recommended goal-setting framework:

1. The company's mission and vision
2. The company's overarching goals
3. Your organization's mission and vision
4. Your employees' goals
5. The strategies that describe how those goals will be achieved

6. The tactics that will be used to execute the strategies
7. The day-to-day activities that support the tactics
8. Measures of success for each goal
9. Goal measurements for each measure of success

You may want to consider one additional step when setting goals. We encourage managers to develop a weighting of importance for each goal. Weighting goals serves to clarify which goals deserve the most attention throughout the performance year, and helps your employees focus on what is most important. Weighting also helps in the evaluation of performance. Simply stated, if one of your employees had two goals, one weighted at 65% and the other at 35% (adding, of course, to a total of 100%), the performance delivered against the goal weighted 65% would account for, or "weigh" more heavily in, the evaluation of overall performance.

Table 4.3 shows a sample page from one of our client's performance appraisal forms. As you can see, this part of the form asks you to identify targets or goals, and for each goal to provide the results achieved, a rating, a weighting, and a score. Managers are then asked to compute an overall score for all goals, and to translate that score to a 5-point rating scale. Just to be clear, the only part of the form that managers use during goal setting are the "target/goal" and "weighting" sections. The other parts, of course, will be completed at the end of the appraisal period.

Types of Goals

Recently there has been discussion about distinguishing performance goals from learning goals (Seijts and Latham, 2005; Seijts, Latham, Tasa, & Latham, 2004), with the difference in goals being described as one of mind-set—a focus on either ability or motivation. The authors suggest that setting high or challenging performance goals is effective only when employees already have the ability to perform the task. If they do not have the ability, then a learning goal should be set to acquire the necessary knowledge and skills. The implication is either one type of goal or another. However, we believe that a challenging performance goal can be set *along with* the necessary development goal to ensure effective levels of performance.

The framework we suggest proposes both performance and development goals, and we believe the two work hand in hand. Of course, if one of your employees was not skilled enough to come close to achieving a very ambitious

Table 4.3   Results Evaluation

Instructions: Evaluate year-end performance for stated targets or goals. Rate each target or goal (on a 1–5 scale), and multiply it by its percent weighting to determine each target or goal score. Provide a total score by adding all individual target or goal scores. Also, provide an Overall Results Evaluation Rating at the bottom of the page.

Statement of Target or Goal	Results	(a) Rating	(b) Weighting	(a) × (b) Score

Add all the numbers in the (a) × (b) column to get the Total Score:

Overall Results Evaluation Rating:	1.0–1.9	2.0–2.7	2.8–3.6	3.7–4.5	4.6–5.0
	1	2	3	4	5
	Did not achieve expected performance	Partially achieved expected performance	Achieved expected performance	Exceeded expected performance	Far exceeded expected performance

The signatures below indicate that the appraiser and the employee have discussed the above targets or goals and expected results at the beginning of the performance year.

Appraiser's Signature and Date: _____

Employee's Signature and Date: _____

performance goal, we hope you would not set one! This is where development goals enter, and this is our primary rationale for setting development goals, as you will see below—to enable improved and higher levels of performance.

In general, performance goals can be set for any level of the organization as more or less overarching goals. Therefore, goals can be set at the overall corporation level, the business unit level, the department level, and the like. Here, we focus on individual performance and development goals. We also discuss team goals.

Individual Performance Goals

Individual performance goals are task focused and give your employees control over, and accountability for, achieving them. If aligned appropriately with the company's and your organization's mission, vision, and goals, these goals will contribute to higher level, business-related outcomes or results, for example, increases in customer satisfaction, revenue, operational efficiency, sales, and so on. So it is typically fair to ask Sally, your business unit's financial analyst, to examine and certify the financials in the unit's overall business plan, but you cannot hold Sally responsible for the achievement of the financials in the business plan. Similarly, you can ask your marketing analyst, Bill, to develop a marketing plan for a new product and expect a sound plan as an outcome, but you cannot hold Bill accountable for achieving the planned sales goals for the new product.

Individual Development Goals

What are individual development goals? These are goals you set jointly with an employee to help him or her improve performance in the current job or acquire the skills or knowledge necessary to prepare for future jobs. Development goals, when tied to the current job, should help your employee enhance the skills or knowledge needed to achieve current performance goals. When related to a future job, development goals should be tied to qualifying your employee as a candidate for, or ensuring effective performance in, a designated future job.

Some examples may help. You might set a development goal for Sally, our financial analyst, to help her improve her performance in her current job. This goal might center on improving her understanding of return on investment (ROI) principles and strategies. Typically, you would then expect Sally's analyses to reflect a better understanding of ROI than evidenced before in her work.

Now let's take Bill. Bill wants to work in the finance department in a role similar to Sally's. Because Bill has previous operations experience and several years of experience in marketing, a future-focused development goal for Bill might center on acquiring more financial knowledge by taking a certificate program in finance through a local university. You might measure Bill's success by how well he does in the program, through a direct evaluation of what he has learned, or by his competitiveness for the financial analyst position.

We hope our message is clear: that given the limited resources of time and money, development goals should be set purposefully and evaluated in the context of improved current job performance or in preparation for future jobs. We have come across too many managers who thought a development goal involved nothing more than "attending a communications workshop sometime in the third quarter" and "checking off" on the appraisal form whether or not this actually happened. So we offer the following as an example of a development goal for Sally:

- *Development goal*: "Improved understanding of ROI."
- *Strategy*: "Enroll in a seminar on ROI analysis."
- *Tactics*: "Identify and register for program," and "Attend all classes and complete all assignments."
- *Goal measure*: "Demonstrated improvement in business plan ROI analyses."
- *Goal measurement*: "Business unit manager feedback on business plan ROI analyses."

Team Goals

When you set team goals, you are setting performance goals for a group of employees, either within your organization or across different organizations. Team goals help to foster employee engagement and can be set for any number of reasons. One reason might be to focus on a goal that could only be achieved through teamwork, that is, the combined efforts of one or more of your employees. For example, improvements in customer satisfaction may be critical to the customer service department, which let's presume for the moment that you lead. Although each customer service manager in your department will probably have his or her own customer satisfaction goals, your team-level goal helps both to ensure greater focus and attention on the need to improve customer satisfaction and to promote and encourage the level of cooperation needed among your customer service managers to achieve this goal. On the other hand, still in your role as the leader of the customer service department, you might be charged with the effort and need to set a team goal around the successful launch of a new product, involving employees from manufacturing, sales, marketing, finance, and other departments. Although each employee and each department may contribute uniquely, setting a team goal elevates the focus of attention to above and beyond mere individual and departmental contributions and interests.

If you decide to utilize team goals, just be sure that all employees on the team understand their specific responsibilities, as well as how each of them contributes to the successful achievement of the team goal.

Goal-Setting Process

You might ask, "Do I need to set goals jointly with my employees, or can I just assign goals to them?" When you set goals jointly with your employees, research shows that the goals you set tend to be more difficult than if you merely assign goals, and these more difficult goals lead to higher job performance (London, Mone, & Scott, 2004). Why? When you engage in joint goal-setting discussions, you promote an information exchange, for example about strategies to achieve the goals, and these discussions tend to increase your employee's self-confidence in his or her ability to achieve the more difficult goals and meet higher performance expectations.

In this section, we discuss a process for setting performance and development goals jointly with your employees—and let us remind you that setting goals jointly with your employees is important to driving employee engagement. Although we present this process in a logical sequence, the day-to-day realities of organization life may not always allow you the luxury of all of these steps in the sequence we suggest. The process we are recommending is based on our experience working with leadership and management teams in setting direction and goals for their organizations. The steps in the process are as follows:

1. Tell your employees that you are starting the goal-setting process for the upcoming performance year, and indicate the time frame in which you want to have the goal-setting process completed. Outline the process for them.
2. In preparation, advise your employees to do the following to create a context for current goal setting:
   A. Reread the mission and vision for the company.
   B. Reread your organization's mission and vision.
   C. Review their job descriptions.
   D. Review their current goals, strategies, and tactics.
3. As the manager, you should identify any new overarching goals, and develop a working draft of team goals for your department, if necessary.
4. Share the overarching goals and team goals, if any, with your employees. Also share any other strategic messages that may be important for your employees to consider.

5. Using the above information, ask your employees to develop drafts of their performance goals, strategies, tactics, and development goals.
6. Meet with each employee to review and discuss his or her goals, strategies, and tactics. During this meeting you will want to ensure that the employee's performance goals are aligned with the overall direction of the company and your department, challenging and meaningful, and realistic. Ensure that the employee's development goals will help him or her to improve performance in the current job or to acquire the skills or knowledge necessary to prepare for future jobs.
7. Once the goals, strategies, and tactics have been finalized, ask each of your employees to develop the measures of success and measurements.
8. Meet with each of your employees to review the proposed measures and measurements. Discuss and finalize the measures and measurements.
9. Review your employees' goals, strategies, and so on with your supervisor, as necessary.
10. Communicate and discuss any changes with your employees, and revise as necessary.
11. You and each of your employees "sign off" on the agreed-to goals, strategies, and so on, and each of you should keep a copy for your files.

Driving Motivation to Achieve Goals

Victor Vroom's (1964) classic expectancy theory still provides a useful way for understanding how your employees will approach goal achievement. According to the theory, three distinct questions will be raised and answered by your employees to determine their overall level of motivation to perform:

1. If I put in the effort, will I achieve the goal? (Expectancy)
2. If I achieve the goal, will I get the reward I am after? (Instrumentality)
3. How important or valuable is the reward? (Valence)

The idea, as indicated in Table 4.4, is that your employees consider the probability of achieving their goals by taking each of these components into account. The theory suggests that motivation is a multiplicative function of all three, and the probability of expectancy, instrumentality, and valence can range from zero to one. You can see immediately that if any of the three components has a probability of zero, there will be no motivation to perform.

Table 4.4   Expectancy Theory and Employee Motivation

Employee Motivation =	*Expectancy × Instrumentality × Valence*		
	Perceived probability that effort will lead to goal achievement	Perceived probability that goal achievement will lead to the desired reward	Perceived value of the reward

So, what can you do as a manager to capitalize on what expectancy theory has to offer and to enhance the motivation of your employees? Table 4.5 describes some actions and strategies that you can use to increase expectancy, instrumentality, and valence.

Table 4.5   Strategies for Increasing Employee Motivation

When It Comes to Increasing **Expectancy**	*When It Comes to Increasing* **Instrumentality**	*When It Comes to Increasing* **Valence**
• Be sure your employees have or can acquire the skills necessary to do their jobs and achieve their goals.	• Act in ways that demonstrate your trustworthiness, helping your employees to believe they will get the rewards desired.	• Help reinforce the value of the rewards by showing your employees how the rewards are consistent with their:
• Provide the necessary resources.		*– Preferences*
• Reassure your employees—tell them you have faith in their ability to achieve their goals.	• Clarify how pay policies and plans work.	*– Needs* *– Values* *– Goals*
• Do not set goals that are too difficult to achieve.	• Help employees see the connection between goal achievement and rewards.	
• Make it clear that your employees can control the extent to which they achieve their goals and, therefore, that they can effect the expected outcome.	• Don't make promises you can't keep.	

The Goal-Setting and Performance Evaluation Conundrum

The conundrum or challenge facing all managers when setting goals is deciding on the level of performance that defines the achievement of the goal. In our model, this level of performance is the measure of success. But what is the challenge? We believe that there is a difference between setting goals for motivation and setting goals for performance evaluation. The goals you set should be motivating. Earlier in this chapter, we indicated the importance of setting challenging or "stretch" goals. The most common definition of *challenge* or *stretch* refers to a goal that has between a 50% and 75% chance of being attained. Obviously, when there is little expectation of achieving a goal—say, a 10% chance—the odds are certainly against your employee, and there will be little motivation to try to achieve it. When the goal can be easily attained—say, a 90% chance—then the goal is not very motivating. Although achievable, higher levels of expected performance would have been preferred.

With some discussion, you and your employee can certainly come to an understanding of what makes for a challenging goal. The difficult part is when it is time to evaluate performance. The following presents the conundrum: If the goal is challenging, and your employee does not meet it, is he or she evaluated as not meeting performance expectations? In other words, say that you expect one of your employees to increase sales revenue by 25% this year, but all forecasts are for a down market. What if your employee increased sales by 10% and beat all industry averages? How would you evaluate him or her? As a failure? As a success? We would argue that your employee was successful. A 25% increase in sales revenue was certainly a very challenging goal, and given market conditions, a 10% increase appears to indicate stellar performance.

How do you resolve the conundrum? First, you should be clear when you are setting goals about the degree of stretch involved, as well as how the goals will be evaluated. When setting the measures of success, both you and your employee should clearly know whether achieving those measures equates to falling below, meeting, or exceeding expectations. So, in the example above, you and your employee might have agreed that anything close to a 25% increase in sales is really exceeding or far exceeding expectations. You might have also agreed that meeting expectations was exceeding the industry average.

Second, at the time of your employees' performance evaluation, you should consider important environmental factors (e.g., substantial changes in your own company and organization, the industry, the general business climate, the national or world economy, etc.). Again, the level of the expected performance may be hampered significantly by conditions outside the control of your employees. We are not suggesting that any change in the environment drives an adjustment in the level of performance expectation, but what we are suggesting is that you judiciously consider these changes for their possible impact.

Consider what Seijts and Latham (2005) have said on the subject, as well:

> The assignment of ambitious goals without any guidance on ways to attain them often leads to stress, pressures on personal time, burnout, and [in] some instances, unethical behavior. It is both foolish and immoral for organizations to assign "stretch goals" and then fail to give employees the means to succeed, yet punish them when they fail to attain the goals. (p. 124)

In conclusion, if you are clear with your employees about how expected levels of goal attainment impact the evaluation of their performance, if you provide them with the means to achieve their goals, and if you take environmental factors into consideration, you will be in the best position possible to fairly and objective evaluate your employees' performance.

Conclusion

Effective goal setting leads to more challenging and meaningful work, and a greater sense of empowerment. Goals establish a working contract between you and your employees—and between you and your manager. They establish expectations, create motivation, and drive employee engagement. Your employees' goals should reflect the purpose of your organization and your employees' jobs and should be aligned with the overall goals of your department and company. Begin formulating your own goals by reviewing the overall mission and vision of the company and how that relates to the specific functions of your organization. Then, working with your manager, outline performance expectations for yourself (hopefully your manager has read this book, too). Engage in the joint goal-setting process with your employees. Set goals for individual performance, individual development, and team performance. For each goal, be specific by articulating strategies, tactics for accomplishing the strategies, activities for each tactic, measures of success, and measurements.

The goal-setting process should be conducted at least annually. You may want to revisit your employees' goals periodically, say every 6 months, because conditions change. Sometimes the goals may remain fairly stable, but you and your employees might need to change the strategies, tactics, or activities depending on the situation. That means you need to monitor your employees' performance and provide your employees with frequent feedback. Feedback, then, becomes a central, continuous ingredient in the performance management process. However, as we said in the first chapter, giving feedback is a part of the performance management process that managers tend to avoid, and receiving feedback, let alone actually seeking it, is a part of the process the employees tend to avoid. We turn to the topic of feedback in the next chapter.

Chapter 5

Meeting the Feedback Challenge

From the perspective of employee engagement, your feedback is a form of communication that can help your employees understand how their work contributes to the success of their teams, your organization, and the company. Your feedback also promotes employee engagement when you use it to direct and improve employee performance. And when you deliver positive feedback, it is seen as recognition. In fact, at XINC we found that helping employees understand how their work supports the company's efforts and providing ongoing performance feedback and recognition were positively related to employee engagement.

Feedback, then, is a critical part of the performance management process. It can be informal, as it may take place almost anytime, for instance, after an important event or simply in passing conversation. It can be formal, for example, when you write a year-end performance appraisal and have an appraisal feedback discussion with one of your employees. Your feedback may also be a part of an informal appraisal, which we recommended (in Chapter 2) you should conduct at least quarterly. And, as you will learn in Chapters 7 and 8, 360-degree feedback and coaching can also be instrumental components of this phase of the performance management process. However, if you tend to shy away from your responsibility and avoid giving feedback directly, your employees will be left with only your indirect feedback, that is, how you treat them, the assignments you give them, and the like—but the problem is that they may or may not interpret these signals correctly.

The challenge for you is to provide feedback in a way that engages your employees and motivates them to improve their performance. In some cases, the challenge is recognizing burnout in one of your employees and providing feedback that renews his or her energy rather than exacerbating what your employee perceives as overwork and lack of opportunity. (In Chapter 10, we discuss how you can help prevent and alleviate employee burnout, as well as how to help your employees become reengaged.)

In this chapter, we focus on helping you understand the importance, value, and nature of feedback as a crucial component of the performance management process and a driver of employee engagement. We show you how to improve your ability to deliver effective feedback and how to handle the more difficult feedback conversations.

Assessing Yourself

Before going further, spend a few moments on the following self-assessment. Because no one but you will see this assessment, feel free to write in your responses. If you think the statement is true, write a *T*; if you think the statement is false, write an *F*. If you are undecided, write a *U*.

1. Giving feedback to employees is an important part of my job.
2. I believe feedback can change an employee's behavior for the better.
3. I will not lose my employee's loyalty if I give negative feedback.
4. Giving feedback to employees is a valuable use of my time.
5. I will not lose my employee's friendship if I give negative feedback.
6. I know how to give feedback effectively.
7. I feel comfortable giving positive feedback.
8. I feel comfortable giving negative feedback.
9. I plan sufficient time in the day to give employees feedback.
10. I am always trying to improve my ability to give effective feedback.

Statements 1 through 5 reflect your personal beliefs about the value of feedback. If you don't believe that feedback is worthwhile, we hope you will change your mind by the time you finish reading this chapter. Statements 6 through 10 are skills based, and your responses depend on your experiences and training in giving feedback.

Why Give Feedback?

Giving feedback benefits both you and your employees. For example, consider the following benefits (adapted from London's [1995] summary of research). Your feedback

- Helps you direct an employee's behavior, keeping it focused on achieving what is important to the work group.
- When positive, lets your employees know they are appreciated, as well as where they stand—both of which can increase their motivation to do better next time and support engagement.
- Helps your employees monitor and improve their performance as they learn to keep in mind what you feel is important and the standards of excellence you expect.
- Influences future performance as it suggests how much and where your employees need to improve.
- Helps target what your employees need to learn or just do differently in order to improve their performance.
- Helps your employees realize that they can be even more successful than before as they learn about what needs improvement.
- May help your employees know what levels of performance lead to promotions or pay increases.
- Helps your employees to take control of their own performance.
- Increases your employees' feelings of engagement when they see how they contribute to your department's goals and their efforts are in alignment with larger organizational goals.

Overall, your feedback is important to managing performance because it helps in a number of ways. It affects the direction of your employees' behavior, clarifies what actions lead to rewards, outlines a path for promotional opportunities, increases your employees' self-awareness and their ability to monitor their own performance, and encourages your employees to evaluate themselves and take responsibility to change their own behavior.

What to Consider When Giving Feedback

Before giving feedback, think about how the following factors can influence the value of your feedback (adapted from Kluger & DeNisi, 1996):

- The amount of information your employees need to understand and process the feedback and think about themselves from others' perspectives.
- Your employees' sensitivity and willingness to listen to the feedback, because this will affect their ability to hear the feedback and to learn.
- What is happening in your organization, that is, the context of the situation. For example, your employees will respond to feedback more favorably when their jobs are secure and there is no threat of a layoff.
- How you will measure or know if your feedback was acted upon or resulted in an improvement in performance. Without some type of an accountability mechanism in place, your feedback may have less impact.
- The support you can provide and the resources available to your employees for acting on the feedback, including coaching, role modeling, counseling, training, and challenging assignments.

Tips for Giving Effective Feedback

To make the information you provide more effective and productive, you may want to incorporate the following tips when preparing to give feedback:

- Your feedback should be clear, easily understood, and palatable; don't complicate the message.
- Your feedback should focus on how well your employee performed and *what* he or she did to bring about the outcome. The *what* concentrates on behaviors that can be changed to enhance future performance.
- Don't provide too much information. Too much feedback at once can cause your employees to misunderstand or ignore your feedback.
- Your feedback should be frequent—a regular occurrence—and should be provided as a normal part of how you run your business.
- Give your feedback sooner rather than later—when the issue is fresh in your mind and your employee's mind.
- Take into consideration all the factors that affected performance, including factors that were both beyond and within your employee's control.
- Focus your feedback on the elements of performance that contribute to your employee's success and that are under his or her control. Focusing on factors that are beyond your employee's control can be demoralizing and frustrating.
- If you are providing feedback based on hearsay (someone else's direct observation), be sure the source is credible.
- Be ready to go beyond just the facts as providing feedback usually requires your explanation, patience, and encouragement. Furthermore, don't assume that your employee will know how to use the feedback to improve performance.

Finally, realize as well that the most important person in the feedback interaction is your employee, the person receiving the feedback, not you, the manager giving it. Although this may come as a surprise, it is more important that the feedback be "heard" rather than "told." In other words, the emotional and psychological needs of your employee, the person receiving the feedback, are more important than those of the person—you—giving it. In practical terms, this means that you should

- Not give feedback based solely on when it is most convenient for you to do so;
- Share your feedback when your employee is most likely to be receptive to it; and
- Only give feedback when you can be available for follow-up questions or further discussions after the feedback session.

What Is Constructive and Destructive Feedback?

The terms constructive and destructive have been applied to feedback for some time. Actually, the terms constructive and destructive apply to the way in which you package and deliver the feedback. *Constructive* feedback is easy to understand, fair, honest, and not threatening. It recognizes factors beyond your employee's control and highlights specific actions that your employee can do something about. Constructive feedback does not make your employee feel bad (ashamed, despondent, or otherwise unhappy) or attack your employee personally (e.g., "You're lazy"). It shows what could be done to change performance outcomes (e.g., "Here's what you could do differently next time"). *Destructive* feedback makes your employee feel threatened or attacked personally. It causes your employee to defend his or her actions or attribute blame to external factors ("It wasn't my fault"), or it causes your employee to psychologically withdraw, ignoring your feedback altogether.

When in the actual situation of giving feedback to your employee, you may want to practice and remember the following strategies:

- Conduct the feedback meeting in a private setting—respect your employee's privacy and need to maintain his or her self-esteem.
- Don't try to give feedback if your employee already appears frustrated, angry, or tired—these feelings won't be conducive to processing your feedback effectively.
- Be sure to allow ample time for discussion—it is hard to predict an employee's exact reaction and how much time he or she needs from you to process your feedback effectively.

- Encourage introspection and self-evaluation—particularly to support learning and to overcome defensive reactions.
- Initially be descriptive rather than evaluative—describe what happened clearly so you and your employee know exactly what is being evaluated.
- Try to present factual information instead of opinions—especially when your feedback is about performance improvement versus recognition.
- Show that you have collected adequate information—again, this helps to deal with possible resistance and, in general, just shows that you have the full story.
- Focus on behavior, not your employee's personality—you are not going to change an employee's personality, but you can help him or her to learn new behaviors or reinforce positive ones.
- Encourage input from your employee—be sure you get his or her point of view, as providing feedback is not a one-way street and your employee has a valid perspective that can add insight to the situation, whether or not it is a positive or negative situation.
- Review the consequences of improving if the feedback is about weaknesses versus strengths—which can serve to help motivate your employee to change and take action.
- Demonstrate your genuine interest in, and concern for, your employee—this is accomplished both by what you say, as well as how you say it and your behavior overall; don't deliver feedback when you don't have the time and energy to be constructive in your approach.
- Summarize what was discussed and check for understanding—you want to be sure that your message was heard, the implications are clear, and you are in agreement about any possible actions.

Your Employees' Receptivity to Feedback

Think about what can happen when you give an employee feedback. Your employee is likely to try to determine whether your feedback is valid and, particularly if it is perceived as "bad," whether he or she can attribute the problem to factors beyond his or her control. For instance, if your feedback is perceived as unfavorable, your employee might say, "There was nothing I could do about it," or "My people are unhappy with me because there were no pay raises last year."

There are two main reasons why some employees are more receptive to receiving feedback than others. The first is the extent to which an employee tends to monitor his or her own behavior and performance. The second depends on the employee's self esteem. An employee who is good at self-monitoring and high in self-esteem will be more receptive to your feedback. How can you determine an employee's receptivity?

Being Good at Self-Monitoring

The following describes employees who are considered effective self-monitors. The more these characteristics describe your employees, the more receptive they will be to receiving your feedback. Good self-monitors are

- Attuned to what you, the job, and the company expect of them—they are clear about their goals and alignment to overall objectives;
- Likely to change their behavior to meet your demands or the demands of the work group;
- Sensitive to work group norms and the different roles that people have in the work group;
- Likely to compare themselves to others;
- Very sensitive to feedback—your feedback will never be ignored; and
- Attentive to your motivation and ability to deliver feedback.

In contrast, employees who are low in self-monitoring don't change their behavior from one situation to another (Caldwell & O'Reilly, 1982). See Table 5.1 for a short list of descriptive statements that may provide additional insight and help you to determine the extent to which your employees are self-monitors.

Table 5.1   Self-Monitoring Views

If Low in Self-Monitoring, Employees Tend to Agree With the Following	If High in Self-Monitoring, Employees Tend to Agree With the Following:
• I find it hard to imitate the behavior of other people. • In a group of people, I am rarely the center of attention. • I am particularly good at making other people like me.	• I can make impromptu speeches even on topics about which I have almost no information. • I guess I put on a show to impress or entertain others. • In different situations and with different people, I often act like very different persons. • I may deceive people by being friendly when I really dislike them.

Source: Based on Snyder (1974; reprinted in London, 2003, p. 41).

Being High or Low in Self-Esteem

The following will help you distinguish employees in your organization with high self-esteem from those with low self-esteem. The higher an employee's self-esteem, the more receptive he or she will be to your feedback.

Employees with high self-esteem are

- Readily able to adapt to changing situations;
- Likely to feel good about themselves;
- Resilient when trouble occurs, bouncing back from setbacks quickly and positively;
- Self-confident;
- Likely to see themselves as effective and capable of handling challenges and overcoming barriers; and
- Confident in their ability to make good things happen.

Furthermore, employees who are high in self-esteem are likely to believe the following (based on Fedor, Rensvold, & Adams, 1992):

- I'm a person of worth, at least on an equal basis with others.
- I have a number of good qualities.
- I am able to do things as well as most other people.
- I take a positive attitude toward myself.
- On the whole, I am satisfied with myself.

On the other hand, employees with low self-esteem are more likely to

- Be down on themselves;
- React emotionally to feedback they perceive as unfavorable; and/or
- Feel overwhelmed by setbacks and barriers to accomplishing their goals.

And in contrast to the way those with high self-esteem think about themselves, employees low in self-esteem are likely to believe the following:

- I am inclined to feel that I am a failure.
- I do not have much to be proud of.
- I wish I could have more respect for myself.
- I certainly feel useless at times.
- At times, I think I am no good at all.

In addition to using the above descriptors to help you better understand the level of self-esteem an employee may hold, see Appendix 5.1 at the end of this chapter for a short, researched-based assessment that can be used to determine levels of self-esteem. You can copy the assessment, and ask your employees to complete it and, if comfortable, to discuss their results with you. You may also use the assessment yourself to more formally, based on what you know and have learned about your employees, estimate your employees' levels of self-esteem. Of course, this may be hard for you to do, but it could not only provide you some insight about your employees' receptivity to feedback but also alert you to other possible concerns that you may want to raise in coaching sessions with your employees.

And What About You?

Because asking for feedback is not always easy, we offer you this short self-assessment to help you determine your own comfort in seeking feedback from your manager. To what extent would you agree with the following statements?

1. If I asked my manager how I was doing, he or she would become more critical of me.
2. I would look incompetent if I asked my manager for feedback.
3. I tend to get embarrassed when asking my manager for feedback.
4. It takes too much effort to get my manager to give me feedback.
5. My manager would think worse of me if I asked for feedback.

Typically, if you agree with one or more of the above five statements, you are just reluctant, if not somewhat resistant, to approaching your manager for feedback. In essence, these are excuses for not asking for feedback. Do some introspection and ask yourself what it will take for you to ask for feedback. Then make it happen.

Giving Feedback: A Case Study

A manager, Fred, wanted to conduct an exit interview with an employee, Sally, who was leaving the organization. Fred knew that Sally's last day was the following Thursday, but because he was going to be on vacation that week, he chose to conduct the interview on the Friday morning before he left.

During the interview Fred heard some disconcerting things about Sally's supervisor, Mike. Sally was highly critical of Mike, and this was surprising to Fred. In essence, Sally told Fred that she could no longer work for Mike and that Mike was the primary reason for her leaving.

This left Fred with a dilemma. Should he take some action? What should he say to Mike? Fred decided to meet with Mike, and he arranged for this meeting later in the day (Friday afternoon). Fred's attitude was that "where there is smoke, there must be fire." In other words, Fred took Sally's word that there must be a problem with Mike's performance. Mike was totally shocked. Mike tried to be open and to listen to the feedback, but the events that were being recounted were quite distorted. In fact, some were just "unbelievable." Again, because Fred was implying wrongdoing on the part of Mike, the session left Mike shocked and depressed. And, because this feedback session was held at the end of the day, Fred soon left to prepare for his early morning departure and start his vacation.

During the subsequent days, while Fred was away, Mike started to sort out some of the feedback, and actually put a plan in place to get more feedback from others in the work group. Mike wanted to really understand what was happening and truly wanted to get to the bottom of the situation. After a good deal of self-reflection, Mike had a flurry of personal insights about the situation. With these insights, along with the feedback from others in the work group, Mike was sure that Fred would now see the situation differently. As the facts unfolded, Mike realized that most, if not all, of Sally's remarks about him were severe distortions of the truth; some were outright lies. This was a relief to Mike, and he felt vindicated.

Because Fred was still on vacation, however, none of what Mike learned could be shared with him. This was troubling, as Mike was growing tense about the overall situation and its potential implications, and wanted to have, as soon as possible, the chance to "correct" Fred's perception. Mike had a reasonably good reputation and did not, for one more minute, want it to be tarnished. However, Mike was left to wait in frustration.

Now, if you were Fred, what would you have done?

Giving Performance Feedback: A Sample Discussion

The following is an example of a feedback session. It is a relatively short discussion between a manager and an employee. The focus of the feedback is the employee's behavior, which the manager had just witnessed in a meeting with the employee and one of their internal customers.

Manager (Sam): Ann, I want to talk with you about what went on in that meeting. Do you have some time now?

Employee (Ann): I am free for the next half hour, but I'm not sure what you want to talk about.

Sam: Well, Ann, I want to understand a little bit better some of your behavior toward Pat (the internal customer) and give you some feedback. I am not sure that was the best way to handle the situation.

Ann: OK, but I'm not sure I know what you're referring to, so can you tell me what the problem is?

Sam: Well, first I wanted to ask you what you thought about the meeting.

Ann: It seemed like a typical meeting, and as usual Pat pushed us for specifics on the project timelines. Pat can be annoying with his desire for details. But I think the meeting went well.

Sam: It seems like we might have the same thing on our minds. I think the meeting went well too, but how do you think you handled Pat's request for the project timeline that would detail the key activities over the next 2 months?

Ann: I agreed to give it to Pat, didn't I?

Sam: Well that's true. Do you have any thoughts about how you acted toward Pat at that time?

Ann: I don't think I did anything wrong. What's on your mind?

Sam: Well, when Pat requested the timeline, you tried to convince him that the overall project goals and milestone dates were good enough for tracking the project. Pat acknowledged your comment, but said that because this project is under the close scrutiny of his senior management, he needed more detail. Do you remember that?

Ann: Yes, I remember that.

Sam: Do you remember what you did next?

Ann: Ahhh! I think I know what might be your concern.

Sam: And?

Ann: Yes, I then said, "Pat, that's your problem, not mine."

Sam: And why might that be an issue?

Ann: Well, Pat is our customer, and Pat's request, although making more work for me, is really pretty reasonable given the situation.

Sam: I think you're right. That remark was really not that appropriate. I don't think Pat deserved it. What do you think?

Ann: I agree. I guess I just let my frustration come through. I'm really very busy now, and I didn't want to spend any more time on doing another timeline.

Sam: I think you've got it. Why don't we set up some time for more discussion about this? I think perhaps a little coaching on how to help you better handle your reactions and working through some alternative approaches might be useful. We can develop some strategies for you to use with all of our customers. What do you think?

Ann: Thanks, Sam. That sounds like a good idea. I know my review is coming up soon, and perhaps we can strategize then.

Sam: Fair enough.

This example was not meant to be textbook perfect, but our manager, Sam, did do a number of right things.

1. Sam did not assume Ann had time to talk at that moment.
2. Sam stated clearly what he wanted to discuss.
3. To make the learning more effective, Sam used a style of getting Ann involved, asking for input. This helped Sam to understand how aware Ann may be of her behavior.
4. Sam affirmed Ann's perception that the meeting went well overall.
5. Sam kept the focus on behavior, or in this instance on what Ann said. Sam did not try to label the behavior, for example by saying Ann was insensitive.
6. Sam also asked Ann to evaluate the impact of the behavior, rather than trying to tell Ann its consequences. Remember, Sam asked, "And why might that be an issue?"
7. Sam also offered to help Ann with some follow-up coaching, and checked her receptivity to it.

Although many authors offer extensive detail on how to structure a feedback conversation, we are more concerned that as a manager, you demonstrate your sincerity, your caring, and, if the situation warrants it, your willingness to help your employee further develop. Given that, a structure that we often recommend is similar to the one used in the sample discussion above:

- Ask for permission, and assess the readiness of your employee to receive feedback.
- State the purpose of the feedback and the specific situation that you want to discuss.
- Begin by asking your employee for reactions and comments about the situation.
- Continue in discussion until the behavior in question is clear to both you and your employee.
- Ask your employee to examine why the behavior occurred, and discuss as necessary.
- Ask your employee to assess the impact of the behavior.
- Help your employee, as necessary, to put the impact into perspective.
- Ask your employee if the situation could have been handled differently, and if so, ask for examples of "how."
- Offer to help your employee further develop the skills necessary to be effective in similar situations.

Feedback for Reinforcement

The previous example and our discussion of feedback so far have focused on feedback for performance improvement. Again, this is usually the most difficult to deliver, which is why we devoted a significant portion of our attention to it.

There is, however, feedback that you may want to give to an employee with the intent of positively reinforcing a particular action or behavior; providing this kind of feedback or recognition, in fact, will foster engagement. Although you may be surprised, there are ways to make this kind of feedback more effective, even if you usually find it easier to give this kind of feedback than feedback focused on performance improvement.

We have two major points to make. First, most of what we have said so far about feedback, if not all of it, pertains to giving and receiving feedback for reinforcement. Second, be specific. Managers, generally speaking, don't make clear what they are trying to recognize. Employees usually only hear phrases, such as "Nice job," "Good work," or "Strong presentation." So, if you delivered a 30-minute presentation to a group of customers and your manager just said, "Well done," what conclusions would you draw? Did she like absolutely everything? Was it the way you handled questions? Was it the actual flow of the presentation? Was it your sense of humor? In reality, she might have liked everything, she might have liked something, or maybe she was just being nice!

The following simple example should illustrate the point. Remember, you need to be specific if you want your feedback to effectively promote and encourage similar behaviors or actions in the future.

In the scenario below, Carol is Tom's manager, and she just watched Tom deliver a presentation to a room full of customers.

Carol: Tom, do you have a minute?
Tom: Yes, I do.
Carol: I wanted to give you some feedback on the presentation you just gave. Good job. Can you come back into the conference room with me for a moment?
Tom: Sure, thanks, but is anything wrong?
Carol: No, not at all.
Tom: OK.
Carol (*Now both are seated in the conference room*): As I said, you did a good job on this presentation. I know you worked hard to get it in shape for today's customer meeting.
Tom: Yes, I guess I did.
Carol: I specifically liked the extensive detail you had on the new proposal. That was very impressive. First of all, I didn't think you had enough

time to incorporate all that detail given such short notice, and second, that detail really helped them see the merits of the new proposal. Actually, you were pretty much in control throughout the whole presentation. You can tell that you had their attention. Your answers to their questions were always clear and honest. That was good.

Tom: Thanks. I'm glad it worked out.

Carol: Well, that's it. I just wanted to let you know how I felt and that you did a good job today. Keep it up.

Tom: I'll certainly try to do my best. Thanks.

How to Handle the More Difficult Conversations

You know from your experience that conversations involving performance feedback can be difficult at times, due to either the nature of the feedback or your employee's personality. In this section, we first provide advice for what you can do when your employee's behavior shows he or she is having a difficult time processing your constructive feedback. We then discuss a variety of personality characteristics that may make it difficult to have feedback conversations in general, whether your goal is to reinforce behavior or to improve performance.

Handling Difficult Responses to Constructive Feedback

No matter how well you prepare for giving constructive feedback to one of your employees, you may encounter some difficult situations. Your employees may become defensive, combative, or emotional. So during the course of the feedback conversation, be aware of the dynamics that may surface and, in general,

- If a difficult situation arises, acknowledge it.
- Be prepared to shift your planned agenda to address the situation.
- Be open to the possibility that you may be contributing to the performance problem or the difficult response.

In Table 5.2, we offer you strategies for effectively responding to the more difficult reactions or responses—including hostility, silence, and defensiveness—you can expect to your constructive feedback.

Table 5.2　Strategies for Handling Difficult Reactions to Constructive Feedback

Difficult Reaction …	Don't …	Do …
Hostility or anger: Your employee becomes angry, lashing out at you.	Counterattack or become defensive.	Imagine yourself in your employee's "shoes." Consider how would you feel and react. Acknowledge the angry feelings, and ask for your employee's feedback. Also, you may need to clarify that the feedback is about behavior and results, not about the employee's character or personality. **Example:** "It sounds like you're angry about this feedback. Can you tell me more about why you're angry?" Or "It sounds like you're angry about this feedback. I just want to emphasize that this feedback is not about evaluating your worth as a person, but about specific behaviors."
Defensiveness or denial: Your employee denies the accuracy of your feedback, or tries to deny its importance.	Ignore the employee's viewpoint, or get involved in an "I said, you said" conversation.	Confront and describe the conflicting views, and discuss them openly. Accept the possibility that your employee may know something you don't; ask for specific, observable evidence. Be ready to (re)state the evidence on which you based your feedback. **Example:** "It seems like we have a different perspective here. Can you pinpoint what in my feedback you find inaccurate or unfair?"

(continued)

Table 5.2   Strategies for Handling Difficult Reactions to Constructive Feedback (continued)

Difficult Reaction …	Don't …	Do …
Passing the buck: Your employee externalizes the blame for poor performance on, for example, the lack of tools, assistance, resources, time, support, or the like.	Ignore the complaints, or let your employee avoid responsibility for his or her performance.	Use active listening to indicate your "hearing" and understanding of your employee's perspective. Acknowledge the concerns, and encourage your employee to focus on what he or she can control. **Example:** "It sounds like you have some frustrations. Why don't we address them now? Then we can focus on what is under your control."
Silence: Your employee is uninvolved in the conversation, saying very little or nothing at all.	Keep talking as if everything is OK.	Acknowledge your employee's silence, express your concern, and ask for his or her thoughts. Try to detect "unspoken" causes or issues. **Example:** "I notice you're not saying much, and I'm concerned that there's something on your mind. What can you tell me about it?"
Despair: Your employee feels inadequate and/or discouraged as a result of the feedback.	Ignore your employee's feelings, or tell him or her to "Grow up."	Acknowledge your employee's frustration or sadness, and give him or her the time to talk about it. Remind your employee that the feedback is about specific behavioral issues, not his or her value as a person. Look for opportunities to create small successes. **Example:** "It must be hard for you to hear this. I value your contribution, and this feedback is not meant to reflect on you as a person."

Handling Difficult Personalities

In your management career, sooner or later, you will have the opportunity to provide feedback to an employee who, one way or the other, makes it more difficult to do just because of who he or she is. Loosely speaking, the problem seems to stem from his or her personality, and his or her responses to feedback—whether reinforcing or constructive—are less than productive. Well, no one ever said performance management and providing feedback were going to be easy.

The following are six challenging, personality-related characteristics that you may encounter. For each characteristic, we suggest techniques to use to make your feedback conversation as valuable as possible:

1. **Having an inflated view of self**: Your employee believes his or her way is the best way.
   - Encourage your employee to think about how others might approach the same situation.
   - Provide specific examples of day-to-day situations that have a variety of alternative solutions.
2. **Having a deflated view of self**: Your employee thinks he or she cannot do anything right, and often has low self-esteem.
   - Simply listen and show your understanding.
   - Point out examples of success and positive achievement.
3. **Always making a competitive or comparative view**: Your employee consistently compares his or her performance to others, rationalizing why his or her performance is better.
   - Listen to your employee's concerns and maintain a neutral position.
   - State your desire to help.
   - Keep the focus on your employee's actual behaviors and results related to set goals and performance expectations.
4. **Being overly emotional**: Your employee gets caught in his or her emotional reactions and has a hard time holding a rational perspective.
   - Acknowledge the emotion while keeping an objective point of view.
   - Stick to the facts of the discussion.
   - Give specific examples of behaviors or results.
5. **Being overly controlling**: Your employee likes to take control of the situation.
   - Structure the feedback ahead of time, and follow your plan during the conversation.
   - Keep the discussion tightly focused on specifics.
   - Ask questions that require direct responses.

6. **Being passive**: Your employee is not engaged in the conversation and says little or nothing.
   - Ask open questions to explore the lack of involvement.
   - Ask your employee to provide thoughts on his or her current performance, then help him or her to reflect on that performance.
   - Give direct, specific feedback.

Conclusion

Giving and receiving feedback are important for engaging employees and are critical to effective performance management, although at times this may be difficult to provide due to an employee's reaction or personality. Feedback is part of the formal performance appraisal process. But, perhaps more importantly, it is an informal process that occurs frequently—whenever some critical event or performance outcome occurs. Consider your own comfort with giving face-to-face feedback. Maybe by realizing the value of feedback, you will do more to incorporate giving (and, for that matter, seeking and receiving) feedback as part of your daily managerial activities. We summarized a number of reasons why feedback is important. For instance, it helps you to focus your employees' behavior, as well as your own, on what is important. It expresses your appreciation for good performance and goal achievement, and suggests the need and means for redirection when performance falls short of expectations. When giving feedback, you need to consider how much information to provide and how to provide the feedback in a constructive, nonthreatening way. Remember, you are not judging a person's character. You are focusing on behaviors that affect performance outcomes. It helps to be specific, focusing on what your employee did to affect certain outcomes. You also need to be sensitive to each individual's privacy and need to save face. Otherwise, you will just engender defensiveness and avoidance.

Now that you understand the importance of helpful feedback, consider the value of asking for feedback for yourself, even if your own manager is not immediately forthcoming with feedback. Ask your manager, peers, employees, and customers how you are doing. Create an environment in which people feel comfortable giving you feedback and talking about performance improvement strategies. They, in turn, may become more comfortable receiving feedback and will start to ask for it themselves.

In Chapter 6, we discuss how you can use recognition—another form of feedback—to support and promote successful behaviors and performance. Then in Chapter 7, we discuss an increasingly popular management tool and process—360-degree feedback surveys—that you can use to help your employees make the most of feedback.

Appendix 5.1: Assessment for Measuring Self-Esteem

The assessment is given here and instructions for interpreting results follows.

Assessment for Measuring Self-Esteem

Instructions:

Use the response scale below to indicate your agreement or disagreement with the following statements by placing the appropriate rating (1–5) next to each statement.

Response Scale:

1	2	3	4	5
Strongly Disagree	Disagree	Neutral	Agree	Strongly Agree

Statement	Rating
I am confident I get the success I deserve in life.	
I rarely feel depressed.	
When I try, I generally succeed.	
I complete tasks successfully.	
Even when I fail, I feel positive about myself.	
I have no doubts about my competence.	
Overall, I am satisfied with myself.	
I determine what will happen in my life.	
I feel in control of my success in my career.	
I am capable of coping with most of my problems.	
Things never really look pretty bleak and hopeless to me.	
Most of the time, I feel in control of my work.	
Total Score (Total of All Ratings)	

Source: Judge, Erez, Bono, and Thoresen (2002). This measure is nonproprietary (free) and may be used without permission.

Instructions for Interpreting Results of the Assessment for Self-Esteem

Your score for this assessment can range from a low of 12 to a high of 60.
Broadly speaking:

- Scores ranging between 48 and 60 indicate a high level of self-esteem.

- Scores ranging between 36 and 47 indicate a moderate level of self-esteem.

- Scores ranging between 12 and 35 indicate a low to moderate level of
  self-esteem.

Chapter 6

Recognizing Employee Performance

Managers typically have at their disposal a variety of ways to recognize employee performance. From a compensation perspective, chances are you can provide your employees with a base-pay merit increase and, depending on their roles in the organization, some sort of bonus. This bonus can be either discretionary, that is, solely determined by you, or more structured—say, for example, as part of a unit- or company-wide incentive plan that is clearly tied to organization metrics, with fixed payouts based on those metrics. In fact, today compensation is considered as one major aspect of the "total rewards" package that organizations offer in exchange for employment. What else is part of the total rewards package? In general, total rewards will include the following: the range of company benefits (retirement, health care, vacation time, etc.), learning and development opportunities, work experience, and recognition and awards (financial, honors, and public statements of appreciation).

If you recall, at XINC, we found that total rewards was a direct predictor of employee engagement. As a manager, you have somewhat less control over two of the more corporate-driven aspects of total rewards, the range and depth of benefits and the kind and type of compensation plans administered. Given this limited discretion, we won't go into detail here about how you can use those components to drive employee engagement—just be sure you administer them fairly and equitably. However, we previously addressed how goal setting, feedback, and appraisal can help your employees to maximize the value of their work experiences; and we also discussed what you can do to support individual

105

and team learning and development opportunities. In this chapter, we focus our attention on recognition—an important driver of employee engagement, satisfaction, and retention that is largely under your control.

In Chapter 5, we positioned recognition as positive feedback, and noted that providing recognition is a critical component of the performance management process. We also stated that providing performance feedback and recognition is important to building a culture of employee engagement. In addition, our work with one Fortune 500 organization in the telecommunications industry has shown repeatedly that satisfaction with the overall quality of performance management, as well as with the recognition received from managers, contributes significantly to overall employee satisfaction.

Research with another client, a Fortune 500 company in the entertainment industry, revealed the impact of recognition on employee retention. The results of the company's employee opinion survey over 2 years showed that "lack of recognition" was a major reason for leaving this company of more than 20,000 employees. Out of 15 possible choices, it ranked second only to "on the job stress." It even ranked higher than "compensation," "lack of advancement opportunity" and "heavy workload."

Recognition is one of the most important factors contributing to employee satisfaction, ahead of pay and benefits (Buckingham & Coffman, 1999); it also has a positive impact on retention, engagement, productivity, and profitability, and it can increase employee morale and pride. Recognition helps to build career resilience, as well, by encouraging employees to set challenging goals for themselves, find innovative ways to meet those goals, overcome setbacks because they assume they can, continually seek new opportunities, and enjoy responsibility and managing their own work.

Why, then, is recognition underutilized in today's workplace? What do you think? In the entertainment company mentioned above, a follow-up survey identified four major obstacles to using recognition:

1. *Lack of knowledge*: Managers didn't know what to do or how to do it.
2. *Time constraints*: Simply, managers reported having no time to do it.
3. *Perception*: Fear of being seen as showing favoritism.
4. *Budget constraints*: Recognition costs too much.

Gostick and Elton (2007) also discussed a number of obstacles they see as preventing managers from recognizing their employees. We present some of the more significant ones below, and suggest actions you can take to overcome them. These obstacles include the fear of

1. *Not having enough time to recognize employees.* Frankly, it does not take a lot of time to use recognition wisely; as a manager, much of your recognition can come as part of your day-to-day performance management in the form of feedback—offering a genuine "Thank you for …" can be accomplished in less than 60 seconds.
2. *Being inconsistent and showing favoritism.* Actively look for opportunities to recognize each of your team members, and if you do, you can always find at least a small achievement or demonstration of the right behavior that you can recognize; it is up to you both to help your employees succeed and to be there to recognize their successes.
3. *Recognition losing its meaning.* There are various ways to recognize your employees; use different forms of recognition, reward appropriately to the achievement, and do it on a timely basis to help your employees see your recognition as important and valuable.
4. *Using other than cash awards, because only cash awards matter.* Remember, feedback is an important form of recognition—it is free—and feedback is important to engagement and overall performance management.
5. *Embarrassing your employees.* Ask your employees how they would like to be recognized—publicly or privately—and then honor their wishes.
6. *Recognizing an employee who is not meeting expectations 100%.* In fact, recognizing employees for their successes may help them gain the confidence to improve in other areas by showing them that their successes are important and do matter; remember that providing recognition and positive feedback helps to build career resilience and increase overall career motivation.

In our experience, we have often found that managers do not give much thought to how to recognize employees. When they do think about it, they are not sure what to do, how to do it, when to do it, and how much it should cost.

What Is Recognition?

Think of recognition as a message of appreciation or positive reinforcement tied to an employee's behavior or accomplishment of a specific task or goal.

Recognition falls into two broad categories: formal and informal. Formal recognition is usually programmatic and company-wide, and includes length of service, birthday, employee of the month, safety, and attendance awards. Other formal recognition programs, such as a CEO award, are designed to recognize a relatively small number of employees and offer highly valued rewards. These rewards can include all-expense-paid vacations, expensive watches, rings or plaques, large cash awards (for example, greater than $1,000), and the like.

Informal recognition is typically less programmatic. It provides opportunities for rewarding greater numbers of employees, but the rewards are usually of lesser value (financially) than those found in the more formal programs. Coffee mugs, theater or cinema tickets, gift checks, and acknowledging an employee at a monthly staff meeting are examples of informal recognition.

What Do You Recognize?

Because compensation in the form of base pay and bonus is designed to reward those who meet or exceed expected annual or long-term performance objectives, you should use informal recognition to reward key behaviors or specific results important to your organization.

Although you are free to recognize any employee achievement, we suggest focusing on those efforts that are aligned with the strategic direction of the business. That is, recognize employee performance that is consistent with your department's and the company's mission, vision, values, and goals. This helps to keep your employees focused on what is most important. For example, we worked with one company that encouraged managers to establish local or informal recognition programs to reward employees whose behavior was clearly consistent with the company's newly articulated values: respect for others, dedication to helping customers, and the highest standards of integrity, innovation, and teamwork.

You can also recognize your employees who are demonstrating excellence or significant improvement in the behaviors used in your company's 360-degree feedback process. As your will see in Chapter 7, we suggest that you use an employee's 360-degree feedback results as input for setting development goals. During the performance year, you can use informal recognition as both a motivator and reward to ensure progress toward these goals and then use the performance appraisal to evaluate their overall attainment.

Another source of behaviors for recognition may well be found in your company's appraisal process. Many appraisals include an evaluation of key behaviors important to the success of the business. Although you will evaluate your employees on these behaviors as part of the appraisal process, you may still want to recognize an employee, or a team of employees, for outstanding demonstration of these behaviors.

What do employees have to say? We have conducted surveys, focus groups, and interviews asking employees about what types of behaviors and outcomes they believe should be recognized. They cite the following: going "above and beyond," being proactive, taking responsibility, offering good ideas, loyalty and commitment, teamwork, and overall performance.

What should you recognize? In addition to the ideas we suggested, try discussing the topic with your employees. You will probably get relatively good input and a few surprises.

How Do You Recognize Your Employees, and What Does It Cost?

So now that you are convinced that recognition is worthwhile and you have identified the performance outcomes or behaviors you want to reinforce, the next step is to determine how to do it. The following are a number of actions you can take to informally recognize one or more employees with basically no financial cost to your organization:

- You can
  - Send an e-mail.
  - Write an acknowledgment and thank-you letter.
  - Invite an employee to a senior management meeting.
  - Provide the chance to make a presentation to senior management.
  - Assign a new, exciting project.
  - Arrange for an employee to join an important committee.
  - Invite an employee to act in your place when you are away (e.g., on vacation).
- You can ask your senior management to
  - Place a phone call.
  - Write a letter.
  - Send an e-mail.
- You can publicize an achievement
  - In your company newsletter.
  - On your company's Web site.
  - On department bulletin boards.

Consider the following as just a small sample of the many recognition possibilities available to you that will have just a minor impact on your budget:

- Certificates
- Letters of recognition
- Floral arrangements or gift baskets

- Cell phones, MP-3 players, digital cameras, and other small electronics
- Lunches or dinners
- Theater tickets
- Movie tickets
- Gift certificates
- Gift checks
- Afternoons off
- Pen and pencil sets
- Watches, rings, pins, or other jewelry
- Company coffee cups, T-shirts, jackets, or the like
- Reserved parking spaces
- Best-selling books or magazine subscriptions

The following are some high-cost ideas, although often these are associated with more formal recognition programs:

- Domestic airline tickets for two
- International airline tickets for two
- Weekend hotel stay
- Large cash awards

Simply Say, "Thank You"

Yes, simply saying, "Thank you," can be a powerful form of recognition. How long has it been since you sincerely thanked and recognized one of your employees for his or her efforts? If you did so just last week and do so often, you are probably in the minority. Most managers have a difficult time just saying, "Thank you." Look at some of the reasons offered:

- I feel awkward saying thanks.
- My employees already know I appreciate what they do.
- They are adults; they don't need to be told "good job."
- I pay them well—they know I appreciate them.

Saying, "Thank you," is simply a habit you can learn. If you need further convincing, research shows that when your employees don't receive recognition, they tend to feel inadequate, resist job challenges, look for direction from others, hide their mistakes, blame themselves when things go wrong, and generally become disengaged from their work and the company.

How Do You Make Your Recognition Effective?

Based on our experience and drawing from a short work by Rosalind Jeffries (1996), we have pulled together the following strategies to help you make your recognition as effective as possible.

1. **Be inclusive**: Be sure to recognize everyone involved in an accomplishment. Don't only think about the star performer; consider those in "the back room" who are providing support. For example, if you want to recognize the efforts of a sales team, include not only the sales professionals but the administrators and coordinators as well.

2. **Be universal**: Although we focused primarily on how to use recognition as part of the process of managing employee performance, you can use informal recognition with your peers, your boss, and your customers.

3. **Be varied**: Even if you have a favorite of your own, try using a number of recognition methods with your employees. You may use an e-mail on one occasion, offer your thanks on another, and maybe offer a cup of coffee on yet another.

4. **Be spontaneous**: Unexpected recognition, such as stopping by your employee's office or giving an employee a call to say thanks, can be even more effective than the expected informal recognition you would provide at your monthly staff meeting.

5. **Be frequent**: To make recognition a habit, build it into your daily activities list. Put it on your schedule. If you don't reserve the time for giving recognition, chances are you won't do it. Also, take the opportunity to reward efforts at project milestones, as some projects may take several months to complete. Don't wait too long.

6. **Be sincere**: Be open and honest with your recognition. Dig a little deeper than normal. Let your employees know that you really appreciate their efforts and that it makes you feel good to see them be successful.

7. **Be proportional**: The recognition should fit the achievement. Don't give T-shirts to a team of star performers who worked on a 6-month project and saved the company a significant amount of money, and don't provide domestic airline tickets to your assistant who worked late three nights in a row to get a report ready for an important client.

8. **Be specific**: As we highlighted in our discussion of feedback in Chapter 5, be specific about what you are recognizing. This helps you to reinforce the behavior that you desire. Therefore, instead of just saying, "Thanks for the report," you might say, "The extensive detail you provided in the report made it very easy for me to convince senior management of the importance of this project."

9. **Be timely**: Because informal recognition is under your control, don't let time pass between the accomplishment and your recognition of it. Recognition is more effective when it occurs closer in time to the acts or behaviors you want to reinforce. Waiting a week to tell an employee that he or she delivered an excellent presentation to the project team leaders will not be as effective as if you did it immediately following the presentation.

10. **Follow the Platinum Rule**: "Treat others as they wish to be treated." Try to tailor your rewards to meet the needs of the person you are recognizing. For example, as we mentioned earlier, some employees may prefer your praise in private, whereas others desire recognition in front of their peers. This is an important point. You want your recognition to be effective. You do not want your attempt at recognition to backfire, to turn into some form of punishment rather than reward. We know of one instance where a senior group of managers considered "dinner with the vice president" as the best form of recognition for a group of front-line employees. Fortunately, they tested the idea before they formalized the reward. The employees did not even want this option on the list of recognition possibilities!

What Are Your Next Steps?

This is easy. Start today. If you consider yourself good at recognizing your employees' efforts, we congratulate you and encourage you to continue what you are doing. We would also urge you to try new strategies and approaches.

If you are not actively using recognition, there are some simple steps that you can take. Saying, "Thank you," is one of them. Then develop a plan for how you can begin to strategically drive and reinforce the behavior and results you expect from your employees.

Lastly, consider some good advice offered by Deeprose (1994) for being sure that your recognition meets the needs of your employees.

■ **Ask your employees**: Let your employees know that you want to recognize their recent efforts. Suggest the rewards you had in mind, and ask whether or not something else may be more meaningful.

■ **Offer some suggestions**: Providing alternatives to choose from will help your employees to make appropriate choices without fear of offending you.

■ **Observe**: Without asking directly, rely on your familiarity with your employees to determine what might be an appropriate reward; ask yourself what this person talks about, likes, enjoys doing, and so on.

■ **Confirm your observations**: Check out your recognition ideas with your employees' colleagues or friends.

■ **Don't be afraid to get it wrong the first time**: If your employees do not seem as excited by the rewards as you thought, don't take it personally. Try again another time to make the rewards more meaningful.

Recognition as a Reinforcer

In Chapter 3, we emphasized the importance of creating a climate of trust and empowering your employees. Empowered employees act with autonomy and discretion, and generally are motivated by the activity of the work itself rather than by external rewards. In other words, they are intrinsically motivated. Deci (1980; Deci & Flaste, 1995) stated that intrinsically motivated employees are, by definition, driven to fulfill their need to feel competent, and they are also self-determining, meaning they feel that they control their own fate (their perceived locus of causality is internal). As a result, when you empower your employees and provide meaningful opportunities and challenges that foster intrinsic motivation, you help create the conditions that allow for a natural building of their sense of competence. Your employees then reinforce and continue to build their own sense of competence in a cyclical way as they set out to meet and succeed at subsequent opportunities and challenges.

As a manager, you also strengthen your employees' sense of competence and achievement through your positive feedback and recognition of their success. This brings us to an important point. You don't have to be concerned about overly recognizing your employees for their achievements when they are intrinsically motivated—that can actually decrease their feelings of self-determination and minimize the benefits of intrinsic motivation. So think of your recognition as a reinforcer—something that lets your employees know they are on the right track. Don't position your recognition as a motivator—a way to drive or set up expectations. If you do, you are more than likely shifting the balance to extrinsic motivation, positioning the external reward as to what is important. This diminishes the positive feelings of competence and self-determination that accompany intrinsic motivation, which is the most effective form of motivation in the long run.

Conclusion

Recognition, like feedback, is an often overlooked part of performance management—a part that many managers feel uncomfortable doing. Recognition has the ability to positively affect your employees' engagement and satisfaction, morale, pride, productivity, and profitability. There are many simple, nonfinancial ways to recognize performance and, as a result, enhance motivation. Recognize key behaviors and the short-term tactics and activities that help achieve goals in the long run. You can recognize employees who, for instance, stay late to finish a project or are proactive to point out ways of improving team performance. Recognize good ideas, loyalty, and teamwork as well as overall performance.

We offered a number of suggestions for giving recognition. Simple e-mail messages or phone calls will do, but of course, an in-person "Thank you" is always appreciated. More public means of recognition also go a long way to demonstrate to others that certain behaviors are valued. This may be accomplished with articles in the company newsletter or bulletin. Small, unexpected bonuses, gift certificates, and time off are often much appreciated and demonstrate to employees that you notice and value their extra efforts.

Finally, empower your employees and provide challenging and meaningful work to foster intrinsic motivation, and use the recognition at your disposal to reinforce the behaviors, efforts, performance, and outcomes you desire.

Chapter 7

Learning About 360-Degree Feedback

Consider the following: You encouraged one of your management employees to attend a week-long leadership development program run by a well-known university business school. You receive a packet in the mail asking you to complete a 360-degree feedback survey about your employee's performance. You also learn that your employee will distribute the survey to his or her own employees, peers, and key customers. All of these people, except you, as manager, complete the form anonymously. Your employee will receive the report of the results on the first day of the training program.

Consider another scenario: Your company is growing by leaps and bounds. Qualified people are hard to find, and the company needs to retain its best people and give them opportunities for development so they can be ready for more responsibility and to help grow new areas of the business. To support all this, the company is increasing its investment in development activities. One of these activities is a 360-degree feedback survey. You learn that each of your employees who manage others will now be evaluated not only by you but also by their direct reports, peers, and customers. All the ratings except yours will be anonymous—so your employees will be able to tell how you evaluated them. HR considers the results confidential, so technically only your managers will get the results, and although they are encouraged to do so, they don't have to share their results with anyone else, including you. The whole purpose of the survey process is to give your employees feedback about their performance and to help them think about what they need to do to improve.

One more possible situation: You read in a memo from the human resources department that your company is implementing a new performance appraisal process. In addition to you rating your employees once a year, your management employees will be rated by their own direct reports and peers as well. In fact, the ratings from these different sources will be available to you prior to completing the "official" performance evaluation. So now you have more input that can serve to increase the accuracy of your performance evaluations and any subsequent administrative decisions, such as merit increases.

What Is 360-Degree Feedback?

Chances are that you have encountered, or will soon encounter, 360-degree feedback. This is a survey about management behavior and performance completed by a manager's employees, peers, immediate manager, and possibly higher-level managers, and customers, who may be inside or outside the company. Managers are typically asked to rate themselves, too. Then the manager receives a report of the results. The survey includes items that focus on important aspects of behavior and performance in your organization and company. Each item is rated on a scale that might range from 1 (low) to 5 (high). Some surveys use rating scales with fewer points, and some more. In scoring the survey, the items are averaged for each group (all employees, all peers, and all customers). The report presents the results for each item so that managers can see how their self-ratings compare to how others see them. In addition to the ratings, the survey may provide a space to write in comments or explanations. These would be transcribed so that handwriting cannot be identified. Often these are general comments so that no one individual can be identified, or the comments are edited to ensure anonymity and confidentiality. After a manager receives the report, he or she might meet with his or her own supervisor to discuss the results. Managers are also encouraged to hold a meeting with their employees to talk about what they learned and what they plan to do about it. The results are supposed to help managers identify skills and knowledge areas that need development in order to improve job performance.

A 360-degree feedback survey, like feedback in general, is a form of communication, conducted more systematically. Targeted to provide managers with feedback about their behavior and performance—depending on the items or questions in the survey—it can also help managers to determine whether or not they are fostering engagement for their employees. In fact, with some modification, the employee opinion survey questions used at XINC can be used in a 360-degree feedback survey to determine, for example, the overall level of engagement, as well as the strength of the direct and indirect predictors of engagement in a manager's organization.

The 360-Degree Feedback Process

360-degree feedback is more than just a survey; it is also part of a process. For you, as the manager of other managers, the process consists of helping your management employees to identify people to assess their behavior and performance, discussing the feedback report with your managers, using the results to help your managers formulate goals for development and performance improvement, ensuring your managers carry out the activities necessary to achieve those goals, evaluating changes in your managers' performance, and engaging in goal setting for further development.

360-degree feedback is typically used as a development tool as part of an overall performance management process. It provides, you, the manager, with information about your management employees that can lead to identifying development areas and development goals. As a result, 360-degree feedback can play a key role in development planning.

How Is a 360-Degree Process Developed?

In most companies, the approach for creating and implementing a 360-degree feedback process includes

- Analyzing managers' jobs to identify the key performance areas that will be assessed in the survey;
- Determining specific behaviors that relate to successful performance in those areas;
- Developing survey items that reflect these behaviors;
- Implementing the 360-degree process in the organization;
- Collecting and analyzing the results from the process for all managers;
- Preparing a report for each manager;
- Providing guidelines and support, maybe formal coaches, to help managers digest the results and set goals for development and performance improvement; and
- Providing ways to help managers achieve their development goals, for instance, identifying appropriate training programs, or assigning managers to special projects (for example, working on a task force to develop a new product).

360-Degree Feedback Surveys Differ From Employee Opinion Surveys

Typical attitude surveys ask employees to indicate how satisfied they are with various aspects of their experience at work. This might include their feelings about the company, top management, their pay and benefits, the work they do, as well as their supervision. The responses are usually summarized across all employees in the company, then by division, and then by department. In contrast, 360-degree feedback asks about the behavior and performance of a specific manager. Results are grouped and averaged by those who complete the survey, and the manager is provided a report that addresses his or her own behavior and performance. The feedback is all about the manager, so it is hard to ignore.

The Value of Feedback From Different Perspectives

The value of 360-degree feedback is that it provides pointed information about a manager from various people who have different roles or relationships to that manager. What do we mean? Although some of the items may be rated by all the people the manager asked to complete the survey because those items reflect general behaviors and performance (for instance, the degree to which the manager is organized, communicates clearly, and meet deadlines), other items may be addressed to people in a given role. For example, only a manager's employees have had the experience to determine if sufficient time is spent providing them with career guidance and coaching about how to improve their performance. Some of the managers' peers may have observed this behavior or have heard the manager's employees talking about it, but they wouldn't have had direct experience with it and so should not be asked to evaluate performance in this area.

However, a manager's peers are probably in the best position to evaluate the extent to which the manager cooperates and collaborates with colleagues in other work groups on team projects, contributes new ideas at group meetings, and seeks advice from coworkers who have different expertise. The manager's customers are in the best position to evaluate the extent to which the manager is sensitive to their needs (for example, their specifications for quality of service or products). You, as the manager's supervisor, would have direct information about your manager's ability to produce outcomes expected for your department, such as meeting revenue goals, staying within budget, and demonstrating continuous improvement.

Participating in Designing the Survey

You might wonder why we suggest asking managers, like yourself, whenever possible, to help write the survey items. Involving managers helps your human resource department to ensure that the items reflect elements of performance that are important both to you and to the company. In addition, the items will appear more realistic, because the items will have been written by you or your peers—those actually doing most of the rating. Managers will also be more likely to pay attention to the results because they will know that (a) the items reflect elements of performance that are important to the company, (b) their fellow employees worked hard to design the survey, and (c) their colleagues took time to provide the ratings.

Frequency of Administering the Survey

In most companies, the survey is usually administered once or twice a year; in others, as often as every quarter. In addition, an informal process can be set up so that you can initiate a 360-degree feedback survey for one of your managers, or they might do it for themselves, whenever there is a reasonable need for feedback, perhaps to check how others saw them cope with a tough situation.

Why Is 360-Degree Feedback So Popular?

Virtually every Fortune 500 company has used, or is considering using, 360-degree feedback. Indeed, a number of large firms have made it an ongoing part of their performance management process. Many small firms have also adopted 360-degree feedback. So why is 360-degree feedback so popular? Why not just rely on managers, like you, to evaluate their employees? After all, you are called on to make administrative decisions. Don't you decide who receives a raise and how much, who attends training and when, who is ready for advancement, and so forth?

Actually, 360-degree feedback doesn't change your role in this regard. When 360-degree feedback results about your employees are available to you, you have more input with which to make your decisions. This input has become especially valuable because of the increased complexity of work and the impossibility of one manager, like you, knowing everything important about an employee's performance. Consider that in today's increasingly complex corporations, managers don't feel they are able to know everything there is to know about how an employee is performing. With flatter corporate structures and broader spans of control, managers have more employees in their departments, and they don't work closely with any one of them. Also, other people (employees, peers, customers) have different perspectives and concerns about a given manager's performance. For instance, employees are able to evaluate their manager on the extent to which the manager provides support for their training and development. Peers are able to evaluate their coworkers on the extent to which they contribute to teamwork. Customers understand a manager's responsiveness to their needs. Each of these groups has a unique perspective on the manager's role—a view that you, the manager's supervisor, do not have.

Should Survey Feedback Results Be Used to Make Administrative Decisions About Managers?

360-degree feedback surveys, when first introduced into the organization, can be threatening to everyone involved in completing the surveys. Employees who are rating a manager, as well as colleagues of that manager, may fear that the manager will know what they said and retaliate if their opinion is unfavorable. The managers being rated may fear that some employees and peers may be out to get them, and may believe that the evaluation role should be limited to their supervisors. These managers may also be concerned about the accuracy of their results if there has been substantial turnover in their work group and if their peers and others have not had a chance to know them well enough to make a judgment about their performance. As the supervisor of the manager, you may be concerned about the facts that your ratings stand alone in the report and that your manager will really want to know why your ratings may not be as high as his or her self-ratings.

These are reasons why many companies use 360-degree feedback survey results solely for developmental purposes. That is, the results are given to managers to help guide their training and development. The information suggests strengths that managers should enhance and weaknesses that managers should correct. Knowing that the results will be used solely for development, rather than as input for administrative decisions such as pay increases and promotions, those rating the manager are likely to be more honest in their assessments. The idea in these companies is to encourage everyone to be involved in the development process, not just you and your employees. Over time, as everyone becomes used to the feedback process—perhaps over a period of 2 or 3 years, administering the survey annually—a company may shift to using the survey for administrative purposes.

Other companies do not want to use the results just for feedback. They believe that the results should be incorporated into the formal appraisal process and be used to make important decisions about people. In these companies, the survey is introduced with this in mind right from the start. These companies provide results reports to both the managers and those who supervise them and expect the supervisors to use the reports to guide their performance discussions with the managers and to set goals for development.

What Is the Rationale for Using 360-Degree Feedback Results for Making Administrative Decisions?

Many experts and organization leaders believe that managers will not pay attention to their own feedback results unless they are used to make decisions that the managers care about. If the results are provided only to the managers, and their higher level supervisors don't have access to them, then why should managers act on the results? Of course, diligent managers are likely to see the value of the results, and others may at least feel obligated to use them, but there is no certainty that all managers will use their results. Therefore, the full investment in 360-degree feedback may not materialize.

The difficulty with using 360-degree feedback to make administrative decisions, at least when the survey process is initially introduced, is that managers may feel threatened. Many managers have told us that they feel that their employees should not evaluate them. They say they need to be free to make important administrative decisions about their employees without worrying about how they will be evaluated in return (we touched upon this point in Chapter 2). These same managers expressed similar concerns about their peers. They say that although they generally work together in a collaborative fashion, they sometimes are in disagreement and may have to take a course of action that their peers may not like. If they need to be concerned about how their peers will rate them, then the managers say that they may not take certain actions, even if those actions are in the best interest of the company.

On the other hand, managers have told us that their employees and peers can provide valuable feedback, and that they can benefit from their honest assessments. So if ratings are used only for development, and no one in the company other than the person rated will have the results, threats go away and people feel free to rate the manager as accurately as possible.

One way companies decide how to use 360-degree feedback is to use surveys and/or focus groups to ask everyone involved what they think about the process. If there is uncertainty and some distrust, then the best approach is to introduce 360-degree surveys for development only.

Typical Reactions When Introducing 360-Degree Feedback

Whenever we have implemented a 360-degree survey process in a company, we start by conducting meetings with groups of managers, who will be targeted to receive feedback, to describe the process. The reaction is invariably the same. Managers have all kinds of reasons why the process won't work for them. For instance, they say:

- I just reorganized my department and made some unpopular decisions. My people are not happy with me, and this will come out in how they rate me.
- Employees don't understand what it takes to be a manager here.
- It's not up to my people to evaluate me. I evaluate them!
- My peers don't have enough information about my job. They don't know everything I do, and I don't know everything they do.
- I have new people in my work group. They can't be expected to evaluate me. They don't know enough about me yet.
- My employees will do anything they need to do to get a raise. The only feedback I'll get will be flattery. I'll feel good, but I won't learn anything.

These are all legitimate concerns. Timing is important for introducing 360-degree feedback. The time may not be right if the organization just underwent a major downsizing and restructuring. Or the company may have just merged with another firm, and people are learning each other's corporate cultures, integrating staffs, and getting used to new ways of doing business. In such cases, it may indeed be better to wait until things settle down a bit before implementing a 360-degree survey process. However, unless there has been a major change throughout the company, no time is likely to be exactly right for everyone. Introducing the feedback process as a developmental tool can be a way to diffuse everyone's concerns and focus attention on performance improvement. The idea is to engage people throughout the organization in the performance management process and make feedback an ongoing way of learning about performance and identifying directions for improvement.

The Need for Clear Communication

Whether a company plans to use 360-degree survey feedback for development alone or for development and administration, employees and managers need to be crystal clear about the purpose and how the process will work. If this is a company-wide or division-wide initiative, group sessions should be held with managers about how the survey will be administered. Separate meetings should be held with employees without their managers present. Usually, a member of the human resources department conducts these meetings and addresses all issues and concerns openly.

Questions Your Managers May Have About 360-Degree Feedback

The following are the typical questions we tend to hear from managers who will be receiving the feedback. These questions may be addressed to you, as well, by your own managers if they are about to go through the process. Feel free to modify our answers to best fit your needs and situation.

How Do I Know the Feedback Will Be Fair and Accurate?

The feedback will be anonymous. Everyone rating you will know there is no way they can be identified. Also, the items are written to be as clear as possible, so there shouldn't be any confusion about meaning. This should help accuracy. In addition, everyone will be asked to evaluate areas of your performance that they know something about. If they haven't observed your performance on a particular behavior, they can usually respond, "No chance to observe."

Half of My Employees Have Been With Me for Only 3 Months: How Can They Evaluate Me Accurately?

Surveys don't have to be given to your employees who have been with you for only a short time. I can help you decide how short is "too short," although I may leave that up to you. Remember that if fewer than three of your employees in a group evaluate you, you will not receive the results. So you don't want to limit your feedback by not allowing for participation.

Even if all of your employees are given a survey, regardless of their tenure, they can indicate they have had "No chance to observe" on any item. You need to trust that your employees will try to be as accurate as possible and not evaluate you on items they really don't know about. If most people in a group (for instance, your employees or your peers) evaluate you and you are certain that many do not know you very well, then let's take this into account when interpreting your feedback. In other words, we may not give the ratings as much credence as we would if the people in that group all knew you well. However, we may still ask why the results emerged as they did and what you might do to change your behavior, enhance your performance, and change perceptions for the next survey.

We Just Went Through a Major Budget Cut, and None of My People Received Raises. I Don't Think This Is a Good Time to Ask Them to Evaluate Me. Do I Have to Participate in the Survey?

Everyone in the company experienced the same budget cut, so if a negative attitude prevails, it will affect how managers are rated across the board. Also, your employees will rarely blame you personally for tough economic times. In any case, we can take these conditions into account when we interpret your results. We need to judge the extent to which your results are due to your behavior and performance (perhaps how you handled the budget cutting) or due to the external pressures and decisions you were forced to make.

My Employees Don't Understand Half of What I Do. How Are Their Ratings Going to Help Me?

Again, if your employees don't feel they know enough to evaluate you on an item, they can indicate this. However, keep in mind that the items your employees evaluate you on are elements of performance that are related to manager–employee relationships. Similarly, items your peers evaluate you on are elements of performance that are related to peer relationships. For instance, peers don't have to rate you on how clearly or frequently you communicate with your employees if they have never seen you communicate with them.

Do I Have to Use the Feedback Report?

I hope you will take the feedback seriously, but ultimately, it is up to you. Our challenge will be to incorporate the feedback into other information we have about your performance and use our best judgment to set goals for performance improvement. Everyone can work on enhancing strengths if not correcting weaknesses. We will want to identify areas for development, set priorities, and take actions to improve your performance.

Questions Employees May Have About 360-Degree Feedback

When introducing the 360-degree feedback process for the first time, we have found that employees who will be rating their managers also have a number of questions. The following are some of the key questions, with answers that you can use and share with your managers who will be engaged in the process, to help them respond to their employees' concerns.

Will You Be Able to Tell How I Rated You?

No. Your responses will be averaged with those of other employees in our work group.

Suppose I'm the Only Employee in This Group Who Responds to the Survey. Or Suppose Only Two or Three of Us Respond. Won't You Be Able to Guess Who Said What?

No. A report of results will not be provided on items for which there are fewer than three raters. So, if only two of you respond, or if there are only two raters in any category that respond, then all of my results will be averaged together.

Will You Want to Talk to Me About the Ratings?

I have been asked not to talk to you or anyone else completing the survey about their ratings before or after the survey is administered. However, I will bring you together in a group to discuss and interpret my results, and talk about ways of improving. Although this is an optional step in the process, research shows that if I review my results with you, I am more likely to improve my job performance than if I don't (see, for instance, Walker & Smither, 1999).

Do I Have to Complete the Survey?

No. There is no requirement. I will only know how many of you, as well as my peers, customers, and so on, responded.

Will Your Pay Depend on My Responses?

Note: The answer to this obviously depends on how your organization intends to use the results. There are two possible answers, as explained here. If the results are for development only, then your answer is emphatically "No." If the results are to be used for administration, then the following response may apply: "My manager will take the results of the survey along with other information into account in appraising my performance and will use the appraisal to make pay and other decisions."

Ways Companies Administer the Survey

Companies administer 360-degree feedback surveys in several ways once it is decided which managers will participate in the process. Some companies send all involved a survey in the mail—perhaps to their home address in order to emphasize the private nature of the assessment. Others use online or Web-based surveys, and all involved are usually contacted by e-mail. With this method, surveys can be completed on a laptop or desktop computer and returned electronically for speedy analysis.

Another method is to ask managers to distribute the surveys themselves. One disadvantage of this method is that it may make others feel obligated to rate them favorably because of the power of the face-to-face interaction. Another disadvantage of this method is that some managers may be inclined to give the surveys to people they believe will rate them favorably. However, if the purpose is solely for development and this is clear to everyone, people should, and probably will, be honest in their evaluations.

Just-in-Time, Do-It-Yourself 360-Degree Feedback

Another technique is to allow managers to administer a survey whenever they feel they need it. This is easy to do with Web-based technology. Typically, the computer software asks the manager to select items for evaluation from a list of possible items, or to write his or her own. Basically, the manager would select or write items that are relevant to his or her job and development needs at the moment. For example, the manager may use the survey when he or she is facing a critical problem at work and wants some immediate feedback. Or the manager may use the survey before establishing goals to guide his or her development activities during the coming months. Or the manager might have returned from a leadership development program and wants to know how well he or she is doing in areas of particular focus.

After deciding on the items, the manager would typically use the Web-based system to provide a "survey coordinator" the e-mail addresses for the individuals who should receive the survey. An e-mail is then sent electronically with a link to the survey Web site. The e-mail describes the purpose of the survey, explains that it is a confidential process, and expresses the manager's thanks for their cooperation. Everyone will have a certain window of time to respond (say, a week). In most cases, after the elapsed time, the computer system automatically generates and sends the manager an electronic report.

The Feedback Report

The feedback report usually lists average ratings for each item rated. The report might also present the range of the scores (the lowest rating, the highest rating) for each item or the number of people giving each rating (for example, the number of employees rating the manager 1, 2, 3, and 4—assuming a 4-point rating scale). The report may include normative data from the company, that is, the average rating received by all managers for each item, which allows the manager to compare his or her ratings to those received by others. As a result, the manager can better calibrate whether his or her results are high, moderate, or low compared to those of other managers. Low ratings on an item may not be so bad if everyone was rated low on that item. This may say more about the corporate culture than it does about the manager's specific behavior. Of course, as the supervisor of the manager receiving the report, this information when shared with you will be extremely useful.

Ways Companies Tend to Deliver the Report

Companies vary in the way they deliver the feedback report. Consider the following methods.

Desk Drop

This is when the human resources department simply sends the report to the manager in a sealed envelope marked *Confidential*. How would you react? You might be tempted to slip the unopened envelope in the bottom drawer of your desk and tell yourself that you will get to it when you have more time. Then you don't notice the envelope again until you clean out your desk when you're transferred to your next job! However, if you are very interested in your results—and believe they will help you with an immediate concern—you will be more inclined to use them.

Feedback Workshop

This method asks managers to attend a feedback workshop facilitated by someone from the human resources department. Typically, the facilitator opens the workshop, reviews the survey process, describes a sample report, and then distributes the individual reports. Managers then have a chance to review their own results.

The facilitator usually guides the group in how to use the report to set goals. If one of your managers was attending this workshop, he or she would probably work independently without divulging his or her results to other group members. For instance, the facilitator may ask the manager to first look for the five items for which his or her employees provided their most favorable ratings, then the five items they rated most unfavorably. Then the facilitator may ask the manager to compare these ratings to his or her self-ratings. The manager might be guided through a process based on a set of questions similar to the following:

- Did you rate yourself higher than your employees saw you? If so, why?
- Could they be right?
- Did your peers see you in the same way your employees did?
- What are the implications for changes you might make in your behavior?
- According to the results, what are your strengths?
- What are your weaknesses?
- Can you list five goals for changing your behavior?
- Can you describe what you will do (for instance, training courses you will enroll in) to achieve each goal?

When the results are unclear or more information could be helpful, the facilitator may encourage the manager to meet with employees, peers, or you, as his or her supervisor, to share the results or at least seek additional feedback, and then set development goals.

Receiving the Results From a Coach or Trainer

Some companies use internal coaches or hire external coaches to work with managers one-on-one to review their feedback reports and formulate plans for development and performance improvement. The coach's role is to encourage the manager to take the feedback seriously and to process it deliberately. Why?

People have a tendency to look for what they expect to see, conclude that the feedback confirms their self-perception, and ignore or explain away information that does not meet their expectation. For example, some managers, in line with attribution theory, may rationalize that a low rating was due to some external event ("My employees were unhappy with their pay raises this year" or "We were under tight deadlines, so there was no time to work on career development"). A good coach won't let this happen. A coach will help a manager reflect on the results, and then ask the manager to consider whether his or her explanations are just rationalizations. A coach will also help a manager to synthesize the results, identify the really important feedback, and set priorities for development and performance improvement. We say more about coaching in Chapter 8.

Does 360-Degree Feedback Work?

There is a growing body of research on whether managers learn from 360-degree feedback and improve their performance as a result. A general finding from a number of studies is that managers see themselves more favorably than their supervisor, peers, and employees see them. Also, these other raters tend to agree on their perceptions. If one of your managers evaluates him or herself, for example, more highly than others do, this is likely to be a problem, especially for areas of performance where others see the manager as needing significant development. So as long as the manager doesn't rationalize away the feedback, there is likely to be something valuable to learn. (For more information, see Mount & Scullen, 2001; Murphy, Cleveland, & Mohler, 2001; Smither, London, & Reilly, 2005; Walker & Smither, 1999).

Does 360-degree feedback help managers improve over time? Smither, London, Flautt, Vargas, and Kucine (2002) summarized 13 longitudinal studies of the extent to which 360-degree feedback helps managers improve performance one or more years after receiving the feedback. The results generally showed that managers who received feedback improved over time and improved more than managers who did not receive feedback.

Not surprisingly, managers improved most in the areas in which they were rated most unfavorably and initially overrated themselves. Personality also seemed to make a difference. Managers who believed more strongly that they were effective in being able to improve their performance and who were more favorably disposed to receiving the feedback to begin with were more likely to improve, compared to managers who were doubtful that they could change or were cynical about the company in general and the survey in particular. In addition, managers who met with raters to talk about their feedback generally improved more than those who did not discuss the feedback with the raters.

Tracking Changes in Behavior Over Time

360-degree feedback can be used to help you track changes in your managers' performance over time. Ideally, if the feedback was useful, one would expect that areas that others viewed as weaknesses would improve. This would happen because your managers accepted the feedback about these areas and exerted more energy in trying to develop them.

Over time, one would expect that your managers' self-ratings would more closely match others' ratings. This would happen because the feedback focused their attention on the gaps between the ratings, and they would become more sensitive to others' views and would be somewhat likely to change their own ratings consistent with those views. In addition, if they were high in self-monitoring, they would be more likely to change their self-ratings to match how others see them than if they were low in self-monitoring.

There are three concerns to be aware of when comparing ratings over time:

1. People rating your managers may change their standards, being more or less stringent the second or third time. They may expect more or less, and so will be more or less likely to use the high or low ends of the scale.
2. People may change their definitions of the scale points. Each level of performance may take on new meaning, perhaps because they have seen others use the scale points differently (for example, they learned that the top rating was used very sparingly by others, or low ratings were more frequently used, or the highest ratings were reserved for extraordinary performance).
3. People's definitions of the behavior and performance dimensions may change over time.

These are concerns because any changes over time may be due to these factors rather than actual changes in your managers' behavior or performance. A way to overcome these problems is for the HR department to be precise in defining dimensions and scale points and to remind everyone that these definitions should be reviewed prior to completing the survey. Sometimes the HR department will ensure that the behavioral expectations are listed next to scale points to communicate examples of behaviors that reflect each performance level. In any event, it is helpful if discussions about standards occur prior to administering the survey so that everyone will have a common view of the type of performance that constitutes each level of the rating scale.

Sample Upward Feedback Survey and Report

So, after all this discussion about 360-degree feedback, what does a survey look like? See Figure 7.1 for a sample survey, and see Figure 7.2 for a sample feedback report.

FORTX ENTERPRISES INCORPORATED
FEEDBACK REQUESTED FOR

[Name of Manager]

YOUR RELATIONSHIP TO INDIVIDUAL REQUESTING FEEDBACK

☐ Employee   ☐ Peer   ☐ Supervisor   ☐ Customer   ☐ Self

INTRODUCTION

The behaviors in this feedback survey detail expectations for managers and above in all of FORTX Enterprises' business units. They were selected to focus management performance and development efforts in support of business success and the attainment of the company's vision.

Developed by FORTX Enterprises' senior leadership in conjunction with the Organization Development Department, behaviors in this survey will serve as the foundation for future innovations in the areas of feedback, development, training, and performance management.

General Instructions for the INDIVIDUAL Being Rated

After reviewing the general instructions below, turn to and complete only the part of the survey titled YOUR section.

General Instructions for RATERS

This survey is designed to collect feedback regarding an individual manager's behavior. The results of this survey will be used to help that individual understand how his or her behavior supports the achievement of FORTX Enterprises' corporate objectives and to target areas for individual development.

Please complete ONLY the items that pertain to your relationship with the manager being assessed, as well as those items described as FOR ALL.

Please take the time to rate each behavior carefully and honestly.

Your rating should be based on your **Satisfaction** with the level of competence demonstrated in each behavior using the following scale definitions.

Please refer to the definitions provided and use the full range of ratings as you complete this survey.

Figure 7.1   Sample 360-degree feedback survey.

Rating Scale and Definitions

Satisfaction Rating	Definition
Very satisfied	Demonstrates an outstanding level of competence in this behavior. Far exceeds expectations.
Satisfied	Demonstrates a high level of competence in this behavior. Exceeds expectations.
Moderately satisfied or dissatisfied	Usually demonstrates an average level of competence. May at times perform this behavior more or less competently than others.
Dissatisfied	Demonstrates a weak level of competence. Performance of this behavior does not quite reach expectations.
Very dissatisfied	Demonstrates an ineffective level of competence. Exhibits a very strong need for improvement.
No opportunity to observe	Don't have enough information. Probably have not observed this behavior, or do not have enough experience working with this person to provide a fair and meaningful rating.

General Instructions

Using the Rating Scale

Using the scale below, please **place a number next to the items** that best correspond to your satisfaction with this individual's competence.

Satisfaction Rating Scale

Don't know	Very dissatisfied	Dissatisfied	Moderately satisfied or dissatisfied	Satisfied	Very satisfied
0	1	2	3	4	5

If you were satisfied with the competence demonstrated, you would place a 4 in the box next to the item, as shown below.

4	1. Treats me with respect.

Figure 7.1   Sample 360-degree feedback survey (continued).

Providing Written Feedback

If you are a RATER, you will find space for your comments, if you choose to provide them. **Your written comments will be combined with others' in a single report to ensure confidentiality and anonymity.** Try to make your written feedback as specific as possible.

Reporting of Results

Self- and supervisor feedback results will be reported separately. All other feedback results will be reported by rater category; however, if there are fewer than three respondents per category, results for those categories will be reported in the aggregate to help ensure rater confidentiality and anonymity.

Complete the following items if you are an EMPLOYEE who works for the individual being rated:

Employee Items

	Jointly sets performance objectives with me.
	Supports me in developing my career plans.
	Motivates me to do a good job.
	Gives me authority to do my job.
	Provides the support necessary to help me do my job (e.g., advice, resources, or information).

Complete the following items if you are the individual's PEER:

Peer Items

	Understands the work to be done within my department.
	Is available to me when needed.
	Participates productively in staff meetings.
	Lets us know what's going on in his or her workgroup.
	Communicates the reasons for his or her actions.

Figure 7.1   Sample 360-degree feedback survey (continued).

Complete the following items if you are the individual's SUPERVISOR:

Supervisor Items

	Participates productively in staff meetings.
	Has the subject matter knowledge to do the job.
	Represents the group effectively to others (e.g., to clients, to senior management, etc.).
	Uses company resources effectively.
	Is always looking for ways to learn.

Complete the following items if you are the individual's CUSTOMER:

Customer Items

	Keeps commitments.
	Listens to my concerns.
	Understands my needs.
	Strives for quality in spite of time pressure.
	Communicates the reasons for his or her actions.

FOR ALL—complete the following items if you are an EMPLOYEE, PEER, SUPERVISOR, or CUSTOMER.

Items for All Raters

	Treats me with respect.
	Encourages innovation.
	Is flexible.
	Is cooperative.
	Is willing to put in extra effort.

Please provide your additional feedback below.
[A blank space would be included for this purpose.]

Thanks for completing this survey.
Send your completed survey to the Organization Development Department.

Figure 7.1 Sample 360-degree feedback survey (continued).

YOUR Section: Instructions for the individual being rated in this survey.

*Complete the following items in terms of **how satisfied you are with the way you engage in behaviors directed toward** your employees, peers, supervisor and customers:*

Employee Items

	Jointly set performance objectives with your employees.
	Support my employees in developing their career plans.
	Motivate my employees to do a good job.
	Give my employees authority to do their jobs.
	Provide the support necessary to help my employees do their jobs (e.g., advice, resources, or information).
	Treat my employees with respect.
	Encourage innovation.
	I am flexible.
	I am cooperative.
	I am willing to put in extra effort.

Peer Items

	Understand the work to be done within their departments.
	I am available to them when needed.
	Participate productively in staff meetings.
	Let them know what's going on in my workgroup.
	Communicate the reasons for my actions.
	Treat my peers with respect.
	Encourage innovation.
	I am flexible.
	I am cooperative.
	I am willing to put in extra effort.

Figure 7.1   Sample 360-degree feedback survey (continued).

Supervisor Items

	Participate productively in my supervisor's staff meetings.
	Demonstrate the subject matter knowledge to do the job.
	Represent the group effectively to others (e.g., to clients, to senior management, etc.).
	Use company resources effectively.
	I am always looking for ways to learn.
	Treat my supervisor with respect.
	Encourage innovation.
	I am flexible.
	I am cooperative.
	I am willing to put in extra effort.

Customer Items

	Keep commitments.
	Listen to my customers' concerns.
	Understand my customers' needs.
	Strive for quality in spite of time pressure.
	Communicate the reasons for my actions.
	Treat my customers with respect.
	Encourage innovation.
	I am flexible.
	I am cooperative.
	I am willing to put in extra effort.

Thanks for completing this survey.
Send your completed survey to the Organization Development Department.

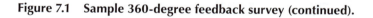

Figure 7.1   Sample 360-degree feedback survey (continued).

FORTX ENTERPRISES INCORPORATED
360 MANAGEMENT SURVEY REPORT FOR

GEORGE LINCOLN

INTRODUCTION

There are several things to notice about this report:

- There is a lot of information.
- The report includes the average (mean) score and the range (lowest rating and highest) for each item.
- The norm is the average of ratings for the item for all managers in the company.

HOW TO READ THIS REPORT

Results are presented separately for

- Employees
- Peers
- Your supervisor
- Customers

At the end of the report, you will find the written feedback from all raters.

READING THE RESULTS TABLES

The following are the definitions of the abbreviations used in column headings in the results tables:

- SR: Your own rating
- MR: Mean or average rating for the rater group
- LR: Lowest rating on the item
- HR: Highest rating on the item
- #: Number of raters responding to the item
- N: Norm or average rating for all managers at FORTX

Figure 7.2   Sample 360-degree feedback report.

Employee Results

Items	SR	MR	LR	HR	#	N
Jointly set performance objectives with your employees.	5	3.6	2	4	7	3.8
Support your employees in developing their career plans.	4	2.8	1	3	6	3.6
Motivate your employees to do a good job.	5	4.0	2	5	7	4.2
Give your employees authority to do their jobs.	5	3.4	2	4	7	3.7
Provide the support necessary to help your employees do their jobs (e.g., advice, resources, or information).	5	4.2	3	5	7	4.5
Treat your employees with respect.	5	4.5	4	5	7	4.7
Encourage innovation.	4	2.8	1	4	6	4.1
Is flexible.	4	3.3	2	4	6	4.5
Is cooperative.	5	4.4	3	5	7	4.7
Is willing to put in extra effort.	5	4.7	4	5	7	4.7

Peer Results

Items	SR	MR	LR	HR	#	N
Understand the work to be done within their departments.	5	4.5	3	5	5	4.8
Is available to them when needed.	4	4.2	3	5	5	4.3
Participate productively in staff meetings.	5	3.9	2	4	5	4.6

Figure 7.2 Sample 360-degree feedback report (continued).

Peer Results (continued)

Items	SR	MR	LR	HR	#	N
Let them know what's going on in my work group.	5	3.3	2	4	5	4.5
Communicate the reasons for my actions.	5	2.7	1	4	5	4.2
Treat my peers with respect.	5	4.2	4	5	5	4.5
Encourage innovation.	5	3.9	1	4	5	4.1
Is flexible.	5	4.4	2	4	5	4.8
Is cooperative.	5	4.4	3	5	5	4.6
Is willing to put in extra effort.	5	5.0	—	5	5	4.6

Supervisor Results*

Items	SR	MR	N
Participate productively in supervisor's staff meetings.	4	4	4.6
Demonstrate the subject matter knowledge to do the job.	5	5	4.8
Represent the group effectively to others (e.g., to clients, to senior management, etc.).	5	5	4.4
Use company resources effectively.	5	4	4.6
Is always looking for ways to learn.	3	4	4.3
Treat my supervisor with respect.	5	5	4.8
Encourage innovation.	5	4	3.7
Is flexible.	5	4	4.2
Is cooperative.	5	5	4.5
Is willing to put in extra effort.	5	5	4.8

* Please note that because there is only one rating per item by the supervisor, the MR rating is also the LR and HR ratings, and therefore, these columns do not appear in this table.

Figure 7.2 Sample 360-degree feedback report (continued).

Customer Results

Items	SR	MR	LR	HR	#	N
Keep commitments.	5	3.3	1	5	9	4.2
Listen to my customers' concerns.	5	3.7	2	5	9	4.3
Understand my customers' needs.	5	3.8	2	5	9	4.4
Strive for quality in spite of time pressure.	5	3.8	2	5	9	4.2
Communicate the reasons for my actions.	4	2.7	1	4	9	3.9
Treat my customers with respect.	5	3.2	4	5	9	4.1
Encourage innovation.	4	3.4	1	4	7	4.3
Is flexible.	5	3.5	2	4	7	3.9
Is cooperative.	5	3.7	2	5	9	4.2
Is willing to put in extra effort.	5	3.9	2	5	9	4.5

WRITTEN FEEDBACK RESPONSES

- I want to advance, but there seem to be no opportunities, and no one cares, least of all George.
- I don't feel that my goals are clear.
- The watchword around here is don't do anything out of the ordinary.
- My manager goes all out to get the job done.
- I wish I knew more about what's happening in George's department. George is a team player.
- I have only good things to say about George.
- I talk until I'm blue in the face, and it doesn't seem to matter. I'll take my business elsewhere if this doesn't change.

Figure 7.2   Sample 360-degree feedback report (continued).

> ■ I've been disappointed before. I can't depend on George to meet deadlines. I don't know if it is George's fault or is this just how the company works. I don't really care. I just want George to get the job done on time and done well.
>
> **Please contact the Organization Development Department if you have questions about this report.**

Figure 7.2 **Sample 360-degree feedback report (continued).**

Interpreting the Sample Report

Although the sample report shown in Figure 7.2 was developed for a manager we will call George Lincoln, if this was your report, you might conclude the following.

Looking at your employee ratings, you were more satisfied with your relationship with your employees than they were with you. You received favorable ratings, similar to those of other managers in your company, on your cooperativeness, on your willingness to put in extra effort, and on treating your employees with respect. However, you were lower than others in your company on encouraging innovation and flexibility, and supporting your employees' career development.

Looking at your peer ratings, again, you were slightly more satisfied with your relationship with your peers than they were with you. In fact, you rated yourself very satisfied on all but one of the items. The norms indicate that peers in your company rated each other very positively on all items. However, your peers rated you lower than the company norm, and lower than your self-rating, on communicating reasons for your actions and letting your peers know what's going on in your work group. This suggests you should concentrate on keeping your peers better informed of activities in your department and the decisions you make.

Looking at your supervisor ratings, both you and your supervisor were very satisfied with your demonstrated competence on almost all items. You saw yourself as a little weak on looking for ways to learn. Your supervisor was a bit more favorable, but still saw room for improvement. Also, your supervisor was not quite as satisfied as you were in your flexibility, encouraging innovations, and use of resources. Also, both of you feel you could improve somewhat in staff meetings. Still, your supervisor clearly has a positive view of your performance, judging from the norms.

Looking at your customers' ratings, you seem to have a major problem. You indicate you are quite satisfied with your relationship with your customers. They, on the other hand, see problems. Some rated you very low, and others very high. However, the averages tended to be below the averages received by all managers in your company. So you can't argue that customers, in general, tend to be critical. Yours are critical, though. They especially see you as not communicating reasons for your actions. You have a lot to work on here.

Overall, you should be working on communicating more clearly and being more responsive to your customers and peers. For employees, a top priority is giving more attention to the support they need for career development. Your supervisor thinks highly of you. Maybe this is because your revenue is high. Or maybe it is because your supervisor does not yet have good information about how your customers and peers perceive you. Rather than divulge all your ratings to your supervisor at this point, you might ask your supervisor for suggestions on how to enhance communications and be more responsive to customer requests and needs.

Conclusion

360-degree feedback is a formal, systematic process of communication, and it can play a significant role in performance management. It is not a one-time event limited to conducting a survey and receiving a feedback report. The process encourages participation of a manager's supervisor, direct reports, colleagues, and customers in performance management.

Managers may also participate in the process by helping to develop items for the survey, rating themselves and others, and receiving and processing feedback. Different views are indeed valuable, and the supervisor's judgment alone, as the sample report showed, may not be thorough or sufficient to understand what is happening. Receiving the report is just the start for development and improvement. The information needs to be interpreted, goals need to be set, and actions need to be taken. Depending on the nature of the items in the feedback survey, managers can learn a great deal about the extent to which they are effectively managing performance and fostering an environment of employee engagement.

Companies often engage internal or external coaches to help managers analyze their 360-degree feedback results and develop action plans for improvement. However, coaching is more than that, as you will see by our discussion of coaching in Chapter 8.

Chapter 8

Coaching for Success

Coaching can be thought of as helping employees to become the best they can be by making the most of their overall capabilities. Coaching positions employees to work more effectively and cohesively in their environments, whether working with individuals, teams, or leading organizations. A survey of more than 200 companies in 19 countries describes the state of coaching in organizations today (Morgan, Harkins, & Goldsmith, 2005):

- Coaching is most often used for developing leadership capability.
- Coaching, by and large, focuses on behavior change.
- The top reasons for coaching are to enhance current performance and to correct performance issues.
- When coaching is chosen over other development methods, it is largely because coaching can be tailored and customized to meet individual circumstances.
- The use of internal coaches has been institutionalized in most organizations, whereas the use of external coaches for senior executives is on the rise.
- Internal coaches are generally rated more effective than external coaches.
- Coaching can be targeted to any level of management or leadership, from lower levels in the organization to its most senior executives.
- The success of coaching is most often measured by achieving agreed-to changes in behavior and performance.
- 360-degree feedback is the most frequently used tool in conjunction with coaching.

In this chapter, we discuss coaching from two perspectives. We provide you, the manager, with a how-to guide for coaching your employees. We describe a coaching process and the actions you can take to be as effective as possible in your coaching role. We then present an overview of the use and role of professional internal and external coaches. Finally, we discuss how you can make the coaching experience a success.

Defining Coaching

Coaching can be defined in a number of ways. Three definitions that we have found useful are as follows:

- Coaching is "an on-going, one-on-one learning process enabling people to enhance their job performance" (Harris, 1999, p. 38).
- Coaching is "a process that fosters self-awareness and that results in the motivation to change, as well as the guidance needed if change is to take place in ways that meet organizational needs" (Dotlitch & Cairo, 1999, p. 2).
- The coach "works in partnership with the client to discover solutions together, finding them through careful listening, provocative questioning, enlightened guidance, and the right level of prompting at the time. To a great degree, the coach's goal is to enable the client to find the right answers by him or herself" (Morgan et al., 2005, p. 26).

In the first definition, it is clear that coaching is focused on learning, and that learning should lead to performance enhancement. What we like about the Dotlitch and Cairo (1999) definition is that it focuses not only on increasing self-awareness but also on the motivation to change in the context of meeting organization needs and demands. As a manager, when you coach your employees, your overall goal, of course, is to help them improve their performance in light of their goals and the organization's expectations. The same would be expected of you if you were being coached by your own manager or, perhaps, by an external coach.

When you coach your employees, the act of coaching alone helps them feel more engaged. However, you may also coach your employees on specific behaviors that will help them become more engaged, such as increasing their sense of empowerment, ability to speak up and challenge the status quo, and ability to ask for the resources they need to do their job. As a result, in the context of overall performance management, formal coaching contributes not only to increased development and improved performance but also to raising the level of engagement.

In the Morgan et al. (2005) definition, we begin to see that the process of coaching is not about just providing feedback in general or telling your employees what to do. It is about mutual exploration and, in the end, helping your employees to find the right answers on their own. (This point is also emphasized by Flaherty, 1998, in his how-to volume on coaching for performance excellence.)

By the way, a question we are often asked is "What is the difference between coaching and mentoring?" Simply put, from the employee's or mentee's perspective, mentoring relationships are usually with someone who is senior to you and outside of your direct line of management. The relationship typically focuses on issues of career advancement or increasing overall performance. A mentor acts as a confidant, someone who will listen to the mentee's concerns and help him or her to develop solutions. Mentors will also share their own knowledge and experiences, more so than a coach. However, both coaches and mentors need strong interpersonal and communication skills, and at times, may use similar techniques to foster growth and development.

The Manager as Coach

We consider coaching a powerful tool for helping you build a high-performance, empowered, and engaged team. As a coach, you engage in dialogue with your employees about specific aspects of their performance. Together you explore how to bring that performance to the next level of excellence. Your coaching can focus on a number of areas, including leadership development, behavior change, or business issues, such as strategy and innovation. When performed successfully, coaching becomes a self-directed interaction, one in which you primarily provide support by encouraging reflection; you will provide guidance more than answers. In the end, this will help your employees to accept solutions that they, in essence, would have developed mostly on their own.

Finally, as a coach, your goal is to shift the worldview of your employees in a way that opens up new possibilities for action. By listening and making inquiries, observations, and reflections, you help your employees to identify their values and passions and align them with their professional or personal goals. By asking powerful, thought-provoking questions that tap into the inherent wisdom and creativity of your employees, you allow them to discover answers from within themselves.

Areas for Coaching

Table 8.1 outlines some possible areas of focus for coaching, broadly categorized as helping employees adapt, improving performance, and developing potential. You can use this as an initial guide for thinking about how you might use coaching for your employees.

Before entering a formal coaching relationship with one of your employees, you should do some preliminary planning by asking yourself the following questions:

1. Do I know the overarching needs and desires of the employee I will be coaching?
2. Do I know the specific coaching concern, issue, or opportunity and its impact?
3. Have I determined how I will approach the contract for coaching?
4. Have I decided the methods I will use to collaborate on actions and measures?
5. Do I know how I might be able to provide support and encourage reflection?
6. Have I determined a possible time frame for evaluating progress?

Table 8.1   Focus of Coaching

Helping an Employee Adapt	*Helping an Employee Improve Performance*	*Developing an Employee's Potential*
• Understand the impact of external changing demands. • Facilitate acceptance of changing business trends. • Deal with new business issues. • Transition to the requirements of the new organizational culture.	• Improve performance to meet expectations. • Address a performance problem. • Address a problematic situation. • Address the level of engagement. • Address a behavioral concern.	• Maximize potential in a current role. • Create development assignments. • Facilitate the adjustment to a new role or position. • Overall leadership development.

Finally, in general, there are those things we would call *don'ts*—the behaviors you should avoid when in the coaching role. These behaviors are listed below (and are further described in Table 8.2):

- Not sharing your intuition
- Being overly self-disclosing
- Overadvising
- Coaching each employee the same way
- Not hearing what's being said (or not being said)
- Getting sidetracked
- Playing the expert
- Not being yourself
- Making unwarranted assumptions
- Being judgmental

Table 8.2 Coaching Don'ts

Don't...	Example and Description
Not share your intuition	If you have a hunch, test it with your employee.
Overly self-disclose	Use self-disclosure only when you cannot draw further insight through questioning or for empathetic reasons. Make it brief.
Over advise	Don't tell; ask. Your role is to help your employee find his or her own solution. Sometimes he or she won't be able to find an option. However, before giving advice, ask, "Would you like me to offer you one possible option?"
Coach everyone the same way	It is important to adjust your approach to fit the employee you are coaching. While maintaining your own individual style, focus on using the tools, concept strategies, and advice that most benefit the employee.
Not hear what's being said (or not being said)	You might stop listening because you know what your employee is about to say. Show respect for your employee. Pay attention to 100% of the message.
Get sidetracked	When employees don't want to face something, they might create diversions. You need, however, to press your employees to persevere and complete what they have set out to achieve. Of course, don't allow your own issues to sidetrack you.

(continued)

Table 8.2 Coaching Don'ts (Continued)

Don't...	Example and Description
Play the expert	When you play the expert, it can create a dependency and can be disempowering to your employees.
Not be yourself	As long as you are putting the interest of your employee first, be yourself.
Make unwarranted assumptions	Points take some time to "sink in" and be understood. When making an important decision to act or change, allow your employee time to "digest." Repeat and rephrase to ensure both you and your employee understand the same thing.
Be judgmental	Take care not to measure your employees against your own personal standards and values.

Power Coaching

In our work with organizations, we have branded an approach to coaching that we call *power coaching*. Power coaching emphasizes the following in coaching relationships for managers and their employees:

- *Increase self-awareness around business results*: You and your employee will set coaching goals that consider the need to change from as many as three possible perspectives:
  - Your perspective: based on your assessment of your employee's performance, behavior, and potential
  - The employee's perspective: based on his or her own desire to improve performance, build new capabilities, or advance his or her career
  - Your company's perspective: based on the changing needs of the business and the ability to adapt to those needs and meet new challenges
- *Formulate an action plan*: Your employee agrees to accomplish specific tasks and set goals for acquiring new skills, performance improvement, and behavior change. The key issue here is accountability. Your employee is accountable for achieving the goal. You are accountable for providing guidance.
- *Structure the coaching process*: Coaching unfolds in a logical, orderly manner (the process is outlined in the next section).
- *Emphasize reflection*: You and your employee are engaged in conversations that focus on reflecting on the employee's actions, behaviors, attitudes, and so on, leading to fresh perspectives and views, and a deepened understanding of performance and behavior.

The Coaching Process

Figure 8.1 displays the power-coaching process, outlining the five major steps you and your employee will follow. Here is what each step entails:

- *Step 1: Identify the concern, issue, or opportunity and its impact*: Help your employee understand what the concern, issue, or opportunity is that may be affecting him or her, you, the team, the department, and/or the organization, positively or negatively. Describe the positive impact that taking action will have on the employee, customer, team, and so on.
- *Step 2: Develop a contract for coaching*: Clarify the purpose of coaching and what you and your employee want to achieve. Explain that the coaching process is a series of conversations, through which you will help your employee reach the agreed-to goal. The goal can range from improving relationships with key customers or stakeholders to achieving a new, higher level of performance. Ensure your employee is committed to moving forward.
- *Step 3: Collaborate on actions and measures*: In a collaborative conversation, determine the actions necessary to meet the agreed-to goal for coaching. Following the goal-setting framework discussed in Chapter 4, make sure any goals set are specific and measurable, and identify necessary resources and a time frame. Discuss, agree to, and document how you will measure results. Also consider any available feedback, including

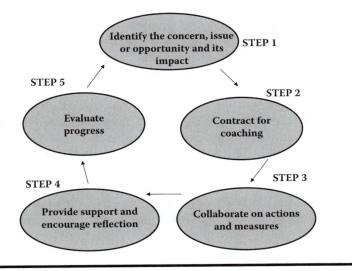

Figure 8.1. The power-coaching process.

360-degree feedback, to help you target the desired results and identify metrics by which you will measure progress against the goal.

■ *Step 4: Provide support and encourage reflection*: Your employee needs your support to meet his or her goals. Support can be as simple as listening while your employee figures out a difficult situation, or helping him or her to gather required resources. In a collaborative conversation, decide what actions are necessary to meet set goals.

- Consider asking key stakeholders for feedback throughout the coaching process. Feedback is important if you want to help your employee make significant changes or achieve dramatic performance leaps. Either your or your employee can collect the feedback so that you can mutually determine if any changes in course or strategy are needed. Schedule one-on-one sessions to provide the opportunity to discuss feedback and monitor overall progress. Remember, coaching is a process that involves a series of conversations over time.
- However, in order to change behavior, your employee needs a balance of taking action and time for reflection. In fact, fostering reflection may be the most beneficial support you can provide your employee. Reflection will help your employee to see things differently, both while in the process of taking action and after results are achieved. Some sample reflective questions include the following:
  • What major assumptions have you been making about this project?
  • Is this the same way you have approached this type of situation in the past?
  • Why did you take that approach?
  • What are some of the other ways of viewing this problem?
  • Who else might you have considered asking for input or feedback?
  • Given what we know now, what can you do differently going forward?
  • How do you feel about your progress, and why?

■ *Step 5: Evaluate Progress*: At an agreed-to point in time, you need to make a final assessment of progress. The assessment should consider the actions and measures that were established in Step 3. Also review other potential areas of impact, such as those related to the employee's sense of self, the team, the department, and the organization. Strongly consider going back to the same stakeholders you solicited feedback from earlier in the process, and see how their perceptions have changed. Take time to reflect on and celebrate success.

Table 8.3 expands on this process by stating what transpires in each step in the form of specific actions to take, making it easier for you to follow the

Table 8.3   Power-Coaching Process and Suggested Actions

Power-Coaching Step	Suggested Actions
Identify the concern, issue, or opportunity and its impact.	• State the issue, concern, or opportunity, and identify the implications of the current state or level of performance. • Describe how the current level of performance impacts the employee, team, customer, organization, and so on. • Describe the positive impact that taking action will have on the employee, team, and organization. • Get agreement to the issue and its impact.
Contract for coaching.	• Describe the coaching process as a series of conversations. • Overview the steps in the coaching process. • Explain the need to establish a coaching goal and measures. • Clarify mutual expectations. • Ask your employee to commit to the coaching process.
Collaborate on actions and measures.	• Clearly establish the coaching goal. • Identify the specific goal metrics. • Clarify the results your employee is expected to achieve. • Identify the resources your employee may need to achieve expected results. • Solicit feedback from key stakeholders, as needed, to help sharpen the picture of the results expected, as well as for specifying metrics. • Build an action plan by identifying key tasks and time frames. • Explore potential obstacles and brainstorm solutions to those obstacles. • Document the goal.

(continued)

Table 8.3   Power-Coaching Process and Suggested Actions (continued)

Power-Coaching Step	Suggested Actions

Provide support and encourage reflection.	• Schedule one-on-one meetings to discuss progress on the action plan. Always listen carefully and actively.
	
	• Help your employee work through challenges by, for example:
	  – Role-playing conversations with customers or key stakeholders.
	  – Demonstrating how you would handle the situation (e.g., a reverse role-play in which you act as your employee and your employee acts as his or her stakeholder).
	  – Talking through "what if" scenarios to help identify obstacles and build confidence.
	
	• Asking reflection questions to guide your employee to think about the process and results achieved. Reflection questions begin with phrases such as the following:
	  – "What if …?"
	  – "Tell me about …"
	  – "How would you …?"
	  – "What is the potential impact of …?"
	  – "What would happen …?"

Evaluate progress.	• Consider the following questions as you evaluate progress:
	  – Have the results been achieved?
	  – What has the employee learned in the process?
	  – How does the employee think that he or she has changed?
	  – How do others perceive that the employee has changed?
	  – How have the changes impacted the team and the organization?
	  – How satisfied are you and your employee with the results achieved?

overall process. Once again, we want to emphasize the importance of helping your employees reflect on their experience, guiding them to the best answers versus telling them what they should do to solve their problems or address their concerns. We consider this the hallmark of excellent coaching.

The Pros and Cons of Professional Coaching

The popularity of using professional, external coaches as a management and leadership development method emerged during the fast-paced boom of the 1990s. Managers and executives alike wanted personal attention, and they didn't want to risk divulging their weaker points to people in the company who controlled their destiny. A coaching industry was being created. Much of the early work in this area focused on senior-level executives, so the process of coaching when using an external coach was initially marketed as *executive coaching*. Several authors have recently provided good insight into the world of executive coaching (see, for instance, Hollenbeck, 2002; Kilburg, 2000; Kilburg & Diedrich, 2007; Morgan et al., 2005). Today, professional internal and external coaches are used in most organizations at various management levels (Morgan et al.). In fact, we believe that the definition put forth by Kilburg (2000) for executive coaching is applicable to managers at all levels and, perhaps, situates the coaching relationship more contextually within an organizational framework than the earlier definitions we offered:

> Executive coaching is defined as a helping relationship formed between a client who has managerial authority and responsibility in an organization and a consultant who uses a wide variety of behavioral techniques and methods to assist the client to achieve a mutually identified set of goals to improve his or her professional performance and personal satisfaction and consequently to improve the effectiveness of the client's organization within a formally defined agreement. (pp. 65–66)

Although this definition seems to limit coaching to those with "managerial" responsibility, we would definitely extend the use of a professional coach to individual contributors who have sufficient accountability and responsibility within their organizations.

Of course, even with a professional coach, coaching is a process that occurs over a period of time—generally involving multiple meetings and phone calls during the course of several months. And if the coach is external, he or she can come from a variety of backgrounds. Typically, external coaches are organization development specialists, industrial/organizational psychologists, counseling or clinical psychologists, human resources professionals, or former general business executives. Internal coaches, usually equipped with similar backgrounds, are most often found in the Human Resources department.

If you decide that one of your employees is best served by a professional coach, this does not mean that you no longer have to worry about your employee's performance and career development or that you are not responsible for continuing to coach the employee, too. Your experience and perspective are still vital, whereas the professional coach can provide an objective viewpoint and fresh ideas from experiences in other environments.

Why decide to use a professional coach for one of your employees? Professional coaching can be valuable and effective because

- Your employee will like the personal attention—it is hard to ignore the coach because the focus is on the employee, and this generally increases the employee's motivation to work with the coach.
- The coach will develop a personal relationship with your employee, different than that of your relationship with him or her.
- The coach will be able to focus on your employee's actual business problems and interpersonal issues, and will stand by your employee as he or she experiments with new behaviors and examines how these new behaviors impact results.
- Unlike a packaged training class, coaching is tailored to your employee's specific needs—becoming a highly efficient use of time.
- Feedback is important, but it must be used to be of value to your employee, and coaching facilitates the use of feedback.
- The coach will provide ongoing support and reinforcement.
- The coach provides a chance for your employee to talk openly to an objective third party about his or her concerns.

Objectives of Professional Coaching

The general objectives will not differ significantly from those you might choose to work on when acting as a coach with your employees. A key difference is that the professional coach might be able to bring a greater level of expertise to help your employee with his or her specific objectives and goals. We highlight some of these general objectives below, keeping in mind that you, when acting as a coach, can accomplish much of the same—perhaps just in a different manner.

Professional Coaches Can Help Your Employee Understand and Use Feedback

As a follow-up to 360-degree feedback, a coach can help your employee to review the results of the survey, hopefully in a constructive way. The coach doesn't do the work for your employee, but rather asks him or her to consider possible interpretations. The coach provides a sanity check on whether or not your employee is ignoring key results or rationalizing problems, falsely attributing unfavorable information to factors beyond his or her control. The coach keeps your employee honest. Finally, the coach will encourage the use of feedback results for a good purpose—setting goals for development and tracking whether the goals are met and ultimately whether your employee's performance improves.

Professional Coaches Strengthen an Employee's Accountability for Using Feedback

A coach won't let your employee avoid feedback. The coach will encourage your employee to take personal responsibility for using the feedback. Although an employee may try to rely on his or her coach too much, for instance by asking the coach to write his or her development goals, good coaches won't let themselves be used as a crutch. They establish ground rules for the relationship at the start, and they give your employee tasks that they expect will be completed prior to each meeting. Also, they won't let your employee postpone or interrupt coaching meetings, calling attention to such avoidance behavior and, if necessary, breaking off the coaching relationship.

Professional Coaches Focus on Management and Leadership Development

The goal of coaching, like the goal of any other development process, is to enhance competency. When linked to 360-degree feedback, coaching may be targeted to helping your employee process the feedback and set goals for development. The coach can generally go further to involve working with your employee on behavior change and helping him or her to learn how to learn. Moreover, by being a role model for coaching behaviors, the coach is demonstrating to your employee how to be a more effective coach to others.

Professional Coaches Help With Career Development Planning

A coach can help your employee review career experiences and career goals and set new goals for the future. A coach can suggest alternative career directions. Also, coaches will generally speak honestly to your employee about whether to stay with the company or consider leaving.

Professional Coaches Help Deal With Interpersonal Problems

A coach provides a safe haven for talking about other people. Sometimes a coach will interview members of your employee's team or colleagues to understand their perspectives and gather information that will help your employee interpret a given situation. Your employee can also talk through relationship issues and possible options with the coach, as well as practice different behavioral approaches with the coach before trying them out in the workplace. The coach can also provide tips for how to be clearer, more sensitive, more authoritative, or more participative, depending on what is needed.

Professional Coaches Can Help With Team Development

Coaching does not have to be focused on your employee alone. The coach can attend your employee's group meetings as well as meet with group members individually, with the intention of promoting group interaction and helping members understand each other better.

Professional Coaches Help With Managing Problem Performers

A coach can work with your employee on how to deal with people who are creating problems. For example, the coach can suggest management strategies for dealing with people who don't have the skills or the motivation to do their work. Suppose the workload has increased, and one of your employee's direct reports simply doesn't work as hard as necessary to get the job done, or suppose the technology has changed and someone on his or her team hasn't adapted. These are common problems, but there are no easy solutions. The coach can help your employee to be a better manager by identifying problems and thinking through alternative approaches. The coach becomes an advisor in how to cope with these difficult interpersonal issues.

Professional Coaches Help With Business Issues

Coaches can also help your employee address larger business issues and concerns, such as driving organization change, creating a culture of innovation, or leading a strategic planning process. For example, we know of one external coach working with the CEO of a Fortune 500 company who is helping that CEO to create a legacy of leadership development.

What Happens During Coaching?

So what do professional coaches actually do? Professional coaches can goad employees when they procrastinate. They don't let interruptions get in the way. They help employees focus on what's happening around them and within their own minds. More specifically, these coaches

- Address performance problems.
- Deal with emotions.
- Manage resistance and defenses.
- Analyze and consider ways to resolve conflicts.
- Get the issues on the table.
- Use feedback, and encourage the employee to own up to the effects of his or her actions.
- Emphasize what will work most effectively with the best long-term outcomes.
- Confront tantrums and acting out.
- Help the employee learn, solve problems, and communicate with creativity and energy.

Meetings With a Professional Coach

Coaching is likely to take place during private meetings once every 2 weeks for 2 or 3 months, although it has been reported that the average length of a coaching assignment can be from approximately 6 to 14 months, with senior executives having the longest time frames (Morgan et al., 2005). However, the meetings could be more or less frequent, and contact with the coach may include telephone calls or e-mail messages in addition to the in-person, one-on-one meetings.

Fundamentally, professional coaches follow a process similar to the one we outlined for managers. So here we describe the process—or what happens in the coaching relationship—in the context of a series of meetings over the course of several sessions (based on Weinberger, 1995, and cited in Kilburg, 1996):

- Session 1 (2 hours): Develop an intervention agreement. This includes establishing the focus and goals, time commitment, resource commitment, methods, confidentiality constraints, and payments. It also includes building a coaching relationship, which encompasses establishing the alliance, managing transferences, preserving containment, and creating expectations of success.
- Session 2 (2 hours): Discuss business problems facing the employee.
- Session 3 (2 hours): Discuss feedback—focus on favorable and unfavorable results, and identify and prioritize areas for development.
- Session 4 (1 hour): Set goals for development, discuss action plans, and establish a situation for the employee to demonstrate new skills and knowledge.
- Session 5 (1 hour): Provide feedback and further practice.
- Session 6 (1 hour): Evaluate the coaching—what worked, what didn't.

Getting the Coaching Relationship Off to a Good Start

Your employee and the coach have certain, basic accountabilities that are necessary for making the early phases of the coaching process effective.

The Coach Should …

- Establish a contract—an agreement with the employee about how much time will be devoted to the coaching.
- Clarify what the employee can expect from the coaching process.
- Describe what is likely to occur.
- Set the agenda to keep the employee focused on what is important to him or her, and not let distractions intervene.

The Employee Should …

- Keep his or her commitments to the coach.
- Allot sufficient time for the coaching, avoiding all possible interruptions.
- Do promised homework (e.g., formulating goals for development for discussion at the next meeting).
- Set the agenda to keep focused on what is important, and not let distractions intervene.
- Take the work seriously.

How Do You Help Your Employee Get a Professional Coach?

In most organizations, coaching as a process is typically instituted and made available through the human resources department. If that is the case, contact your HR department. You may be offered an internal coach for your employee. If external coaches are used, your HR department will typically fund the first few sessions, usually tied to the 360-degree feedback process. Generally, if you and your employee feel these first few sessions are worthwhile, you will probably want to continue the process. At that stage, you may need to contract with the coach to continue the process and pay the external coach from your department funds. In companies where no formal programs exist, or if internal coaches are not available, you may have no choice but to contract for a coach for an employee through your own efforts.

Hiring an external coach could cost $2,000–4,000 or more for a half-day meeting. Preparation time and time for collecting performance information may be extra. Still, coaching can be more targeted to your employee's needs than a typical, week-long leadership development program (which may cost $10,000 or $15,000 and several thousand more for travel, room, and food).

Selecting the Right Coach

Quite possibly, some coaches are more effective than others, given their different backgrounds and work experiences. Also, some coaches may be more effective in certain situations. For example, one coach may be more of an expert in coaching for career advancement, whereas another may be more adept at providing advice about organizational change or developing leaders. Although most coaches should have rigorous psychological training, some of the more business-oriented coaches may not. If the decision is to use a business-oriented coach, then before your employee engages in coaching, he or she should undergo a psychological assessment to help determine the extent to which issues may be more psycho-dynamic or competency driven (Berglas, 2002). When selecting a professional coach, ask about the coach's

- Style, basic approach, and areas of expertise
- General background—to determine if your employee can work with this coach
- Experience as a coach—length of time, industry familiarity, and so on
- Process for determining a good coach and employee match
- Philosophy of coaching and development

Effects of Coaching

So far we have promoted the virtues of coaching and described the process. But does coaching really work? What do managers like you think about their experiences with a professional coach, and is there any solid evidence about the effects of coaching on performance? Actually, at present, there are far more "how-to" books than there are research studies. But, fortunately, there are a few studies.

Managers who are coached generally report that the experience was worthwhile (Hall, Otazo, & Hollenbeck, 1999). One study examined the effects of coaching in a public sector municipal agency where 31 managers first participated in a 3-day management development program (Olivero, Bane, & Kopelman, 1997). The 31 managers subsequently worked with an internal coach for 8 weeks. The coaching included goal setting, collaborative problem solving, behavioral practice, feedback, supervisory involvement, evaluation of end results, and a public presentation. The study showed that although both the management development program and coaching increased productivity, the coaching resulted in higher productivity gains in comparison to the management development program alone.

Another study reported on 1,361 senior managers in a large, global corporation. All of these managers received 360-degree feedback, and 404 of them worked with an external coach. More than 280 of the managers in the study responded to a brief online survey that gathered their reactions to the coaching process (Smither, London, Flautt, Vargas, & Kucine, 2002). A follow-up study showed that the managers who worked with a coach were more likely to share their feedback and request ideas for improvement from their supervisors than those who did not, but they were less likely to be seen by their supervisors and peers as having improved. Those who did work with a coach improved more than those who did not.

When Is Coaching Likely to Succeed?

The following are actions you can recommend to your employees in coaching relationships to ensure that their experience with a professional coach is as effective as possible:

- Be and remain motivated to explore your feedback and engage in the coaching process; don't bother if you really don't care.
- Give it a chance. Coaching can help you improve your performance—just give it some time.

- Come to a clear agreement with your coach from the outset about the scope of the coaching, how much time will be spent, and the desired outcome.
- Strive with your coach to move quickly from a discussion about feedback to action plans that can be implemented immediately. As a result, you will see tangible benefits of coaching early in the process.
- Focus on your immediate business issues as well as areas for your professional development. As such, you will be able to address pressing concerns that can have immediate benefit, in addition to establishing development plans that can have a long-term personal benefit for you.
- View your coach as a role model for the coaching process, and use the experience to enhance your appreciation for the value of coaching. You will learn effective coaching techniques such as being on time for the coaching session, holding a private meeting without interruptions, being open and honest without criticizing another's personal qualities, and being accessible to the person you coach between formal sessions.
- Keep your coach engaged when you actually begin implementing your development plan.

Common Obstacles to Effective Coaching

Although a good attitude and commitment to the process increase the likelihood that your employees experience coaching as valuable, a number of obstacles can get in the way. We recommend that you discuss these obstacles with any employee before he or she begins the process with a professional coach so that together you can watch for them, guard against them when possible, or at least recognize their occurrence and how they may interfere with a positive coaching experience. Here are some of these obstacles, typically the result of when your employee

- Has a workload and stress level that overwhelm the coaching process.
- Needs to handle unexpected crises, and starts to view coaching as an unnecessary or unhelpful burden at the time.
- Uses uncertainty in the company about forthcoming mergers or restructuring to focus on job security rather than the more pressing concerns that drove the initial need for coaching.
- Uses coaching as a vehicle for career advancement, and his or her career goals get in the way of focusing on the behaviors that need development to improve current performance.
- Is in search of easy answers.
- Wants the coach to do the dirty work, and expects the coach to take responsibility for delivering any unpleasant messages to others.

- Does not have an accurate view of how he or she is seen by others, and has trouble facing reality.
- Has difficulty seeing the relationship between the competencies he or she needs to develop and the behaviors he or she needs to change. For instance, your employee might recognize the need to be a more strategic leader but may not understand what this means in terms of changing communications patterns and building team relationships.
- Does not meet the coaching commitments made. For example, after an initial discussion about feedback, your employee may not bother to work on a draft development plan before the next coaching session, and indeed may expect the coach to do that for him or her.
- Is not ready to talk openly to someone else about his or her job performance.
- Realizes that the coach does not have the required skills or experience to help solve his or her problems.
- Does not get along with the coach. Styles or personalities clash. In this case, the sooner another coach is found, the better.
- Faces very difficult problems. Some problems are not easily solved during the course of several coaching sessions. These problems may be endemic to the company's competitive situation or the economy. They may also be more personal, for example, your employee may have limited sensitivity to people of other cultures or the inability to make rapid decisions—characteristics that may take years to change and develop.
- Realizes that coaching is not the right development strategy. He or she might benefit more from a training class, for instance, in presentation skills or written communication.

Keep in Mind the Benefits of Coaching

If you have any reservations at this point about offering professional coaching to your employees or the value of professional coaching, we leave you with this list of possible benefits of coaching.

- *Increased behavioral flexibility*: Coaching helps employees take time to analyze their decisions and behaviors. It teaches them to think more deeply before they act. It improves their ability to consider alternative courses of action. As such, coaching can make them more flexible in how they handle a situation, and help them to choose the most effective response.
- *Improved psychological and social competencies*: Coaching gives employees time to think about themselves—both how they react to others and how others react to them. This increases their self-awareness. They are also

less likely to act impulsively out of emotions and unconscious conflicts. Instead, they learn about themselves, and how to acquire more information about themselves, perhaps by seeking feedback. Their capacity to learn and grow increases.

■ *Increased capacity to manage*: Coaching helps employees deal with the stress of everyday business. It helps them recognize that the people with whom they work have different needs, capabilities, and interests. In addition, coaching helps them cope with increased workloads and challenging assignments that may feel more burdensome than enriching, at least at first.

■ *Increased ability to manage turbulence, crisis, and conflict*: Coaching can help employees think through their responses to crises. Just having an impartial person to talk to is helpful during stressful times. Coaching can help them take a more objective, unemotional view of their situation and consider courses of action available to them. Learning how to take two steps back in a tight situation can serve them well later when problems arise and they don't have a coach a phone call away.

■ *Be more planful*: Coaching can help employees understand how to analyze feedback and use it to plan. More generally, coaching can help them appreciate the value of seeking information, using that information to formulate a plan, and using the plan to track their success and make adjustments as the situation changes. Plans can go beyond a focus on immediate business needs to a focus on their careers and, indeed, their life plans—for example, planning for a career change or for retirement.

Coaching Is Not Therapy

Remember that coaching is not the same as therapy. A coach is focused on work issues and job performance. The goal is to examine areas for development and assist an employee in thinking through work-related problems and identifying and evaluating possible responses. A coach will help an employee establish development plans and, if the coaching relationship continues, track success in carrying out these plans. The number of meetings an employee will have with the coach will be relatively few. These meetings may occur every 2 or 3 weeks during the course of several months. Your employee may have some telephone calls and e-mails from the coach to remind him or her to work on development plans, or your employee may call the coach to discuss a business situation that just arose.

This is not the same as long-term therapy with a clinical or counseling psychologist or a psychiatric social worker. A coach will address behavior, and may touch on personality and temperament as characteristics that influence an employee's behavior. As stated earlier, a coach may help an employee deal with interpersonal problems on the job. However, the goal is not to delve deeply into the employee's early life or the psychodynamics of the relationships within his or her family. These may enter into the conversation (for instance, problems at home may be affecting performance at work or vice versa). Expect a professional coach to refer your employee to another professional for private consultations, as necessary.

Conclusion

We defined coaching and discussed how you, as a manager, can become a more effective coach. We articulated a number of coaching considerations as well as "do's and don'ts." We also described an effective, 5-step coaching process we call *power coaching* that you can use with your employees. We emphasized, as well, that the purpose of coaching is to help your employees open up to new possibilities for action.

Although coaching is part of your manager role and is an important component of performance management, coaching can sometimes by accomplished by a professional internal or external coach. We discussed the pros and cons of using a professional coach, helping you to understand what to expect and how to choose a professional coach for your employees. Finally, we described how you can maximize the value of using professional coaches in your organization, should the occasion arise.

Chapter 9

Managing Employee and Team Learning and Development

We define *learning* as the process of acquiring new knowledge, new skills, or a change in perspective, and *development* as the accumulation and application of new knowledge and skills over time, including the capacity to view the world through a more informed, inclusive perspective. The question is, however: Why should you be more concerned today about your employees' learning and development than ever before?

The rapid pace of change in today's world demands continuous learning for ongoing development and performance improvement. For example, you and your employees will need to learn new behaviors as you respond to changes in the environment, shifting circumstances, and new expectations. You may also need to acquire new knowledge and skills to form and implement new ideas or decide on new actions and behaviors. And, at times, you may need to reframe what you and your employees know, learning to see yourselves, your organization, or the world around you in different ways.

As a manager, you can help your employees become continuous learners by working with them to set meaningful work and career goals, coaching them to enhance their performance and expand their professional growth, and encouraging your employees to engage in—and providing opportunities for—training and development. In addition, as found in our study at XINC, your focus on providing performance feedback for learning, setting goals, and having career planning discussions with your employees and supporting their career development efforts will go a long way toward fostering higher levels of engagement in your organization.

Ideally, your employees will take responsibility for their own learning and development, and, of course, you should do the same. Ask yourself: Are you responsible for your own development? You might say, "Who else is if I'm not?" Would your employees say they are responsible for their own development? Perhaps some would and some wouldn't. What would you say from observing them? No doubt, some of your employees are avid learners, and others seem to shy away from learning anything new.

So what is self-development? What type of employee is likely to be a self-developer? What personality characteristics or traits characterize the employee who loves to learn and is likely to be responsive to your support for development, including feedback and coaching? How do you measure an employee's propensity for continuous learning and career development? We address these questions in this chapter. You will also learn about employees who are expansive in their desire for learning and innovation, how to help your employees to acquire knowledge and expertise from their daily experiences, and how to support and promote your employees' ongoing development.

In this chapter, we also address team learning, which most managers know very little about or tend to ignore. We will show you how teams learn in adaptive, generative, and transformative ways and answer the questions "What is team learning?" and "How do I promote team learning?" so that you can strengthen your team's performance and enhance engagement in your organization.

Practical Advice for Helping Your Employees Engage in Self-Development

Let's start with some practical ways you can help your employees to take responsibility for their own development. Here are some actions you can suggest:

- *Seek feedback.* Ask for information about your job performance. Ask about opportunities to try new things on your job. Also, inquire about career opportunities. Ask your peers, other colleagues, and, of course, me, your manager. Don't wait for our once-a-year formal performance appraisal discussion. And don't wait for the company's 360-degree feedback survey!

- *Overcome your reluctance to seek feedback.* Practice asking for feedback from me, your peers, your employees, and your customers. Discover who is good at providing meaningful information.
- *Generate your own feedback by establishing tracking mechanisms.* For instance, collect data about your customers or employees. Create your own feedback surveys.
- *Set learning and performance improvement goals.* In doing so, first review the goals we set, and then focus on how you will meet our objective measures of success, such as new orders, the number of customer contacts, or the speed of implementing a new program or bringing a new product to market.
- *Make goal setting and feedback a continuous process—even a daily process.* As you do so, consider what you are learning from me and others and how you are using this information to enhance your job performance.
- *Learn how to dialogue with yourself.* Think about how others react to you and view your performance, and how changing your behavior affects others' reactions and, more generally, performance outcomes.
- *Don't take your learning for granted.* Consider what you have learned, are in the process of learning, and want to learn. Write down your progress and goals for the future. Set timelines for learning, and collect information to track your progress.

Self-development, in the broadest sense, is a process that occurs throughout our adult years, and your employees will develop the most when they acquire the knowledge, skills, or experiences that help to broaden their perspectives or views of the world.

To help you better understand and evaluate the extent to which your employees are self-developers, we turn now to discussing the continuous learner, career motivation, and the concept of expansiveness.

Characteristics of a Continuous Learner

Although we consider learning the sine qua non of adult development, not everyone is equally motivated to engage in learning activities. For a number of reasons, some of your employees are more likely than others to participate in ongoing self-development. We call these employees *continuous learners*. Are your employees continuous learners? (Are you a continuous learner?)

Consider the following characteristics. Each is indicative of avid continuous learners. How would you answer the following questions about each of your employees? Ask your employees how they would answer them, as well.

- *Openness to experience:* Does he or she look forward to new experiences and, even more so, seek them out?
- *Conscientiousness:* Does he or she work hard and exert more energy, often more than what is really required, in order to be effective?
- *Self-efficacy:* Does he or she have self-confidence and believe in his or her ability to accomplish tasks that bring about positive outcomes for all stakeholders?
- *Uncertainty orientation:* Does he or she acquire new knowledge and learn new skills to reduce uncertainty and manage through ambiguity?

If your employees are continuous learners, they are open to new experiences. They are conscientious and self-confident, and they believe that they can learn and develop, and, in the process, make good things happen for themselves. In this way, they create and sustain a sense of empowerment about their own development, an important feeling that leads to greater degrees of engagement. They also see learning as a way to reduce feelings of anxiety caused by a perceived lack of ability or information. The process of learning becomes a goal in itself, and learning leads to an ever-growing sense of accomplishment and continuous performance improvement.

Career Motivation

Broadly speaking, an employee's *career motivation* revolves around three dimensions: (a) the spark that generates the motivation to further his or her career development, (b) the direction or view the employee has for his or her career goals, and (c) the extent to which the employee is persistent in achieving his or her career goals. More specifically, when you are thinking about your employees' career motivation, consider that

- *Career insight* is the spark. It occurs as your employees recognize opportunities, their own strengths and weaknesses, and their interests in pursuing options that excite them and that they believe can be achieved.
- *Career identity* is the goal direction. This is the vision that employees have of themselves, defined in terms of their career goals, for instance, to be a leader (e.g., CEO of the company), a renowned technical expert, or a respected team member.
- *Career resilience* is the persistence factor. Employees are more likely to be resilient in overcoming career barriers when they believe in themselves. This is more likely when they have a history of accomplishment and success.

These three dimensions form a model of career motivation developed by London (London, 1983, 2003), which also helps us to understand how the propensity for self-development unfolds and can be reinforced throughout our lives. According to the model, resilience leads to insight, which in turn leads to identity. Employees establish a sense of resilience (self-confidence and the belief that they can bring about positive outcomes) early in life, probably even before they started their careers. Their career resilience leads them to be open to new experiences that give them insight into themselves (their abilities and interests) and into the opportunities available to them. This leads them to a meaningful career direction, one in which they have a good chance of flourishing.

Insight and identity grow out of the information employees have about themselves and their environment. As such, insight and identify can be changed with *more* information. Resilience, however, is less easily changed. Why? Resilience is developed and affected by events early in life. However, resilience *can* change, but slowly.

Resilience is a direct outcome of the positive reinforcement received early in life. However, changes in reinforcements for behavior can alter resilience over time. For example, one of your employees, as a young adult, may have received positive reinforcement for leadership behavior throughout his high school years. Another of your employees did not have a similar experience and now has substantial self-doubt about her ability to lead. This may change if she begins to have successful leadership experiences. However, some time and numerous positive experiences with few setbacks may be needed for both of them to be resilient if and when their leadership attempts fail. The bottom line is that your employees need positive experiences in order to enhance their career resilience.

When it comes to building your employees' career motivation and capacity for self-development, and at the same time increasing their engagement, consider the following strategies:

- Support your employees' career *resilience* by identifying and rewarding their positive behaviors, providing them with meaningful recognition.
- Provide your employees with information about career and development opportunities and feedback about their performance, helping to increase their career *insight.*
- Use the goal-setting process to establish meaningful goals and a direct connection between goal achievement and rewards, and to ensure that the goals will provide your employees a sense of challenge, helping to increase their career *identity.*

The Expansive Personality

A third way of looking at and understanding your employees' tendency to engage in self-development, in addition to the lenses of continuous learning orientation and career motivation, is through the lens of *expansiveness* (London & Diamante, 2002). Expansiveness refers to *an unlimited capability for continuous growth with potentially ever-expanding depth and breadth.* This personality type overlaps with those discussed by Macey and Schneider (2008) as important to engagement, including the proactive personality (describing people with the general tendency to create or influence the work environment) and the autotelic personality (describing people who engage in activities for their own sake rather than for specific gain or reward). As a result, employees who are more expansive will also, in general, tend to be predisposed to being more engaged.

Expansiveness suggests a constant striving toward development and a very high degree of motivation. In general, an employee can be described as expansive when he or she is driven and enthusiastic and has a degree of energy and motivation. In addition, his or her goals and challenges will primarily revolve around work and the outcomes or rewards it provides. In terms of orientation toward work, expansive employees are usually either externally or interpersonally oriented; in terms of outcomes, they usually focus on either extrinsic (e.g., financial) or intrinsic (the feeling of fulfillment) rewards. There are two types of expansive personalities—external and internal.

> *External expansive personality*: Employees who are externally expansive are outwardly oriented—focusing on building new organizations or teams or learning and generating new knowledge in their fields. For example, consider those employees viewed as entrepreneurs or thought leaders on your team or in your company. They are driven by the challenge and excitement from learning, developing, and applying cutting-edge knowledge and practices in their fields. This is the overarching theme of their lives. It guides the way they define themselves and most everything they do.
>
> *Internal expansive personality*: Employees who are internally expansive are keenly aware of themselves and how they relate to others. Moreover, they focus on their own self-development, are aware of and recognize their own goals and desires, and are intrinsically motivated to achieve those goals. They want to learn more about themselves, how others react to them, and how they react to others. They also want to learn more to improve their job performance, not just because of the extrinsic rewards that may result (e.g., more money or prestige) but also for the joy of the challenge and the sense of accomplishment (intrinsic reward).

The pressures of our current business environment drive and reward people who are externally expansive. For example, consider most entrepreneurs, and typically those in the field of technology. These externally expansive individuals are adept at overcoming barriers due to technological complexity, change, and organization resistance (e.g., unclear structure and support, lack of resources, and delayed financial gains). However, these same people are likely to struggle in the face of interpersonal difficulties—for instance, resolving conflicts, getting to know newcomers, and managing people who are not performing up to par. Internally expansive people are likely to be more able to overcome these interpersonal difficulties, even if they are confused or frustrated by technological change and organization resistance or lack of support.

Are Your Employees Truly Expansive?

You can evaluate your employees against the characteristics grouped in the three sections below. First you will assess general expansiveness, then you will assess against characteristics of external and internal expansiveness. You can also ask your employees to self-assess using these same questions, and then compare results, which should make for an interesting development and coaching conversation.

> Place a *Y* for yes or *N* for no in the space provided depending on the extent to which the characteristic describes the employee you have in mind. If it mostly describes the employee, rate the characteristic a *Y*; if not, rate it an *N*. If you have given the employee more *Y*'s than *N*'s, then he or she is more likely to fit the given category than not.

General Expansiveness: This Employee …

- Believes he or she has unlimited capability for continuous growth.
- Is constantly striving to learn more.
- Is enthusiastic and passionate about his or her work.
- Is highly motivated.
- Feels continuous joy from his or her work.
- Tries to understand the implications of change.
- Is open to new ideas.
- Looks forward to change.
- Dreams about what could be.
- Is generally trying to make things better.
- Sees barriers as challenges to overcome.

If you have six or more *Y* responses, and you feel they are truly characteristic of the employee you have in mind, then the employee probably is *expansive*.

Externally Expansive: This Employee …

- Feels an unlimited capacity for professional growth.
- Has a driving passion to learn.
- Sets his or her own learning goals.
- Desires to learn about and generate new knowledge in his or her field.
- Is constantly trying to acquire new knowledge and skills.
- Is constantly asking why.
- Is continuously on the lookout for advancements in his or her field.
- Likes to try new ways of doing things.
- Sees possibilities that others do not see.
- Puts his or her ideas into action.

If you have six or more *Y* responses, and you feel they are truly characteristic of the employee you have in mind, then the employee is probably *externally expansive*.

Internally Expansive: This Employee …

- Is on a quest for self-knowledge.
- Strives to learn more about him or herself.
- Frequently ask others what they think about his or her job performance.
- Wants to know more about how he or she affects the world around him or her.
- Wants to know more about how others affect the world around them.
- Strives to understand better what he or she wants from his or her career.
- Strives to understand his or her motivation better.
- Strives to feel better about him or herself.
- Is keenly aware of his or her limitations.
- More often than not, compares him or herself to the way he or she would like to be.
- Tries to understand how others react to him or her.
- Tries to understand if he or she views the world similarly to others.
- Recognizes that words can have a powerful effect on others.
- Tries to improve relationships with his or her coworkers.

If you have eight or more *Y* responses, and you feel they are truly characteristic of the employee you have in mind, then the employee is probably *internally expansive*.

In conclusion, an expansive employee, whether internal or external—and yes, an employee is usually to some degree both internally and externally expansive—is the kind of person who gets thing done. Expansive employees are driven to make things happen, regardless of whether their expected outcome is more external or internal. Expansiveness can and does have a positive impact on individual, team, and organization performance. In fact, many organizations need and rely on expansive individuals. Ask yourself the following questions to determine the extent to which your company requires expansive employees, managers, and executives:

- Is there pressure to adopt new technology, be first in the marketplace with new technological developments, and/or use technology to expand existing markets and lock in market share?
- Is your company always responding to the competition?
- Is your company dependent on its technological wizards and thought leaders?
- Are economic conditions changing? For better? For worse?
- Are business strategies changing because of new technologies and stiff competition?
- Is your company trying to form alliances with other firms?
- Does most work get done in teams? Do these teams pose leadership challenges because members are geographically dispersed, come from different cultural and education backgrounds, and represent different skills and responsibilities?
- Is your company's work environment fast paced?
- Are employees expected to be available to the company 24 hours a day, 7 days a week?
- Are employees treated as if they are only as good as their latest success?

If you answered yes to most of these questions, you are working in a relatively volatile environment that certainly demands expansive personalities.

In summary, we have discussed the motivation for self-development through the lenses of continuous learning orientation, career motivation, and expansiveness.

Next we consider informal learning and show you how to help your employees to create and capitalize on informal learning opportunities.

Informal Learning

Informal learning is the process of learning from our daily activities and experiences. Unlike structured classroom learning or working with a professional coach, learning from experience is an informal, ongoing process. However, what we learn informally may not be apparent unless we make the effort to think about it. As a manager, you can drive employee engagement by helping your employees create and capitalize on informal, typical, on-the-job learning opportunities. For example, you can encourage your employees to learn from

- Considering the guidance or advice they get from coworkers.
- Debating others.
- Listening to what others think of their ideas.
- Watching and observing what others say and do.
- Participating on a project team.
- Doing something new and different.
- Making decisions.
- Making mistakes.
- Creating a new experience or opportunity just to do something different and learn something new.
- Trying to help their colleagues learn something new by coaching them through the learning process and helping them determine what to learn and how to go about it.

Think about the advantages of informal learning. It is cost-effective because the experience is happening anyway. It is "real world," meaning that it focuses on tasks and challenges your employees face in their daily work activities. It is also time effective—your employees don't have to leave their jobs to learn.

Although informal learning may occur naturally, this doesn't make it happen automatically. Why? After all, it's unstructured—no one is there to tell your employees what to learn or when to learn it. And no one is there to verify what your employees learned. Capitalizing on informal learning will require both initiative and self-reflection.

How to Create Opportunities for Informal Learning

There are many opportunities for informal learning. Think about, for example, how and what you have learned from new and different job experiences, as well as the opportunities you have had to get new information or knowledge or broaden your perspective. You can probably also identify a number of people who have helped you learn—good subject matter experts, role models, mentors, or coaches.

Your employees have had and can still have similar opportunities for learning. So in addition to encouraging your employees to learn from these experiences, too, you can also orchestrate other opportunities for learning. For instance, you can form a team to develop a new product or service, method, or procedure. You can also provide your employees with special assignments that will enable them to learn new skills or apply new knowledge. You can also support your employees as they "experiment" with new ways of doing their current jobs.

Basically, then, informal learning is a three-step process that includes, for you, as a manager: (a) establishing learning goals with your employees, (b) identifying activities based on how each of your employees learns best, and (c) helping your employees to reflect on their experiences to process and act on what they have learned. These steps are addressed below.

Establishing Learning Goals and Informal Learning Strategies With Your Employees

Consider the process for establishing goals. If you recall, in Chapter 4, we discussed creating development goals. Development goals, as you know, involve the acquisition of new skills, new knowledge, new behavior, or a change in perspective. You may, for example, help one of your employees to establish a development goal based on 360-degree feedback results. Specifically, you may have both discovered that your employee's peers feel he or she needs to communicate more clearly. As a result, together you can set a goal "to communicate more clearly," with a strategy based on informal learning methods, such as "asking peers for feedback at the conclusion of working meetings." On the other hand, if your employee needed to sharpen a specific knowledge area or skill, such as budgeting, a strategy might be "to review all department budgets with my manager."

In conclusion, once you and your employee have agreed to the learning goals, you will need to identify ways to achieve them. Before we turn to a discussion of how to choose an informal learning strategy, consider that you may also want to include formal learning in your employee's development plans, perhaps as a supplement to on-the-job learning experiences.

Choosing an Informal Learning Strategy

Some of your employees may like to read about concepts and principles, whereas others may prefer to observe role models in action. Still others may like and want to learn by doing. These and most other informal learning activities can be grouped into two broad categories, learning by reflection and learning by doing. Similarly, you can classify each of your employees as either more or less a reflective learner or an active learner.

Employees who are *reflective learners* rely more on thinking when it comes to learning and, in a classroom setting, would largely prefer a lecture style and are usually those who tend to be quiet or ask questions about theories, principles, and the like to further their understanding. Reflective learners

- Like to ponder experiences and think about them from many perspectives.
- Enjoy listening to others discuss new ideas and techniques.
- Pick up new information by watching others and modeling their behavior later.
- Look for reading material and references when they need to learn something new.

Employees who are *active learners* rely more on doing and trying when it comes to learning and, in a classroom setting, would largely prefer activities to lecture, and would be seen as those who volunteer for, or who are being very engaged in, exercises that involve doing. Active learners

- Like "hands-on" learning.
- Seek out and try new experiences.
- Like testing out new concepts, theories, and techniques to see if they work in practice.
- Search out new ideas and experiment with their applications.

As a manager, take the time to work with each of your employees to help them identify their preferred learning styles and those activities that will help them learn best. Urge your employees, as well, to further enhance their own development by trying and learning from activities that are less comfortable for them, so that they broaden their overall capacity to learn. In the end, true learning is about more than being engaged in active- or reflective-oriented kinds of activities; it involves deeper *reflection* on what was learned and putting that learning into practice.

Reflecting on Experience

When we don't reflect on *what* we have learned and how we can *apply* that learning to other current or future situations, informal learning opportunities become missed opportunities for development and growth. So, we present below a number of examples of informal learning opportunities and show you how you can help your employees both to reflect and to act on their learning.

- *Form a development network of informal coaches.* Encourage your employees to include fellow colleagues, team members, and even clients in their networks. Tell them to use their networks to help them interpret events and others' reactions, be a sounding board for their ideas, and support their development. Then, take the feedback, and test out what they learned in upcoming situations.

■ *Think about and discuss events (e.g., client encounters).* Ask each of your employees, after key events, to stop and ask themselves, "What went well and what didn't … and why?" How did his or her actions affect the outcome? What could he or she have done differently to change the outcome? Is there anything he or she can still do to change the outcome? What plan can he or she build and put into practice for handling future events?

■ *Analyze difficult situations.* For example, ask your employees to think about what happened when a client's business stalled, a contract was cancelled, or a customer's business goals changed. What were their thoughts? What were their conclusions? What did they decide to change or do? What action did they take about the situation, or how have they prepared themselves to deal with these kinds of situations going forward?

■ *Analyze barriers.* When running into difficulty completing a project or achieving a goal, ask each of your employees to consider possible barriers and ways to overcome these barriers. Advise them to explore a range of barriers, such as difficult personalities, a win-lose mentality, lack of needed skills or knowledge, poor collaboration, disagreement about actions or timelines, and so on.

■ *Consider ways to add value.* Ask your employees to think about what they can contribute when they are working with a new client or working on a new project with an existing client. Suggest they ask for feedback, and then implement any possible new ideas or take corrective action if necessary, and consider ways to apply their learning with other clients or projects.

■ *Collect benchmark data and best practices.* Remind your employees to seek and collect these data and practices from your own company or other companies. Ask them to use these data to understand the quality and effectiveness of their current practices. If they see gaps and areas for improvement, ask them to take action to apply what they have learned to their own practices and processes.

■ *Seek projects and assignments that will help you develop.* Ask your employees to approach you about assignments or projects they can work on that can provide the opportunity to help them strengthen or gain needed knowledge or skills. Help them to structure the assignments or projects so they can maximize their learning. Tell them they need to monitor their learning and apply what they have learned.

■ *Analyze your competition.* Encourage your employees to engage in competitive analysis—to learn all they can about their competitors—and then analyze the potential impact on their organization and goals. Help them use that information to make needed changes in their strategy and to take action accordingly.

- *Consider ways to change course.* Ask your employees to think about how they can be more innovative, or how they can move a project in a new, more productive direction. Ask them to refine and decide on an approach, test out their ideas, and analyze what worked and what did not work. Then ask them to start the process over again.

- *Engage in critical reflection.* Help your employees, as discussed in our approach to coaching, to examine, in depth, the beliefs and assumptions they hold about themselves, their performance, their employees, their customers, and so on. Also help them to test their beliefs and assumptions with trusted others and to determine the accuracy of those beliefs and assumptions. Decide what actions, perhaps acquiring new knowledge or information, need to be taken, and ensure those actions are taken.

- *Ask others for advice.* Suggest that your employees ask their colleagues and friends at work what they have learned recently; also tell them to ask about the new experiences they have had and to describe in detail any special projects. They should then follow up with questions about the projects when they see them during the next weeks and months. They should make it clear to their colleagues and friends that they want to learn from them, and that they value their expertise and would appreciate their help. To give something in return and build the relationship, tell your employees to offer to describe what they are working on and learning and to invite their colleagues and friends to be sounding boards for their ideas. Tell your employees that they should analyze what they are learning and incorporate their learning into how they think about their work, goals, performance, and development, as well as the actions they take.

Managing Your Team's Learning

Much of today's work is done in teams, but most managers miss the opportunity to actually foster team learning. These managers miss, as well, the chance to use teams and team learning as a way to build employee engagement. But how do you build employee engagement through team learning? When you foster team learning, you strengthen engagement as your employees

- Get information they need to do their jobs more effectively.
- Gain additional recognition for performance.
- Have the opportunity to solve problems in creative and innovative ways.
- Get additional chances to challenge the status quo.

■ Increase their on-the-job learning.
■ Improve overall job satisfaction and meaningfulness.

Certainly there are a variety of teams, from committees and advisory boards, to corporate-wide task forces and quality improvement teams. In this section we will focus on your team of direct reports; however, you will be able to use the advice we offer for managing or leading any team in your organization.

Why focus on your direct report team? We have too often found that managers are not effectively using their direct report teams to solve organization problems and to learn from their experiences as a team. Managers just seem to meet with their direct report teams for reviews or updates on the organization's various projects and initiatives—status meetings more or less—if they meet at all. So we are encouraging you to use your team more effectively. If you do so, you will model the way for your own direct reports to use their teams more effectively, as well, and to promote team learning with each of their teams.

In fact, you should consider all the ideas and advice in this book and apply them to the performance management of your team to help you use your team more effectively and productively. Your team, just like your individual employees, learns and performs, and you can manage team performance in the same way that you manage an individual's performance. For example, you can help your team set and achieve goals, meet stakeholders' expectations, respond to unexpected events, and take advantage of opportunities. You can also provide feedback to shape and improve your team's performance, as well as recognize the team's efforts.

Of course, your team is composed of your individual employees, and when we speak of team performance or learning, ultimately, we are talking about each team member's behavior. However, a team is somehow more than the sum of its individual members. Team performance and learning are functions of how your team members interact with each other, as well as with those outside the team.

We now turn to defining team learning, and then we show you how you can impact and foster your team's learning to increase engagement and improve performance. In our discussion, we are making the assumption that you are the team leader.

If you are interested in a more in-depth look at leading teams and fostering learning at the individual, team, and organization levels, we recommend the Sessa and London (2006) book *Continuous Learning in Organizations.*

Defining Team Learning

Learning in general is the process of gaining new skills, knowledge, and perceptions of the world. Team learning is "the extent to which members seek opportunities to develop new skills and knowledge, welcome challenging assignments, are willing to take risks on new ideas, and work on tasks that require considerable skill and knowledge" (London, Polzer, & Omoregie, 2005, p. 1).

In fact, your team will probably experience three types of learning: *adaptive*, *generative*, and *transformative*. Your team will need to adapt to changes in the environment, generate new ways of working, and sometimes transform itself into a very different team with different goals than it had initially (London & Sessa, 2007; Sessa & London, 2006). As a result, your team will learn adaptive, generative, and transformative patterns of interaction—patterns that become part of their transactive memory. Transactive memory is simply the knowledge your team members share about how they work together and communicate team knowledge to each other and especially to new members (Lewis, 2003). Let's consider adaptive, generative, and transformative learning more closely.

Adaptive Learning

Your team is adaptive when it reacts automatically to environmental changes and pressures. Adaptive learning occurs when you and your team members fine-tune how you interact with each other and make minor changes as events or expectations change. The team learns in an adaptive way as the team members explore and alter their roles in relation to meeting team goals and expectations. In this instance, transactive memory is an adaptive mechanism. The team learns to institute its transactive memory when unexpected events occur.

Generative Learning

Your team engages in generative learning when you and your team members seek and discover information, acquire new knowledge and skills, inform and train each other, and use this new knowledge and skill to improve performance and results. Team members gather information, seek alternatives, reflect on work processes, test assumptions, examine different opinions, and try new ways of working together. Generative interaction patterns build on existing patterns, and generative learning expands the team's capacity in new directions. Generative learning results in the creation of new routines, and transactive memory is reconstructed in useful ways.

Transformative Learning

Your team's learning is transformative when you and your team members recreate the team's purpose, structure, and interaction patterns; team members examine their core values, assumptions, and beliefs as well as the need for change, for example, in team member roles, team structure, and purpose. Transformative learning includes engaging in deep reflection, critical analysis, and deconstruction followed by a rebuilding. It is a process of renewal as divergent views become synthesized and conflicts are resolved through the use of dialectical thinking, not compromise or majority rule (Kasl, Marsick, & Dechant, 1997). This deep reflection can change members' beliefs, attitudes, and emotional reactions. Team members may develop new insights about each other and establish a new transactive memory system about who can do what when unexpected events occur.

Facilitating Team Learning

Here we draw on the work of London and Sessa (2007), who have identified ways that you, as a manager, in your role as team leader, can promote adaptive, generative, and transformative team learning with your direct report team.

> *Facilitating adaptive learning.* Direct your team members' attention toward the stimuli for change. You can also assign roles, and encourage members to try new behaviors and to test new methods while perfecting those that are tried and true. You can outline steps for changes in procedures that will reduce or eliminate external pressures and maintain stability. If your team is relatively new, encourage your team members to talk about themselves and their past experiences related to the team's goals so that members get to know each other and what their capabilities are (London, 2007). You should also provide positive feedback to the team as a whole and to individual members for moving forward the task—for instance, saying, "We're doing a good job," "Thanks for all your efforts," "We're almost there, keep up the good work," and, more specifically, "The data analyses are clear," or "The product tests exceeded our expectations." As the team completes its work, you and the team members can review changes that were made and how well the team responded to pressures and opportunities, and use recognition to show your appreciation for their efforts.
>
> *Facilitating generative learning.* You can create generative learning by locating resources and best practices from other organizations that might apply to your team. You can also provide your team members with a collective training experience, and encourage team members to develop new ideas and try them, creating a climate where failure is OK and recognized as a learning experience. You can give your team time to practice and maintain the team's learning by codifying new approaches. If you make generative learning methods a habit, the outcome should be new procedures to

meet current and future possibilities. You should then incorporate these procedures along with any new skills and behaviors into the team's way of operating. If your team is beginning an initiative or project, set the stage for generative learning by creating plans for learning and evaluation. As the work progresses, you can emphasize the team's strengths, examine best practices from other teams and organizations, and compare interim results with the team's goals. When it is time to evaluate the team's efforts, you and your team members can compare the outcomes to benchmarks of excellence from other teams and organizations or from the team's past performance. This will help your team members to better understand what they learned and how they applied their new knowledge and skills for the benefit of the members and the team as a whole.

Facilitating transformative learning. You can facilitate transformative learning by having a discussion with your team members about group process and by encouraging them to experiment with new ways of working together, try new routines, evaluate their success, and determine ways to improve. You can also help your team members to change and in other ways unfreeze and acquire new skills, attitudes, and perspectives. You can discuss feelings of uncertainty, introduce wholly new behaviors and expectations, and drive the team to adopt new goals. As the team launches new projects or initiatives, you can suggest that members look beyond the team's boundaries, perhaps inviting people from other teams to attend meetings or asking team members to visit other groups or organizations. This will enable team members to discuss commonalities and differences and ways the team can benefit from cooperating with other groups. As the team progresses, encourage the team members to stop periodically for debriefings to reflect on what they have learned and how they are doing, essentially extracting the learning and making it explicit. As the team brings projects or initiatives to a close, ensure that your team members reflect on the past and present state of the team and consider its future potential. The transformation ends as the team achieves a new equilibrium, at least until the next transition.

Conclusion

Employees who are self-developers tend to have certain characteristics. They tend to be continuous learners, have a high degree of career motivation, and be more expansive than not. As a result, employees who are self-developers also tend to be more engaged employees. And as a manager, when you help your employees to capitalize on informal learning opportunities, you not only help to foster engagement but also help drive high levels of development and performance. Together, feedback, coaching, and self-development create a corporate culture that engages employees in continuous development and performance improvement. As a result, performance management becomes everyone's responsibility and an important component of the organization's culture.

In addition, we have encouraged you to apply the techniques of performance management to your team, and emphasized the importance of managing your team's learning as a way to strengthen engagement. We discussed adaptive, generative, and transformative learning; showed the value and contribution of each; and showed you how to facilitate each type of learning with your team.

Today's world calls for continuous learning at all levels in the organization as you and your employees cope with the challenges, expectations, and uncertainties of our global economy. It also calls for paying attention to the health and well-being of your employees as demands upon them continue to grow, often leading to stress and feeling overworked. In the next chapter, we address the issue of what can happen if this stress is prolonged—a condition known as *burnout*—and what you can do to manage and prevent it.

Chapter 10

Managing and Preventing Employee Burnout

So far, we have presented key concepts, best practices, techniques, and tools to help you drive employee engagement through effective performance management. We have focused on the positive concept of engagement and what you can do to help employees feel more engaged at work. In an ideal world, this would be sufficient; however, certain factors and conditions in the workplace can negatively affect employee engagement in your organization, and in fact can lead your employees down the opposite path—to burnout, low performance, and withdrawal. Consequently, it is crucial for you to understand burnout, including its personal and organizational consequences, its major causes, how to undo the damage (alleviate burnout and create a more engaging work environment), and how to prevent burnout. You will find that much of what we have discussed throughout this book in support of employee engagement—the concept, ideas, strategies, techniques, and so on—will be found in this chapter, and are shown to be effective in helping to prevent and eliminate burnout.

Let's begin with the following scenario:

For the most part, you have thought of your employees as being high performing. They generally have a positive attitude and optimistic outlook. They work well together, communicate with each other frequently and clearly, and deliver effective results in a timely manner. However, recently the demands on your employees have increased. They are working harder and putting in more hours. These demands are likely to continue. You have begun to notice that the general climate in your organization is less positive. Some employees have complained about being overworked. They have missed deadlines, and the quality of their work isn't what it used to be.

Does this scenario sound familiar? Do you recognize any of these characteristics in your employees? One of the most striking findings in the literature on burnout pertains to its severity and prevalence in organizations. The leading researchers on the topic, Maslach and Leiter (1997), described burnout as a "crisis" and an "epidemic." The increasing pressures to raise the bar (do more with less, beat the competition, meet tight production deadlines, and so on) are taking their toll. Today, any one of your employees is likely to be doing the work that used to be accomplished by two or three people, working longer hours, and, given advances in technology, "staying connected" 24/7. These changes and increased pressures, in addition to the rising demands of everyday life, may leave many of your employees feeling drained and exhausted, and in some cases burned out.

According to Maslach and Leiter (1997), there has been a clear shift in the paradigm of burnout. Initial thoughts about burnout positioned it solely as an employee's problem and responsibility to address. However, current research and theory reposition burnout as being more organization driven. With this shift in emphasis, many managers have begun to ask about the actions they can take to alleviate and prevent burnout, and to ultimately develop a work environment that fosters employee engagement.

Clearly, you should be concerned about burnout, how to manage it when it occurs, and how to prevent it when possible. If you have any doubt, just consider the following adverse effects burnout can have on your employees, as well as the cumulative impact it can have on the overall success of your organization:

■ Stress-related health issues (e.g., high blood pressure)
■ Feelings of anxiety, depression, lower self-esteem, and so on
■ Negative impact on life at home
■ Job dissatisfaction (e.g., job is no longer challenging or exciting)
■ Less enthusiasm about the organization (e.g., feeling apathetic about positive organization change)
■ Negative impact on coworkers (e.g., by demonstrating cynicism, poor interpersonal relationships, etc.)

- Increased absenteeism or lateness to work
- Reduced productivity (e.g., taking longer to complete routine assignments)
- Decreased effectiveness (e.g., not as innovative, creative, etc.)

Essentially, burnout "takes an emotional toll on the worker and it takes an economic toll on the workplace" (Maslach & Leiter, 1997, p. 154). You can, however, play an integral role in reducing the negative effects of burnout. But before you can successfully do so, you need to fully understand the construct of burnout.

What Is Burnout?

Research in general positions burnout as a physical, mental, and emotional response to chronic and prolonged levels of elevated stress. It is a state of extreme exhaustion caused by the inability to meet ongoing environmental demands such as a heavy workload, tight deadlines, and conflicting personal and professional obligations. Typically, you can associate burnout with feelings such as being exhausted, not getting anything done, being out of the loop, not caring anymore, wanting to give up, being bitter about everything, acting annoyed and angry, and showing resentment.

Although the terms *burnout* and *stress* are often used interchangeably, they are distinctly different in their characteristics and outcomes. *Stress* is a short-term emotional reaction to the demands in the environment that generally causes feelings of worry or tension. Stress is often associated with the fight-or-flight reaction—the adaptive, physiological response you would take to either fight against or attempt to escape stressful situations. Typically, these situations are not long term and can be resolved relatively quickly.

Similar to Maslach and Leiter (1997, 2000), we describe *burnout* (the opposite of employee engagement) as feeling sluggish (rather than energized), having a pessimistic outlook (versus an optimistic outlook), and feeling ineffective (versus enjoying a sense of personal accomplishment). Burnout is a result of continuous, chronic exposure to stress. It develops over time and has long-term consequences and outcomes. It is characterized by varying degrees of *exhaustion*, *cynicism*, and *ineffectiveness*. Note that your goal, as a manager, is to create a climate that safeguards employees against the possible causes of burnout and, in turn, fosters engagement.

Causes of Burnout

Burnout can be triggered by various personal, personality-centered, organizational, and work environment factors (Maslach & Leiter, 1997; Smith, Jaffe-Gill,

Table 10.1 The Personal Causes of Burnout Checklist

There are a number of personal behaviors, attributes, and reactions described below that could potentially lead to burnout over time. Being aware of these potential causes is the first step to alleviating or preventing burnout.
☐ **Experiencing individual changes**: Shifts in your personal beliefs, interests, values, or views of your job that conflict with your current roles and responsibilities.
☐ **Having unrealistic expectations**: Expecting too much of yourself; expecting too much from your job (e.g., anticipating significant opportunities or projects).
☐ **Having idealistic job and career goals**: Setting goals way beyond your current knowledge, skills, and abilities.
☐ **Having an inability to set and maintain boundaries**: Taking on too much and/or not being able to say no to requests.
☐ **Feeling overly responsible for low levels of personal accomplishment**: Attributing an inability to achieve goals to your own actions and not considering inevitable obstacles in your work environment.
☐ **Being a perfectionist**: Constantly trying to reach a level of perfection in all you do.
☐ **Being overly self-critical**: Consistently and regularly criticizing yourself and/or your work; holding yourself to extremely high standards.

Segal, & Segal, 2008). In Tables 10.1 and 10.2 you will find a list of personal and personality-centered factors, drawn from Smith et al. (2008) as well as a number of other sources, that can cause burnout. Through performance management, you may be able to affect some of these causes, such as an employee's unrealistic expectations, idealistic job and career goals, and his or her understanding of the obstacles to success. You may also be able to help your employees to increase their resilience—a personality-centered cause. Recognize, however, that most of the causes listed in Tables 10.1 and 10.2 will, by and large, need to be self-managed by your employees. Therefore, you should primarily focus your efforts on where you can make a direct impact: the organizational and work environment factors—and there are a number of these factors that could trigger burnout.

Organizations, in general, are in a constant state of flux as they strive to be competitive and successful. This flux and attendant pressures are wearing on employees. Although you may not be able to personally control the impact

Table 10.2 The Personality-Centered Causes of Burnout Checklist

Some behaviors that may contribute to burnout are often demonstrated by those who have certain personality characteristics. Although these personality characteristics have been found to be associated with burnout, keep in mind that having several of these characteristics does not necessarily mean you are burned out.
☐ **Having low levels of hardiness:** You typically demonstrate a low level of commitment to everyday activities (e.g., family, work, etc.), feeling like you lack control over life events and that you are being resistant to change.
☐ **Having low levels of resilience:** Generally you find it difficult to deal with setbacks effectively and to bounce back from challenges and stressful situations.
☐ **Demonstrating passive coping style:** You tend to avoid or ignore stressful situations rather than confronting them.
☐ **Demonstrating defensive coping style:** You usually express aggression, anger, withdrawal, and the like when faced with stress.
☐ **Demonstrating external locus of control:** You believe that what happens to you is beyond your control and that your behavior is guided by fate, luck, or other external circumstances.
☐ **Having low self-esteem:** You tend to have low confidence in your abilities and yourself overall.
☐ **Demonstrating type A behavior:** You can be characterized as being tense, impatient, aggressive, hostile, and time sensitive.

of organizational changes and pressures on your employees, drawing from the work of Maslach and Leiter (1997), there are six specific work environment factors that you can influence:

1. **Workload:** The extent to which your employees can manage the work they have to do and feel they have the appropriate and required resources to complete the work successfully.
2. **Control:** The extent to which your employees feel a reasonable level of autonomy over their work and a sense of control over their day-to-day activities and tasks.
3. **Recognition and reward:** The extent to which your employees feel they are receiving appropriate feedback, incentives, and compensation for their performance.

4. **Community**: The extent to which your employees feel they have social support from you and their coworkers.
5. **Fairness**: The extent to which your employees feel that the larger organization's procedures and practices and those of your organization are sensible and equitable.
6. **Values**: The extent to which your employees feel their personal values coincide with the larger organization's values and those of your organization.

If your employees are not satisfied with any or all of the factors, misalignments between their needs and those of the work environment emerge (Maslach & Leiter, 1997). Recall, too, that having the resources to do your job, getting performance feedback, being satisfied with your total rewards, and so on, as highlighted in these factors, were found to be predictors of engagement as discussed in Chapter 1. So let's now consider each factor in more detail as it relates to burnout summarizing and building on Maslach and Leiter (1997, 2008).

Workload

Workload is the most common and understood key driver of burnout. Over time, high demands, standards, and expectations; tight deadlines; consistent crises; and limited or no resources can leave your employees feeling overwhelmed and overworked. If a demanding workload is chronic and not followed by opportunities to rest and recover, it will become extremely difficult for your employees to stay engaged or sustain effective performance.

Control

Control, or feeling empowered, is critical to engagement. Remember our discussion of trust and empowerment in Chapter 3. Failing to provide your employees with high levels of autonomy, independence, and discretion in making decisions and solving problems to achieve results will inhibit their commitment, initiative and innovation, and trust. In addition, micromanaging how your employees' work gets accomplished will hinder morale and engagement and likely lead to burnout. We recognize that giving up control over outcomes for which you are accountable can be stressful. This is where self-management and balance come in. You can learn to balance the amount of autonomy you give your employees with the control you really need. This may be easier said than done. Still, it's worth the effort to maintain employee engagement.

Recognition and Reward

Lack of recognition and reward can leave your employees feeling uncertain about the quality of their performance and, much worse, devalued. These feelings can be very demotivating, leading to burnout. Ongoing positive and constructive feedback and frequent, meaningful recognition are essential to effective performance management. If you don't regularly provide feedback to your employees, you are likely sending a message that they aren't worth the investment of your time and energy. Furthermore, unless you make recognition and rewards salient and tailored to your employees' needs and preferences, they may not fully value and appreciate your efforts.

Community

A poor sense of community can be detrimental to your employees' overall connection to your organization and your company as a whole. As organizations continue to become more complex and global, teamwork and collaboration become more integral to business success. If the social environment and interactions among your team members are not positive and supportive, the likelihood for burnout increases. This can be intensified if you do not treat all of your employees equitably and respectfully. The challenge is even more complex when leading a remote team. If you make little effort to regularly and consistently interact and communicate with your team members, they will feel detached, excluded, and uncertain about their connection to your organization and the company.

Fairness

Fairness is characterized by feelings of equity and balance that result when your employees weigh the time and effort they expended and the recognition and reward they received. Your employees' perceptions of fairness are driven less by the actual positive outcomes they may receive and more by how they perceive the work processes are implemented (Latham, Almost, Mann, & Moore, 2005; Maslach & Leiter, 2008). For example, feelings of inequity can arise when your employees believe the appraisal, promotion, and reward processes are administered based on favoritism, not merit. All in all, if the sense of equity is not maintained, your employees may restore the balance by putting in less time and effort. This is likely to decrease their engagement, productivity, and performance, possibly leading to feelings of burnout.

Values

When there is a misalignment between your employees' personal values and the values held by your organization and the company as a whole, burnout is more likely to occur. For example, when an employee is asked to cover up a mistake or stretch the truth to make a sale, this could potentially cause a clash in values. Persistent value clashes can lead to deep intrapersonal conflict and a lack of engagement.

In summary, you can limit or prevent burnout by managing employees' workloads, ensuring they have the control they need to do their jobs, giving them recognition for excellent performance, building a sense of community in the team, treating them fairly, and making sure that you communicate values that they share.

Identifying Burnout

Because the effects of burnout are exhibited in unique ways, how can you determine if one of your employees is experiencing burnout? Although there isn't an exact formula, there are common signs and symptoms that you can recognize. Generally the more signs and/or symptoms one of your employees is experiencing, the more likely he or she could be burned out, or close to it.

Early Warning Signs of Burnout

There is a range of feelings your employees will typically describe prior to their actually becoming burned out:

- Powerlessness
- Hopelessness
- Drained
- Frustrated
- Detached from people and things around them
- That their work is not meaningful
- Resentful of having too much to do
- Like a failure
- Stuck in a situation and feeling there is no way out
- Withdrawn and isolated from coworkers and friends
- Insecure about their competence and abilities
- Cynical
- Irritable
- Anxious

You may not have insight into the degree to which any of your employees is having these feelings. This is why an open and trusting relationship with your employees is a critical prerequisite to understanding how they are feeling (see our discussion of trust in Chapter 3). In other words, without high levels of trust, your employees may never tell you what they may be experiencing.

Symptoms of Burnout

Symptoms of burnout fall into three basic categories: psychological symptoms, physical symptoms, and behavioral symptoms (Maslach & Leiter, 2008; Smith et al., 2008). The psychological and physical symptoms may be harder for you to detect unless you have a trusting relationship with your employees. However, this doesn't mean you won't see these symptoms; it just means that they may not be as obvious as the behavioral symptoms likely are. For example, psychological symptoms of burnout include loss of care and concern, feeling apathetic, expressions of cynicism and negativity, and an inability to make decisions. Physical symptoms include exhaustion, fatigue, or changes in weight. Appendix 10.1 includes expanded lists of the psychological, physical, and behavioral symptoms of burnout.

The behavioral symptoms of burnout will likely be the most obvious to you, and the most apparent of those include:

■ Decreased job performance
■ Loss of enthusiasm for the work
■ Increased frustration with the job
■ Decreased desire to communicate
■ Tendency to withdraw
■ Tardiness
■ Poor concentration and/or difficulty focusing
■ Forgetfulness
■ Accident proneness

Overall, the rule of thumb for identifying these symptoms of burnout is to look for unfavorable changes in your employees' behavior.

Although your employees may not have come to you with concerns of being burned out, this does not mean that burnout is not a problem. Getting to know the needs and wants of your employees, their typical performance, and their work behavior patterns, as well as becoming aware of, and sensitized to, the burnout signs and symptoms, will help you to recognize and act on any potential changes in employee engagement and performance.

Taking Action to Reduce Burnout

As a manager, you have an essential role in minimizing and preventing employee burnout. The best way to do this is through a collaborative effort with your employees (Maslach & Leiter, 1997). First, let's look at the major strategies your employees can use to alleviate any signs or symptoms of burnout they may be experiencing. These strategies include:

- Practicing effective time management
- Taking breaks
- Setting realistic goals
- Eating well
- Exercising
- Communicating with you, their manager, when they feel overwhelmed and/or unrewarded

You may be thinking that these strategies seem rather simplistic. But if practiced regularly, they can have a profound impact on your employees' health and well-being. Therefore, although these are employee-driven strategies, we recommend that you become familiar with them (see Appendix 10.2 for an expanded and detailed list of strategies, and Appendix 10.3 for a list of tactics to address personality-centered causes of stress). Suggest or recommend these strategies to your employees, as appropriate.

As a manager, you need to determine which work environment factors are having an unfavorable effect on your employees so that you can focus your efforts where they will have the greatest impact. The best way to do this is by talking to your employees—advice we offered earlier. Discover how they feel and what they think. Once you have identified the work environment factors that are causing burnout, work collaboratively with your employees to determine the most appropriate actions. You have to think creatively and capitalize on performance management to essentially do what works best for you and your team.

Drawing from and expanding on Maslach and Leiter (1997, 2008) and Leiter and Maslach (2005), let's now take a deeper look at each factor and consider how you can minimize burnout and maximize employee engagement through effective performance management.

Addressing Workload

Workload is something you can directly impact through good performance management. An essential part of your manager role is structuring jobs so that the work gets done effectively and efficiently and that the most appropriate people are doing the work. This alignment usually takes place during goal setting, when you can adapt the workload to each of your employee's knowledge, skills, and abilities. Further, it's important to ensure availability of adequate and appropriate resources. With effective goal setting, your employees will be able to manage their workloads and become more successful in their jobs.

Managing workload becomes especially important when there are crises to address or when your employees are forced to "fight fires" rather than think more strategically and plan their working time. Burnout becomes a concern when the high-stress, crisis management nature of work becomes chronic and presents little to no opportunities to rest and recover. You may want to consider offering your employees days off following a major deadline or completion of a project. The need to restore balance and have sufficient opportunities to rest after a stressful period at work is critical to promoting engagement and eliminating or preventing burnout.

Addressing Control

Your employees want to have accountability for the work they do and how they do it. Further, they want to be able to solve their own problems and make decisions. It is your job to ensure your employees are empowered and provided with appropriate levels of independence and discretion. Empowering your employees plays a key role in building trust and fostering engagement. Here are some ways to avoid micromanaging the efforts of your employees:

- Do not set policies and practices that are unnecessarily rigid.
- Focus on managing the "big picture" rather than on managing the day-to-day tactical activities.
- Delegate assignments.
- Trust and empower your employees to deliver results and provide guidance, as needed.
- Offer flexibility in the way work gets done.

Your employees will feel more empowered and engaged when they have the opportunity to feel ownership of their performance and results and they recognize how their contributions directly support the goals of the team and the organization.

What are some other steps you can take to ensure you are empowering your employees, demonstrating your trust and confidence in them, and letting them drive their own performance? Consider these few suggestions in addition to those discussed in Chapter 3:

- Bring your employees together to develop and agree to the appropriate levels of decision making and authority.
- Clarify with each employee his or her areas of decision-making responsibility.
- Spell out the range and depth of authority each employee has—set the boundaries and make them clear.
- Ask your employees about the level of involvement they want from you, agree to it, and follow through.
- Ask what you can do to be helpful, but don't usurp your employees' authority, once it is granted.
- When your employees come to you with problems or opportunities, ask for their recommended plan of action and avoid the urge to provide "the answer."

You might also want to consider creating a detailed empowerment plan for each of your employees using the planning tool presented in Chapter 3.

Addressing Recognition and Reward

An integral part of effective performance management is providing your employees with recognition and reward for their performance and development. Recognition and reward are critical to employee engagement, as found in our study at XINC, and they enhance satisfaction, motivation, and morale, as well as sustain effective performance. Essentially, recognition and reward are forms of feedback. One of the most stressful circumstances for your employees is not knowing how their work is perceived by you. Without appropriate amounts of positive and constructive feedback as well as recognition and reward, your employees will generally begin to doubt their competence, feel devalued, and, as a result, reduce their effort. Of course, refer back to Chapter 6 to help you determine the recognition and reward strategies that will work best given your needs and the needs of your employees, and to Chapter 5 for making your feedback as effective as possible.

Addressing Community

A strong sense of community fosters greater levels of satisfaction and engagement, creating a work environment that allows your employees to perform to the best of their abilities. Essentially, if your employees have feelings of abandonment, isolation, conflict, or tension, it will have a negative impact on their satisfaction and engagement, and quite possibly lead to signs or symptoms of burnout over time.

The following ways to build a strong sense of community for your employees rests on a foundation of trust and empowerment:

- Demonstrate ongoing support in all performance and development efforts.
- Defend your employees when necessary or appropriate.
- Treat your employees equally.
- Foster an environment of mutual respect.
- Encourage ongoing relationships among your employees.
- Develop opportunities for open and supportive communication.
- Solicit and act upon your employees' ideas and opinions.

Interestingly, creating a strong sense of community can help you to mitigate the negative impact of the other five workplace environment factors (Maslach & Leiter, 2008). For example, when a team of your employees has to deliver a critical project in a short time frame, in addition to managing their day-to-day responsibilities (creating an overwhelming workload), providing your support and promoting a high degree of teamwork and collaboration will likely ease any potential feelings related to burnout. Essentially, your employees will feel that "they're not in it alone."

Urging your employees to take regular breaks and have some "fun" is another important way to promote a strong feeling of community that helps create opportunities for restoration. Consult with your teams to identify what fun events and activities they would like, while taking into consideration what is acceptable in your corporate culture. Ultimately, you will have to use your best judgment, determine the practicality of employees' suggestions, and begin incorporating them into the day-to-day routine. Be sure to seek feedback on the effectiveness of the events and offer variety to ensure your employees are satisfied and remain engaged.

Addressing Fairness

Being fair and equitable when managing your employees' performance is critical to creating an engaging work environment. Treating your employees with fairness may seem like common sense—we all know we should avoid demonstrating favoritism, applying policies and guidelines unequally, and giving unjustified recognition and rewards. However, sometimes we don't *see* that we may be demonstrating behaviors that could be perceived as unfair. The fact is that research on burnout has shown that this particular work environment factor is the key "tipping point" for experiencing burnout in the workplace (Maslach & Leiter,

2008). If your employees are showing early warning signs of being burned out due to other factors, perceiving the work environment as unequal and unfair could magnify their signs or symptoms and lead to burnout. Remember, too, that treating your employees unequally will diminish the trust they have in you.

What should you do to determine if your employees feel they are treated fairly? Solicit your employees' thoughts on their perceptions of fairness within your organization. You can do this informally or with the help of your HR partner using interviews, focus groups, or an anonymous survey, similar to the Trust and Empowerment Climate Assessment Survey described in Chapter 3.

Overall, keep the following suggestions in mind to ensure that you are managing your team members fairly and fostering a sense of engagement among all of your employees:

- Treat them with respect.
- Treat them equally, avoiding even the appearance of favoritism.
- Make just, fair, and performance-driven decisions regarding workload, levels of independence and discretion, merit increases, and other rewards.
- Extend key opportunities to those who are deserving, and make the justifications clear.
- Follow all organizational policies and guidelines—don't make exceptions for some employees and not others.
- Incorporate your employees' viewpoints when developing or reviewing organizational policies to ensure feelings of fairness.

Addressing Values

"Values are the ideals and motivations that originally attracted people to their jobs, and thus they are the motivating connection between the worker and the workplace, which goes beyond the utilitarian exchange of time for money or advancement" (Maslach & Leiter, 2008, p. 501). Here are some ways you can increase the alignment between your employees' values, your organization's values, and corporate values:

- Help your employees understand the company's core values and how these values apply to them.
- Also help your employees to understand your organization's values; how they align to the corporate values, if different; and how these values align with their own values.

■ Ask your employees how, as their manager, you impact the dynamics, current values, and work ethics of the organization and what changes they would like to see.

■ Engage in ongoing discussions with your employees to ensure that their personal values remain aligned with your organization's values.

■ When interviewing potential job candidates, be sure to provide a realistic job preview and describe the climate, culture, and values of your organization and the company as a whole—checking for the candidates' values and alignment.

Gaining an awareness and understanding of your employees' values, and the extent to which they are aligned with the organization's overall values, will be important to your success in preventing burnout.

In summary, you may have noticed a common theme throughout our discussion of how to address the work environment factors to alleviate burnout in your organization: two-way and continuous communication. As mentioned earlier, creating an engaging work environment requires a collaborative effort between you and your employees, and communication is central to effectively working together. We recommend that you collaborate with your employees, using the Work Environment Checklist in Appendix 10.4, to determine the necessary actions both you and your employees can take to ensure the work environment is supportive of, and fosters, employee engagement.

Thus far, we have focused on how to alleviate the signs and symptoms of burnout, so let's take a look at a more proactive approach, prevention.

Preventing Burnout

At one point or another, you've probably heard the sports idiom "The best defense is a good offense." When you think about this expression in the context of burnout, the importance of proactively managing burnout becomes clear: The best way to manage burnout is not just to alleviate it (defense) but also to prevent it in the first place (offense). As a manager, it is imperative that you take preventative measures that will ensure burnout does not become a widespread issue for your employees and, in turn, your organization as a whole.

How can you do this? The first step probably comes as no surprise: Communicate and work openly with your employees. Understanding the unique needs of each of your employees will help you create the structure and opportunities that will promote employee engagement and prevent burnout. For example, if time management is an issue for your employees, consider online or instructor-led courses, self-help books, and the like. Suggest these educational opportunities as a way of helping your employees gain the necessary knowledge and skills, and, in turn, helping them cope with stress and burnout. In addition, we encourage you to share the following tips with your employees to help them avoid burnout:

- *Keep perspective*: "Don't sweat the small stuff." Try not to let the little things lead you offtrack; concentrate on attaining your goals.
- *Set priorities*: Focus on the tasks that need immediate attention.
- *Be flexible*: As things come up, allow yourself to make adjustments in your schedule.
- *Build in buffers*: Schedule enough time to switch from one task to another in case a task takes longer than anticipated.
- *Stay in touch*: Make time for friends and family.
- *Fuel your creativity*: Find a hobby or a non-work-related activity outside of work that helps you relax and think without pressure.

Conclusion

Your employees are your greatest corporate asset, and unless you help foster an engaging work environment by taking action against burnout, your employees' morale will deteriorate and their commitment and productivity will dwindle. Driving employee engagement through effective performance management takes effort and time, but with ongoing communication, consideration of each employee's individual needs, and collaborative persistence, you will see significant results.

If you are currently on the verge of (or experiencing) burnout, implement the strategies and actions for yourself. Be a role model for your team by managing or preventing your own burnout and maximizing your own engagement. In addition, remember that the appendixes to this chapter (Appendixes 10.1 to 10.4) have tools, checklists, and assessments that will help you structure your own thoughts and conversations with your employees. These resources are intended to stimulate your thinking. You will have to consider your organization, your work environment, your current projects, and the unique needs of your employees and then decide the possible strategies and actions that will be the best, most appropriate steps toward alleviating and preventing burnout, and driving employee engagement.

Appendix 10.1: Symptoms of Burnout Checklist

Burnout Symptoms	The specific symptoms that individuals who are burned out generally experience can be grouped into three basic categories: • Psychological symptoms • Physical symptoms • Behavioral symptoms
As you read through each list of symptoms, consider the extent to which you are currently experiencing them, and focus on those that have recently developed or increased in severity.	
Assessing Psychological Symptoms	Psychological symptoms are expressed in an individual's attitudes and feelings. ☑ *Check all symptoms you are currently experiencing, focusing on those that have recently developed or increased in severity.* ☐ Rigidity to change/loss of flexibility ☐ Loss of care and concern ☐ Feeling apathetic ☐ Cynicism/negativism ☐ Emotional exhaustion/loss of emotional control ☐ Low morale ☐ Loss of patience ☐ Inability to cope with unwanted stress ☐ Feelings of anger/bitterness/disgust ☐ Feelings of guilt/failure ☐ Low confidence and satisfaction with yourself ☐ Loss of idealism (disillusioned) ☐ Inability to make decisions ☐ Suspicion/paranoia ☐ Depression ☐ Alienation ☐ Increased worry ☐ Overly confident/taking unusually high risks ☐ Feeling obligated to satisfy the needs of all people at all times ☐ Loss of charisma

Assessing Physical Symptoms	Physical symptoms are actual changes in physiological functions.
	☑ *Check all symptoms you are currently experiencing, focusing on those not related to a previously diagnosed health condition (although this previously diagnosed health condition may be exacerbated by burnout).*
	☐ Physical exhaustion/fatigue ☐ Change in sleep patterns; insomnia or sleeping more than usual ☐ Headaches ☐ Gastrointestinal problems ☐ Lingering/frequent colds/flu ☐ Weight loss/gain ☐ Shortness of breath ☐ Hypertension ☐ Impaired speech ☐ Teeth grinding
Assessing Behavioral Symptoms	Behavioral symptoms are actions or behaviors demonstrated as a result of burnout.
	☑ *Check all symptoms you are currently demonstrating, focusing on those that have recently developed or increased in severity.*
	☐ Decreased job performance/decreased job satisfaction ☐ Decreased desire to communicate ☐ Tendency to withdraw ☐ Desire to leave your job ☐ Decreased desire to come to work ☐ Loss of enthusiasm for your job ☐ Increased prescription drug or alcohol use ☐ Increased marital or family conflict ☐ Difficulty focusing on your job ☐ Accident proneness ☐ Increased frustration with your job ☐ Forgetfulness/poor concentration

Appendix 10.2: Strategies for Coping With and Preventing Burnout Checklist

Psychological Strategies	If you have been experiencing any of the psychological symptoms of burnout, consider the following strategies.
	☑ *Check each strategy that you plan to implement*:
	☐ **Give yourself time alone:** Regularly set aside some alone time to do something you truly enjoy (e.g., reading a novel, watching a movie, painting, etc.)—make it routine. ☐ **Give yourself breaks:** Take regular 5–10-minute breaks to get away from your desk—leave the vicinity of where you do your work. For example, go for a walk outside to clear and revitalize your mind. When traveling on business, take some time to relax and engage in recreational activities. ☐ **Set realistic goals:** Set work and personal goals (short and long term) that are specific, meaningful, and attainable, and establish a plan to maximize success and minimize the stress associated with failure. ☐ **Increase your self-awareness:** Deepen your understanding of your strengths and weaknesses; this will enable you to develop more effective coping strategies for dealing with stressful situations. ☐ **Practice efficient time management:** Develop your time management skills (e.g., construct a daily to-do list, determine your most productive time of day, and adapt your tasks accordingly) to help you establish better life balance. ☐ **Take a positive perspective:** Look at stressful times as opportunities for you to grow personally and professionally. ☐ **Take a step back from the experience:** Take time to reflect upon your experiences; consider what you can learn from them. ☐ **Stop, think, and then act:** Whenever you're panicked, feel out of control, or are facing a crisis, use the scuba diver's motto: Stop, think, and then act—take a few minutes to stop what you are doing, create an action plan, and then implement the plan. This can help prevent you from doing something you may regret. ☐ **Monitor depression:** If you have a history of depression, monitor your symptoms because burnout could cause a recurrence—consult your doctor if any signs of depression resurface.

Physical Strategies	If you have been experiencing any of the physical symptoms of burnout discussed earlier, consider the following strategies.
	☑ *Check each strategy that you plan to implement*:
	☐ **See your doctor:** Make an appointment for a complete physical, and be prepared to discuss your concerns and symptoms related to burnout. It may be helpful to make a list of all the questions that need to be addressed ahead of time so you don't lose the opportunity for professional advice.
	☐ **Sleep:** Ensure you attain the amount of sleep you need to perform each day effectively. If you have a difficult time letting go of the day's events or tomorrow's to-do list, examine your routine activities that take place an hour before you go to bed. For example, if you watch intense TV programs or work right up until you lay down, try reading a novel or listening to soothing music instead. Also, try to go to bed at the same time each night—this routine will help you fall asleep faster.
	☐ **Breathe:** Close your eyes and concentrate on each breath. Control every breath as you inhale and exhale until you are breathing properly—this will help you relax.
	☐ **Exercise:** Increase your physical activity to gain both short- and long-term health benefits. It can be as simple as stretching, taking a brisk walk, taking yoga classes, or briefly working out in a gym.
	☐ **Eat right:** Follow a well-balanced diet to ensure you obtain the proper nutrients required to provide enough energy for your day. Eating well has a major effect on how you can properly defend yourself against the stress your body is not equipped to handle.
	☐ **Laugh:** Humor can give you a more lighthearted perspective and help you view stressful events as opportunities to learn and grow, making them less threatening and more positive. Laughter brings the focus away from anger, guilt, stress, and negative emotions.

Social Strategies	In addition to developing strategies for the psychological and physical symptoms of burnout, regular and positive social interaction will help you gain a better sense of balance in your life. Consider the following strategies.
	☑ *Check each strategy that you plan to implement*:
	☐ **Nurture your closest relationships:** Your family and friends can give you support and encouragement. Be sure to give these relationships the attention they deserve.
	☐ **Expand your social network:** Become active in your community, or join a group that is personally meaningful.
	☐ **Communicate your concerns about your job:** Talk to your manager or HR representative, and explore options for addressing your concerns.
	☐ **Revisit job and career interests:** Take the time to talk to your manager or HR representative about your current job and career goals—ensure you are satisfied with your job/career and that you are on the right track, and make any necessary adjustments.
	☐ **Practice healthy communication:** Seek out a good listener (e.g., someone who will not judge you), and share your feelings in a professional and constructive manner.
	☐ **Learn to say no tactfully:** Explain your position clearly, and articulate your inability to accomplish a task effectively, given the amount of work you are already committed to completing for current tasks.

Appendix 10.3: Tactics for Addressing Personality-Centered Causes of Stress

Resiliency	Resiliency is the ability to bounce back from challenges and stressful situations.
	☑ *Check the box below if you plan to increase your resiliency*:
	☐ **To increase your resiliency**:
	1. *Network and make social connections*: Developing close relationships with friends, relatives, community group members, and so on can contribute to a sense of well-being.
	2. *View challenges as opportunities to grow*: Try to look beyond the problem, focus on the future, and gain strength from your experiences; leverage lessons learned.
	3. *Accept that change is a part of life*: Embrace change to help you make the most of opportunities and challenges brought about by change.
	4. *Work toward your goals*: Establish a plan, and take steps toward achieving your goals.
	5. *Take action*: Be proactive in your day-to-day activities to help you move toward your goals and to help give you a sense of accomplishment.
	6. *Reflect upon your experiences*: Look for opportunities for self-discovery. Think about your behavior, reactions, feelings, and the like; how they influence the outcome of your experiences; and, as a result, what you might like to change in the future.
	7. *Keep things in perspective*: Try to see roadblocks and setbacks in the context of the "big picture." Face them, work toward overcoming them, and move on.
	8. *Take good care of yourself*: Eat well, exercise, be positive, and spend time with friends and family.

Hardiness	Hardiness is a set of personality characteristics that support your resistance to stress.
	☑ *Check the box below if you plan to increase your hardiness*:
	☐ **To increase your hardiness**:
	1. *Gain control*: Make changes that will help you establish a better sense of balance in your life and increase your control overall.
	2. *Be committed*: Reestablish and sustain your commitment to people, your work goals, and your values.
	3. *Embrace change*: See unexpected change as a positive opportunity rather than as an obstacle.
Coping Style	Proactively coping is an effective strategy for handling the stressors you encounter.
	☑ *Check the box below if you plan to improve your coping skills*:
	☐ **To improve your coping skills**:
	1. *Be assertive*: Face, and directly deal with, the issues that are stressful for you.
	2. *Be proactive*: Implement some of the strategies discussed earlier to help you better cope, for example:
	– Discover what relaxes you, and have fun each day.
	– Take good care of your health.
	– Stay physically active.
	– Develop strong and supportive relationships.
	– Build your self-esteem.
	3. *Be optimistic*: Try to see negative events as minor setbacks to be easily overcome and positive events as evidence of further success and achievement.

Locus of Control	An internal locus of control is expressed when you feel that what happens to you is under your control and the outcomes are a result of your personal effort and ability.
	☑ *Check the box below if you plan to develop a more internal locus of control:*
	☐ **Develop a more internal locus of control:**
	1. *Raise your self-awareness:* Learn more about yourself and leverage your strengths.
	2. *Take accountability for your actions and behaviors:* This can help you feel more empowered and autonomous.
	3. *Gain control:* Analyze situations in which you feel you lack control, and determine what you could do differently in the future to exert more control over these situations.
	4. *Develop a strong understanding of your influence in situations or events:* Focus on the cause-and-effect relationship of your actions and behaviors.
	5. *Recognize and celebrate small successes:* Reflect on each success and how you achieved it to develop a stronger sense of how you personally controlled the situation and outcome.
Self-Esteem	Self-esteem refers to your confidence in your own worth or ability and is key to your happiness and well-being.
	☑ *Check the box below if you plan to increase your self-esteem:*
	☐ **Increase your self-esteem:**
	1. *Empower yourself:* Let others know what you want and how you feel.
	2. *Reward yourself:* Celebrate your accomplishments when you succeed.
	3. *Clarify:* Ask for clarification to avoid any misunderstandings and unfavorable consequences.

	4. *Ask for feedback*: Seek positive feedback about your efforts to learn more about your strengths.
	5. *Build supportive relationships*: Surround yourself with people who are optimistic and encouraging.
	6. *Be nice to yourself*: Treat yourself well, and do things you enjoy.
	7. *Have no worries*: Face your fears, and work to overcome them.
	8. *Try not to dwell on your mistakes*: Learn from these mistakes, and try not to repeat them.

Appendix 10.4: Creating a More Engaging Work Environment

Here we build on Maslach and Leiter (1997) and Leiter and Maslach (2005) and recommend actions you can take to create a more engaging work environment categorized by each of the work environment factors. Focus on the actions associated with the factors you've identified as areas to address with your team.

Ideally you will collaborate with your employees to identify realistic solutions and strategies that will create a more engaging work environment. However, keep in mind that some changes many not be possible within your given environment.

Work with your employees to check each action you plan to implement in the Actions for Employees and Actions for Managers columns.

Factors	Actions for Employees	Actions for Managers
Workload	☐ Talk with your manager if you feel overwhelmed by your workload ☐ Request necessary resources ☐ Seek short-term help from your coworkers	☐ Adapt workload to each of your employee's knowledge, skills and abilities during goal setting ☐ Ensure availability of adequate and appropriate resources

Factors	Actions for Employees	Actions for Managers
	☐ Enroll in training to improve your time management skills and functional skills	☐ Offer your employees additional days off following a major deadline or completion of a project
Control	☐ Discuss with your manager options for increasing your autonomy ☐ Be aware of who makes decisions and for what they are accountable ☐ Seek opportunities to express your opinions and ideas ☐ Take the initiative to solve problems that arise	☐ Avoid setting policies and practices that, in effect, are too rigid ☐ Offer flexibility in the way work gets done ☐ Specify who is accountable for what actions and delegate appropriately ☐ Clarify decision-making responsibility with each of your employees ☐ Empower your employees to solve their own problems
Recognition & Reward	☐ Communicate to your manager what feedback you would like to receive and how often ☐ Communicate to your manager what motivates you and what types of rewards mean the most to you ☐ Suggest fun recognition programs (e.g., company-paid lunch for successful performance) ☐ Discuss any concerns about your recognition and rewards with your manager	☐ Recognize valued actions by providing positive feedback ☐ Utilize formal or informal ways to reward your employees, if warranted ☐ Offer constructive feedback, when appropriate ☐ Appropriately compensate your employees, if possible, based on internal and external market data

Factors	Actions for Employees	Actions for Managers
Community	☐ Develop and sustain relationships with your coworkers ☐ Enroll in training regarding building relationships with your coworkers ☐ Always express respect for others ☐ Raise concerns about feeling secluded or distant from your coworkers with your manager ☐ Engage in open and supportive communication with your manager and coworkers ☐ Suggest out-of-office social activities	☐ Demonstrate ongoing support in all performance and development efforts ☐ Encourage ongoing relationships among your employees ☐ Treat your employees equally and foster an environment of mutual respect and trust ☐ Develop opportunities for open and supportive communication with and among your employees ☐ Solicit and act on your employees' ideas and opinions ☐ Defend your employees when necessary or appropriate ☐ Encourage your employees to regularly take breaks and have fun
Fairness	☐ Treat your coworkers and your manager with respect ☐ Discuss any apparent signs of "favoritism" ☐ Constructively express your discontent regarding organizational policies	☐ Treat your employees with respect ☐ Make decisions that are just, fair and performance-driven ☐ Treat all of your employees equally; don't demonstrate "favoritism" ☐ Follow all organization policies and guidelines — don't make exceptions for certain employees and not others

Factors	Actions for Employees	Actions for Managers
		☐ Extend key opportunities to those who are deserving and make the justifications clear ☐ Incorporate your employees' viewpoints when developing/ reviewing organizational policies to ensure feelings of fairness
Values	☐ Explore ways of aligning your personal values with those of the organization ☐ Discuss with your manager how you feel about the dynamics, current values and work ethics of the team and what changes you would like to see	☐ Help your employees understand the organization's values and how these values apply to them ☐ Ask your employees how you impact the dynamics, current values and work ethics of the team and what changes they would like to see ☐ Engage in ongoing discussions with your employees to ensure that their personal values are still aligned to the work environment and organization ☐ When interviewing potential job candidates, provide a realistic job preview and describe the climate, culture and values of the team and organization

Chapter 11

A Closing Look at Performance Management and Employee Engagement

We conclude the book with a case that confronts key realities of being a manager, effectively applying the techniques of performance management and driving employee engagement.

This case begins with a midyear review of performance goal achievement. The subject of the case, Mark, a manager, was meeting his own manager's expectations, but Mark was not quite satisfied with his own progress and the progress of his team. So he begins to question his own performance and his ability to lead his team, have impact, and keep his employees engaged. As he probes more deeply, he embarks on a journey of seeking more detailed feedback and working with his manager and a professional coach. He becomes more aware of his strengths and weaknesses and discovers ways he can behave differently, especially in interacting with the people who work for him.

The case demonstrates the holistic nature of performance management. All the elements we have been talking about in this book unfold. The levels of trust and empowerment are questioned by Mark and his employees, and are on the minds of his colleagues and manager. The previously high levels of engagement in his organization are at possible risk. Goal attainment is questioned, and goals are reviewed and recalibrated, while goal commitment is renewed. Feedback is sought and internalized. Learning takes place through on-the-job critical incidents and through online courses. Finally, informal and formal reviews provide the framework for effective discussions about both performance and development.

As all this happens, our protagonist, Mark, experiences a major transition in his self-concept. He begins to be more alert to how he affects others and how this influences their performance and his, too. As you read the case, ask yourself what you would do if you were Mark—be reflective. What steps would you take to better monitor and manage your own performance and expectations? How would you empower and foster the performance and development of your direct reports? What steps would you take to ensure your employees remain engaged? What would you ask of your own manager in terms of guidance, coaching, and support?

In addition, consider the following questions, but let us warn you that we leave you with your own answers. Consider yourself empowered!

- Why do you think Mark did not share his feelings of dissatisfaction with John, his manager, during his midyear review? Was he hiding something? Was he just unsure of himself?
- Should Mark have approached John prior to the July informal review about his concerns?
- What fears could Mark have about asking for feedback from his manager; what could hold him back from asking for feedback, in general?
- What strikes you the most about the brainstormed list of causes of performance concerns generated by John and Mark? What seems most important to you?
- At the conclusion of the July meeting, if you were Mark's manager, John, how would you have left things?
- How do you feel about the meeting with John and Mark to talk about Mark's performance on the cross-functional teams? Was it successful? Would you have approached it any differently? Why?
- How do you feel about the decision to launch a 360-degree feedback survey? Was 360-degree feedback necessary? Timely? Too late? Too soon?
- After reading about the categories and areas on the 360-degree survey, what were you expecting as low-scoring items? Of the eight that are identified, which strike you as most critical to employee engagement? Which strike you as the most critical, period?
- How do you feel about the initial outcome of the meeting between Sarah, the internal coach, and Mark? Was it a good start? Were they on track?
- What do you think of the advice Mark got from his peers? Does it seem valid? Does it address the key issues?

- What do you think of the feedback Mark got from his direct reports? Does it seem valid? Does it address the key issues?
- How do you feel about Mark's action plan? Is it comprehensive? If you were John, Mark's manager, would you be satisfied, or would you suggest additional actions for Mark?
- If you were Mark, how would feel about the outcome of the appraisal meeting? Would you feel motivated? Engaged? Ready to move your team forward?

Case Study

It is early September, and Mark, a manager of field service, has been thinking about his performance. The goals that he and John, his supervisor, set at the beginning of the calendar year still seemed fair and reasonable. At his informal midyear review in early July, he and John had a good discussion. As a matter of fact, Mark felt that John truly cared about his performance and was effective in delivering feedback.

What Was Happening Prior to September?

Mark's performance was *meeting expectations* as measured by the objective standards set for him and his department. Mark's ambition, however, was to exceed those expectations. Mark has a high degree of self-efficacy, and believes he should be a top performer. His career identity is also strong—he hopes to advance in his company with the next step being a promotion to regional manager. Although Mark's reaction to the July midyear review should have been positive, he was not totally satisfied. He wanted to further improve his performance. At the time, he gave the impression to John, however, that everything was fine. He did not share his feelings of dissatisfaction. Mark and John ended the midyear review on a positive note and planned to have another informal review in late October.

A couple of days after his midyear review, Mark shared his feelings with a colleague, who wisely suggested that Mark talk to John again to explore more specifically what he could do to further develop and improve his overall performance. Mark took the advice and was able to arrange another meeting with John the next week. This was not easy for Mark to do, as he was not very comfortable asking for feedback about himself. Mark was ambitious, but he was not always strong on monitoring his own performance.

Mark thought a good place to begin was to explore his department's overall service goal. In the past, he was always able to ensure his team provided timely service that resulted in high levels of customer satisfaction. He was not sure why, but his team's performance was not as strong as usual, and the department's service satisfaction levels were just "average."

After another careful review of Mark's progress on all of his goals, John agreed that service would be a good area of focus given that Mark's service satisfaction goal would count for 40% of his overall performance results evaluation. Mark and John had to determine what was wrong and what Mark could do to get his team back on track to deliver higher levels of performance.

Mark and John initially brainstormed a list of possible causes:

- Has there been a major change in the service process or procedures?
- Are Mark's newer employees performing as well as they should?
- Has everyone received adequate training?
- Has Mark set clear goals and expectations for his team?
- Is Mark providing regular feedback to his employees?
- Is his team beginning to show signs of burnout, given customer demands?
- Is Mark communicating enough, in general, about the importance of service satisfaction and its contribution to the bottom line?

As they started to explore these questions, they realized that Mark had been devoting a significant amount of his time to two critical, cross-functional teams, one focusing on the development, sales, and service of a new product, and the other on cross-functional teamwork and process improvement. Both Mark and John felt that these special project teams might be diverting some of his attention away from the day-to-day management of his direct report team. So, John asked Mark to reflect on his own recent behavior. He further asked Mark to think about whether or not he was spending as much time with his team members as they needed. Was he visible enough? Was he monitoring his team's performance? Was he providing feedback?

Mark's basic answer to these questions was "No—I need to be spending more time with them." John then asked if there were really any obstacles in his way to spending more time with his team. Mark said that he just really had to refocus his efforts in the right direction. When John asked Mark if he needed any help to get back on track, Mark told John that because he had a pretty good grip on the problem now, he knew how to handle it and what to do. John knew that Mark was an experienced manager, so he agreed with Mark's approach, but also reminded Mark that he was there if needed.

What's Going On With Mark Now?

Why is Mark thinking about his performance in early September? Since his July meetings with John, Mark has been spending time in the field with his team. His service satisfaction results, however, have not really improved. Mark knows it. John knows it. Mark is thinking of meeting with John. And the informal October review is fast approaching.

Coincidentally, John has just received informal feedback about Mark's performance on the new product team. Although Mark's technical contributions to the team are strong, the team leader told John that Mark has been creating some tension among the team members. The team leader told John that Mark has very strong opinions about how things should get done, and as a result, it appears that Mark does not really value—or seriously consider—the contributions of his peers. In fact, Mark is slowing the team's progress. He seems to be stuck in the role of being a critic and is not helping the team move to generative and transformational levels of learning.

John decided that he should meet with Mark, in essence moving up the informal performance review planned for late October. If what the team leader said was true, then Mark's behavior and performance on the team had to change. John was going to keep an open mind about Mark's behavior on the team until he had a chance to hear from Mark. On the other hand, he couldn't help but think that if what the team leader said was true, this kind of behavior might be causing the problem Mark is having with his own team.

When they met, it was clear that Mark had still been giving his employees' performance more thought, although he was still at a loss for a cause. After they got comfortable, John said, "I want to talk to you about the new product team and how you think it is going. I got some feedback from the team leader the other day, and she said the team is not moving as fast as it could. What's your assessment?"

Mark replied, "In general, it's going OK, but most of the time those people don't know what they are talking about. The team would be better off with fewer people who really knew their stuff and got to it."

John continued the discussion with Mark, and Mark had more to say about his frustration with the team members. For instance, he thought that he was one of only two strong contributors on the team and that the others were not focused on completing the work and didn't realize that the project was taking too much time.

John then said, "Mark, the feedback I got from the team leader, in effect, says that your frustration is showing. You seem to act in a way that implies that only you have the right approach and that your team members can't add any value. Does this make any sense to you?"

Mark replied, "Well, I didn't think she would talk to you, although I told her she could after she and I had a similar conversation. As I said to her, I don't think I'm doing anything other than trying to move the team along—and maybe sometimes my impatience may show."

John offered, "Mark, you may have good intentions, and I know you can make a significant contribution to the team, but in this instance, a number of other people are seeing you quite differently."

Mark was quiet for a moment and then told John this seems to be the kind of reaction he is getting lately from most people. John asked Mark to say more and, in particular, to say whether or not his direct reports were reacting to him the same way.

Mark responded, "You know, you're right. When I'm out coaching my people lately, they don't seem to listen. I'm trying to get their performance up so we can exceed our service goal targets, but when I leave them, they can't seem to deliver the performance I expect."

John reflected back the following observation: "Mark, you seem to be getting similar reactions from a number of people in different situations, and you seem to be having some difficultly seeing exactly how your behavior is impacting others."

Mark struggled with the feedback, but trusted John's assessment even if he did not like the fact that he alone might be the root cause of the problem.

John and Mark decided on two major action steps. The first was for Mark to be particularly conscious of and monitor his behavior, and to try to be more patient and considerate of others' points of view—to explore more than tell or direct. John would also need to work more collaboratively than before. For example, rather than just jumping in with his own ideas, discounting what others on the team had to offer, John advised Mark to say something like "Fred, that's a pretty good idea. I'd like to build on that a little," or "Fred, what do you think of adding a fifth step to the four you suggested?" To help Mark with his own employees, John offered to accompany him on some of his coaching field visits to observe him in action and provide some feedback.

With John's support, Mark also agreed to the second major step: Participate in a 360-degree feedback process, and work with a professional, internal coach.

Why 360-Degree Feedback and a Coach?

John and Mark both agreed that a 360-degree feedback survey could help Mark develop a better picture of how others are seeing him—in essence, help him further develop his career insight and, as a result, develop a more accurate view of himself. They also decided that Mark should work with a professional coach. A coach could help coordinate the overall process and provide Mark with an objective perspective, as well as a confidential sounding board.

Because the company provides internal coaches, John contacted Charlie, the head of the human resources department, to tell him that Mark had his support and approval to work with a coach, as well as to use a 360-degree feedback survey. Charlie recommended Sarah as Mark's coach, and suggested to John that rather than use a vendor-driven 360-degree feedback survey, he might want to offer Mark the opportunity to be one of the first managers to use the company's new 360-degree feedback survey. John knew HR was working on the survey for a company-wide program to be launched in the fourth quarter, but had no idea the survey itself was already available. Obviously, he and Mark agreed to use the company's new survey. Mark also agreed to work with Sarah. Why Sarah?

Sarah is currently the company's director of management development, although before earning a master's in organization behavior about 7 years earlier, she had worked for 5 years in sales management. Most recently, she has been spending about one third of her time in the coaching role. Accepting her as his coach was relatively easy. Mark was favorably impressed with Sarah's professionalism when he had sought her advice in the past on an employee relations issue for one of his own employees and had heard "through the grapevine" that she was a "pretty good" coach.

Because Sarah is a company employee, there would be no direct charge to John's or Mark's budget for her time, although John's budget would be charged for any out-of-pocket expenses incurred by Sarah, which were not expected to be high.

Mark's First Meeting With His Coach: September 15

In Mark's first meeting with Sarah, he reviewed the events to date and expressed his desire to get additional feedback and development support. Sarah agreed to work with Mark and to coordinate the 360-survey process. She defined her coaching role, which included coordinating the survey process, helping to interpret and understand the results, assisting in presenting results to his team and colleagues, and helping to develop an action plan.

By the end of the meeting, they had made the key decisions necessary to move forward. These included:

- Determining the survey participants: John, Mark's direct reports, and all the members of the two special project teams
- Drafting Mark's cover memo that would accompany the survey
- Establishing an aggressive timeline, which included the dates for
  - Distributing the surveys (September 18)
  - Returning the surveys (September 27)
  - The meeting for Sarah and Mark to review the results and formulate a tentative action plan (October 1)
  - Three separate meetings to provide results of the survey to John (October 5), Mark's colleagues (October 7), and Mark's direct reports (October 9)
- Finalizing the action plan (October 14)

Mark and Sarah would not meet again until October 1, when Sarah would be ready to present the survey results.

The Survey Process

Given Mark's reasons for requesting the survey and the fact that the survey was relatively new, Mark and Sarah thought it best to get input from each group of participants on all of the survey's 75 items (described below). Although plans were in place to put the survey online before the company-wide implementation, that option was not available to Mark at this time. As a result, the surveys, along with Mark's cover letter, would be distributed to all participants through inter-office mail. The completed surveys would be returned to Sarah for scoring and reporting purposes. Mark would send an e-mail to all participants beforehand telling them to expect the survey and asking for their cooperation.

Mark's 360-Degree Survey Results

Mark was quite interested in seeing how his results turned out. As Sarah walked him through the results, they were not, to quote Mark, "as bad as I thought they would be." In fact, they were quite favorable. Mark tended to score himself slightly higher on most items compared to how the employees who reported directly to him and his peers rated him. On the other hand, John's ratings of Mark were quite similar to Mark's self-ratings.

This new company survey had three major categories, and each category was composed of five major areas. There was a total of 75 items, 25 per category. The following are the categories and major areas:

- Leading With Purpose
  - Acting With Integrity
  - Leading With Vision
  - Fostering Innovation and Change
  - Influencing With Impact
  - Managing With Conviction
- Leading for Performance
  - Fostering Engagement and Satisfaction
  - Executing
  - Achieving Results
  - Developing Self
  - Developing Talent
- Leading With People
  - Leveraging the Organization
  - Building Relationships
  - Facilitating Communication
  - Working in Teams
  - Leading With Maturity

As Sarah and Mark reviewed the results, it became clear that Mark's greatest strengths, rated 4's or 5's on a 1–5 scale, were in Leveraging the Organization (e.g., works through formal and informal channels to make things happen), Executing (e.g., produces specific and actionable project plans and measures), and Managing with Conviction (e.g., lets people know where they stand through direct and actionable feedback).

In terms of low-scoring areas, Mark got 3's and 2's from most raters (even though he rated himself higher) on the following behaviors, which spanned a number of categories and areas:

1. Brings out the creative ideas of others
2. Knows own personal strengths and weaknesses
3. Seeks feedback; is nondefensive and open to criticism
4. Gives employees the latitude and authority to exercise their own initiative
5. Gives praise and recognition for the contributions of others
6. Actively promotes teamwork and cross-functional cooperation
7. Effectively manages own emotions
8. Understands the effect of own actions on others

Interpreting Mark's Results

Although Mark's results were largely positive, the areas in which he was rated low shed light on his behavior both with his colleagues and with his direct reports. In particular, as Mark and Sarah discussed the results in the context of Mark's recent performance, it seemed that Mark had difficulty recognizing others' contributions. He was not as cooperative and supportive as he could be, didn't manage his feelings well (for example, sometimes showing his frustration with his colleagues), and did not recognize the impact he was having on others. Mark was not fostering his employees' creativity to help solve problems, not giving them enough empowerment to meet their customers' needs, and not being supportive of their efforts by recognizing them for their strong performance, all of which was impacting employee engagement in his organization.

Strategies for Helping Mark

Sarah and Mark talked about potential action steps. One obvious step was to share the results with John. As they talked further, Mark realized that he has very high standards (also rated as one of his strengths—"maintains high standards of performance for self and others"), and that striving to meet those standards may have caused him to overlook and under recognize the value of others' contributions and performance. This behavior can be further explained by Mark's high degree of conscientiousness and his impatience with others, which drives him to take action and do the right thing, at least as he perceives it. It was clear, to Mark, however, that working with Sarah over a few more sessions will help him to develop a better understanding and more control over this particular dynamic.

Sarah and Mark decided that their next step was to prepare Mark for his feedback meetings with his direct reports, his peers, and his supervisor, John, so that he can share his results and ask for suggestions to improve his performance.

Meeting With John

Although Mark felt comfortable meeting with John alone, he asked Sarah to join him just in case John had some unusual questions or concerns.

John was supportive of Mark, and asked whether or not the results gave Mark a better understanding of himself, what was happening, and what actions he might take. Mark answered yes and described some of his own insights. Mark and Sarah then shared their next steps, and John approved.

John also noted the similarity between how he rated Mark and Mark's self-ratings. They discussed the fact that Mark was not demonstrating the same behaviors with John as he was elsewhere, which was probably why John did not have any of his own observations to rely on when he and Mark met to strategize in July.

Meeting With Peers

Fifteen peers rated Mark. Inviting them all to one meeting to share how they rated him would be intimidating. Meeting with each one would be too time-consuming and probably redundant. So Mark and Sarah selected four peers, two from each cross-functional team, and invited them to one meeting. They selected people they thought would be constructive, honest, and friendly, but not necessarily positive. Mark told them that he would appreciate their spending some time reviewing and discussing his feedback results. He noted that this type of session might be something they would consider doing themselves when they received their feedback reports. Because he had Sarah's help and support, both Sarah and Mark thought the session would be just fine.

The process they would follow included these steps:

1. Mark's opening remarks, including introducing Sarah and thanking everyone for their participation
2. Mark's presentation of his results, focusing first on his strengths (higher-rated items), then on his areas for development (lower-rated items)
3. Mark's interpretation of these results in the context of how he sees his behavior on the teams

4. Getting feedback from his teammates on how they see his behavior
5. Asking for recommendations for how to improve or change his behavior
6. Establishing a date by which Mark will communicate his overall action plan
7. Thanking all for their participation

During the discussion of areas for development, three survey items seemed to strike a chord with everyone in the room:

1. "Gives praise and recognition for the contribution of others"
2. "Actively promotes teamwork and cross-functional cooperation"
3. "Effectively manages own emotions"

Their advice to Mark, after some help from Sarah in getting them to be specific, was as follows:

■ Please try to control your emotions and think about what you say before you say it. If you get feedback from one of us in the meeting that indicates you are getting excited, please listen to what we have to say--don't get defensive, and don't get more upset. So if someone says, "Mark, I think you might be getting emotional on this point," please think before you react.
■ You would also get most of us to feel better about working with you if you acknowledge that we are trying to work together, not against you. We know that you bring a lot of talent to the table, more than just in your own area of expertise, but ideas that other people have to offer are also valuable. They can be valuable in their own right, or they may stimulate someone to think of an even better idea, and so on, like brainstorming. So, when someone does offer an idea, we would rather you say something like "That's a good idea" or "Interesting—how do you see that working?" rather than "That's technically impossible" or "That's not an effective way" and then go on to tell us exactly why not.

Mark thought the requests were reasonable—so did Sarah—and Mark told his colleagues that he would do his best to change his behavior in the kind of situations they discussed. He also asked them to be patient with him as his behavior may not be absolutely "perfect" in their next team meetings. He mentioned that he sometimes has difficulty monitoring his performance but that he is committed to making progress in these areas. He told them that if they would continue to be patient and help him see his own behavior, he was sure he could be a more effective team member.

Meeting With Direct Reports

Sarah joined Mark for the meeting, and this time she would play a more active role. Sarah would facilitate getting feedback from Mark's employees on how they see his behavior and asking for recommendations for how to improve or change his behavior. In Sarah's experience, it is sometime easier for employees to offer their feedback when their manager is not directly involved in these steps. It creates a safer environment, and they can speak freely without trying to be "politically" correct. As a result, Mark will actually leave the meeting when Sarah takes his direct reports through these steps. He will then be invited back, and Sarah will present their feedback. Although Sarah will take the lead, any one of his employees will be free to provide comments or suggestions.

Having Sarah handle those steps turned out to be a good idea. Throughout the earlier parts of the meeting, Mark's direct reports had fewer questions and comments than he would have expected. As it turned out, they really like Mark, and they did have some feedback to share, but they did not want to "make him feel bad." This is what they told Sarah after Mark left the room.

Mark's direct reports seemed to be most concerned about the following two items on the survey: "Brings out the creative ideas of others," and "Gives employees the latitude and authority to exercise their own initiative." They said that Mark "used to be like that," but since earlier this year, he seemed to be under more pressure, and he started to take more and more control. They said they didn't quite understand what was going on, but they thought it would "get back to normal" sooner or later.

This is what one employee offered, and all the others concurred:

When Mark came out to the field to work with us, he used to ask us for suggestions and ideas when we faced tough service problems. He would listen to our recommended approach first, and then we would modify it as necessary. But we always had a chance to give our input, and Mark always seemed to help us take our ideas further. Now, he doesn't ask for much input. He usually seems hurried and just tells us what to do. He's been in this business for some time, so his ideas are always top-notch, but it is no fun anymore. We don't feel like our ideas count, and we are not learning as much as we could.

When Sarah asked the group what Mark should do specifically, they thought for a moment, and someone offered a revision of the feedback above:

> He should be like his old self. Ask us for our ideas first. Listen to what we have to say. Help us to understand where we are right and how we can improve. Don't cut us off, or out. We want to be engaged.

As soon as Mark rejoined the meeting, Sarah reviewed his direct reports' feedback and recommendations. Mark took the feedback well. As he was listening to her, he could literally recall doing exactly what they said he did. Mark acknowledged to his team that he understood their feedback, and pointed out a few examples of when he was "controlling." Everyone seemed relieved.

Mark took this opportunity to reinforce with his team that he wanted the department to exceed its service goal, and this is exactly what his employees said they wanted to do. They agreed that if Mark would try to be more supportive, like he used to be, they would put in the extra effort to try to exceed expectations.

Finalizing the Action Plan

Mark and Sarah worked together to finalize Mark's action plan, which laid out activities that would take him to the end of the calendar year. His plan primarily consisted of working with his coach on his behaviors (meeting once every 2 weeks, about five more times before the end of the year), and improving his relationships with his colleagues and direct reports. How would Sarah and Mark work together?

Sarah outlined the approach to Mark. She told Mark that they would identify specific behaviors that he would try with his direct reports and colleagues. For example, Mark would be encouraged to say to an employee he is coaching in the field, "This looks like a challenging problem. How would you approach solving it? What would be your first step?" In this way, Mark would be prepared with a set of behaviors tailored to those situations where he needs to be more effective. Sarah explained to Mark that each session would focus on the challenges and successes he was having with these new behaviors.

Sarah also suggested that Mark try one of the self-paced e-learning courses listed in her department's catalogue of training programs. Because of e-learning's highly interactive nature and Mark's time constraints, she thought that this method would be most appropriate, and Mark agreed. Together they chose a 4-hour program entitled "Managing One's Self in the Workplace."

Mark discussed the plan with John, who gave it his full support. Mark literally launched his plan, on time, on October 14.

End-of-Year Appraisal

Before meeting with Mark on January 6 to discuss his self-appraisal, John contacted some of Mark's colleagues and direct reports to get informal input on Mark's overall behavior and performance. John learned that Mark had improved significantly. This correlated, John thought, to the rise in service satisfaction Mark's department had experienced over the last 2 months. Although his performance on this goal may still be a "Meet expectations," the most recent results were certainly "Exceeding expectations."

The actual meeting with Mark went well. Mark handed John his self-appraisal, and as John read it, he felt that Mark's analysis of his performance and evaluation of his behavior showed he was seeing things more clearly. Writing Mark's appraisal, John thought, will be relatively easy.

When John sat down to write Mark's appraisal, the objective results pointed to an overall "Meets expectations." Although he thought Mark might still be somewhat disappointed, there was a positive message. Mark's most recent behavior and his department's performance were improving significantly.

The Appraisal Meeting

John gave Mark a copy of the appraisal to review on January 10, the day before the appraisal meeting. John started the meeting by asking Mark if he had any major questions or concerns based on what he read, and because Mark had none, John began walking Mark through his rationale for the evaluation.

They spent considerable time talking through the department's service goal results, which John rated a "Meets expectations." John pointed out that in his written summary, he noted that Mark significantly turned around his service results in the last quarter, a major accomplishment. He asked Mark if he thought he could sustain this level of performance going into next year. Mark thought he certainly could.

When the discussion turned to his development efforts this past year, John rated Mark "Exceeds expectations." It was clear that Mark committed a good deal of time and energy to working on his behavior and improving the department's performance, and, fortunately, this effort resulted in positive outcomes in both areas.

Before ending this meeting, they decided to have a preliminary discussion of this year's goals. Because they agreed that Mark's performance goals were not necessarily changing all that much, John asked Mark to think about the measures of success or targets he thought he should set for his performance goals. John also asked Mark to think about his development goals. Mark initially suggested continuing with the plan that was in place—focusing on improving his behavior with his direct reports and his colleagues. John thought that was a good idea, and offered that at some point in the year, if all was going well, they should consider other development areas to pursue and conduct another 360-degree feedback survey.

They planned the follow-up meeting for the morning of January 15. The purpose of that meeting would be to spend the time necessary to finalize Mark's goals, strategies, and measures of success.

John also had something else planned for January 15. He arranged a luncheon for Mark and his subordinates so that he could recognize them for their very strong fourth quarter performance.

Some Final Words

First of all, don't forget to go back and review the questions we posed at the beginning of the chapter now that you have read through the case. This is an opportunity to test your own thinking, learning, and management skill in a safe way. Actually, we suspect that you have done this, and that you have done this well. As a result, we want to recognize your efforts: "Thank you for taking responsibility for your own learning, and ultimately applying your learning to improve and enhance your own development and performance."

Finally, we urge you to "exceed" our parting, overarching expectations:

- Performance management is a business process, and it is an ongoing, continuous process—treat it as such.
- Performance management, effectively applied, well help you to create and sustain high levels of employee engagement, which leads to higher levels of performance.
- The components of performance management work together and create a synergistic outcome, one greater than the sum of it parts—use all the components of performance management to their fullest.
- Trust and empowerment provide a necessary foundation for effective performance management, as well as engagement—remember the drivers of trust and be sure to practice and sincerely demonstrate the managerial trustworthy behaviors.

- Jointly create both performance and development goals with your employees and team: Be sure they are aligned with overall organization and company goals, and make them challenging and meaningful—they set the stage for ongoing performance management and feedback.
- Provide direction, communicating frequently with your employees through feedback about their performance, their development, and the importance of their contributions—help your employees to become experts at monitoring their own performance.
- Development is critical to performance growth and enhancing career success—help your employees to become self-developers and continuous learners, enabling strong performance and fostering engagement.
- Extensively use recognition to reinforce the performance and behavior necessary for success—given what we see in general, most managers don't use recognition enough at all—so use it frequently to drive both performance and engagement.
- At times your employees may need a new perspective, a shift in how they view themselves, their performance, or their career opportunities—empower them through your coaching efforts to help them discover what they need to know, to do, or to change.
- Keep a watchful eye on your employees for any indication of burnout—identify the signs and symptoms of burnout, and take the actions necessary to alleviate or manage it before it negatively impacts performance and engagement.
- Finally, don't forget informal and formal performance appraisals—these are important opportunities to have extended discussions about performance and development. They help you ensure alignment and motivation and explore levels of engagement. The formal year-end appraisal, in particular, also helps set the stage for making fair and equitable compensation decisions, an important driver of engagement.

In closing, we wish you the best of luck and hope we have been able to shed some light on the topic of performance management and how performance management can help you drive high levels of employee engagement, and we also hope that we have provided you "with the resources and tools necessary" to meet our overarching expectations.

References

Berglas, S. (2002). The very real dangers of executive coaching. *Harvard Business Review*, *80*(6), 86–92.

Bersin, J. (2006). *Performance management 2006*. Oakland, CA: A. Bersin.

Brockner, J. (2006). Why it's so hard to be fair. *Harvard Business Review*, *84*(3), 122–129.

Brower, H. H., Schoorman, F. D., & Tan, H. (2000). A model of relational leadership: The integration of trust and leader-member exchange. *Leadership Quarterly*, *11*, 227–250.

Buckingham, M., & Coffman, C. (1999). *First, break all the rules*. New York: Simon & Schuster.

Caldwell, D. F., & O'Reilly, C. A. (1982). Boundary spanning and individual performance: The impact of self-monitoring. *Journal of Applied Psychology*, *67*, 124–127.

Deci, E. L. (1980). *The psychology of self-determination*. Lexington, MA: Lexington.

Deci, E. L., & Flaste, R. (1995). *Why we do what we do*. New York: Penguin.

Deeprose, D. (1994). *How to recognize and reward employees*. New York: AMACOM.

Dirks, K. T. (2006). Three fundamental questions regarding trust in leaders. In R. Bachmann & A. Zaheer (Eds.), *Handbook of trust research* (pp. 15–28). Northampton, MA: Edward Elgar.

Dotlitch, D., & Cairo, P. (1999). *Action coaching: How to leverage individual performance for company success*. San Francisco: Jossey-Bass.

Fedor, D. B., Rensvold, R. B., & Adams, S. M. (1992). An investigation of factors expected to affect feedback seeking: A longitudinal field study. *Personnel Psychology*, *45*, 779–805.

Flaherty, J. (1998). *Coaching: Evoking excellence in others*. Burlington, MA: Butterworth-Heinemann/Elsevier.

Gibbons, J. (2006, November). Employee engagement: A review of current research and its implications. New York, NY: The Conference Board.

Gostick, A., & Elton, C. (2007). *The carrot principle*. New York: Free Press.

Hall, D. T., Otazo, K. L., & Hollenbeck, G. P. (1999). Behind closed doors: What really happens in executive coaching. *Organizational Dynamics*, *27*, 39–52.

Harris, M. (1999). Practice network: Look, it's an I-O psychologist . . . No, it's a trainer . . . No, it's an executive coach! *Industrial-Organizational Psychologist, 36*(3), 38–42.

Hedge, J. W., & Kavanagh, M. J. (1988). Improving the accuracy of performance evaluations: Comparison of three methods of performance appraisal training. *Journal of Applied Psychology, 73*(1), 68–73.

Hollenbeck, G. P. (2002). Coaching executives: Individual leader development. In R. Silzer (Ed.), *The 21st century executive: Innovative practices for building leadership at the top* (pp. 137–167). San Francisco: Jossey-Bass.

Jeffries, R. (1996). *101 recognition secrets: Tools for motivating and recognizing today's workforce.* Chevy Chase, MD: Performance Enhancement Group.

Jones, G. R., & George, J. M. (1998). The experience and evolution of trust: Implications for cooperation and teamwork. *Academy of Management Review, 23*(3), 531–546.

Judge, R. A., Erez, A., Bono, J. E., & Thoresen, C. J. (2002, April). The core self-evaluations scale: Development of a measure. Presented at the annual meeting of the Society for Industrial and Organizational Psychology, Toronto.

Kahn, W. A. (1990). Psychological conditions of personal engagement and disengagement at work. *Academy of Management Journal, 33,* 692–724.

Kaplan, R. S., & Norton, D. P. (1996). *The balanced scorecard: Translating strategy into action.* Boston: Harvard Business School.

Kasl, E., Marsick, V. J., & Dechant, K. (1997). Teams as learners: A research-based model of team learning. *Journal of Applied Behavioral Science, 33,* 227–246.

Kilburg, R. R. (1996). Toward a conceptual understanding and definition of executive coaching. *Consulting Psychology Journal: Practice and Research, 48*(2), 134–144.

Kilburg, R. R. (2000). *Executive coaching: Developing managerial wisdom in a world of chaos.* Washington, DC: American Psychological Association.

Kilburg, R. R. & Diedrich, R. C. (Eds.). (2007). *The wisdom of coaching: Essential papers in consulting psychology for a world of change.* Washington, DC: American Psychological Association.

Kluger, A. N. & DeNisi, A. (1996). Effects of feedback interventions on performance: a historical review, a meta-analysis, and preliminary feedback intervention theory. *Psychological Bulletin, 119,* 254–284.

Laff, M. (2007, September). Performance management gives a shaky performance. *Training and Development,* 18.

Latham, G. P., Almost, J., Mann, S., & Moore, C. (2005). New developments in performance management. *Organizational Dynamics, 34,* 77–87.

Lawler, E. E., & Worley, C. G. (2006). *Built to change: How to achieve sustained organizational effectiveness.* New York: Wiley.

Leiter, M. P. & Maslach, C. (2005). *Banishing burnout: Six strategies for improving your relationship with work.* San Francisco: Jossey-Bass.

Lewis, K. (2003). Measuring transactive memory systems in the field: Scale development and validation. *Journal of Applied Psychology, 88,* 587–604.

London, M. (1983). Toward a theory of career motivation. *Academy of Management Review, 8,* 620–630.

London, M. (1995). *Self and interpersonal insight: How people learn about themselves and others in organizations.* San Francisco: Jossey-Bass.

London, M. (2003). *Job feedback.* Mahwah, NJ: Erlbaum.

London, M., & Diamante, T. (2002). Technology-focused expansive professionals: Developing continuous learning in the high tech sector. *Human Resource Development Review, 1*(4), 500–524.

London, M. and Mone, E. M. (2009). Strategic performance management: Issues and trends. In Storey, J., Wright, P. M., and Ulrich, D. (Eds.), *The Routledge companion to strategic human resource management.* New York: Routledge.

London, M., Mone, E. M., & Scott, J. C. (2004). Performance management and assessment: Methods for improved rater accuracy and employee goal setting. *Human Resource Management, 43*, 319–336.

London, M., Polzer, J. T., & Omoregie, H. (2005). Interpersonal congruence, transactive memory, and feedback processes: An integrative model of group learning. *Human Resource Development Review, 4*, 1–22.

London, M., & Sessa, V. I. (2007). How groups learn, continuously. *Human Resource Management, 46*, 651–669.

Macey, W. H., & Schneider, B. (2008). The meaning of employee engagement. *Industrial and Organizational Psychology: Perspectives on Science and Practice, 1*, 3–30.

Maslach, C., & Leiter, M. P. (1997). *The truth about burnout: How organizations cause personal stress and what to do about it.* San Francisco: Jossey-Bass.

Maslach, C. & Leiter, M. P. (2000). *Preventing burnout and building engagement: Team member's workbook.* San Francisco: Jossey-Bass Inc.

Maslach, C., & Leiter, M. P. (2008). Early predictors of job burnout and engagement. *Journal of Applied Psychology, 93*(3), 498–512.

Mayer, R. C., Davis, J. H., & Schoorman, F. D. (1995). An integrative model of organizational trust. *Academy of Management Review, 20*, 709–734.

Mayer, R. C., Davis, J. H., & Schoorman, F. D. (2007). An integrative model of organizational trust: Past, present and future. *Academy of Management Review, 32*(2), 344–354.

McKnight, D. H., & Chervany, N. L. (2006). An experimental study of trust in collective entities. In R. Bachmann & A. Zaheer (Eds.), *Handbook of trust research* (pp. 29–51). Northampton, MA: Edward Elgar.

Mone, E. M. & London, M. (Eds.). (1998). *HR to the rescue: Case studies of HR solutions to business problems.* Houston: Gulf Publishing.

Moore, D. P. (2000). *Careerpreneurs: Lessons from leading women entrepreneurs on building a career without boundaries.* Palo Alto, CA: Davies-Black.

Morgan, H., Harkins, P., & Goldsmith, M. (2005). *The art and practice of leadership coaching.* Hoboken, NJ: Wiley.

Morrison, E. W., & Robinson, S. L. (1997). When employees feel betrayed: A model of how psychological contract violation develops. *Academy of Management Review, 22*, 226–256.

Mount, M. K., & Scullen, S. E. (2001). Multisource feedback ratings: What do they really measure? In M. London (Ed.), *How people evaluate others in organizations* (pp. 155–176). Mahwah, NJ: Erlbaum.

Murphy, K. R., Cleveland, J. N., & Mohler, C. J. (2001). Reliability, validity, and meaningfulness of multisource ratings. In D. W. Bracken, C. W. Timmreck, & A. H. Church (Eds.), *The handbook of multisource feedback: The comprehensive resource for designing and implementing MSF processes* (pp. 130–148). San Francisco: Jossey-Bass.

Olivero, G., Bane, K. D., & Kopelman, R. E. (1997). Executive coaching as a transfer of training tool: Effects on productivity in a public agency. *Public Personnel Management, 26,* 461–469.

Pastoriza, D., Ariño, M., & Ricart, J. (2008). Ethical managerial behavior as an antecedent of organizational social capital. *Journal of Business Ethics, 78*(3), 329–341.

Poon, J. M. L. (2006). Trust-in-supervisor and helping coworkers: Moderating effect of perceived politics. *Journal of Managerial Psychology, 21*(6), 518–532.

Rynes, S. L., Brown, K. G., & Colbert, A. E. (2002). Seven common misconceptions about human resource practices: Research findings versus practitioner beliefs. *Academy of Management Executive, 16,* 92–103.

Salamon, S. D., & Robinson, S. L. (2008). Trust that builds: The impact of collective felt trust on organizational performance. *Journal of Applied Psychology, 93,* 593–601.

Seijts, G. H., & Latham, G. P. (2005). Learning versus performance goals: When should each be used? *Academy of Management Executive, 19,* 124–131.

Seijts, G. H., Latham, G. P., Tasa, K., & Latham, B. W. (2004). Goal setting and goal orientation: An integration of two different yet related literatures. *Academy of Management Journal, 47,* 227–239.

Sessa, V. I., & London, M. (2006). *Continuous learning in organizations.* Mahwah, NJ: Erlbaum.

Smith, M., Jaffe-Gill, E., Segal, J., & Segal, R. (2008). Preventing burnout: Signs, symptoms, causes, and coping strategies. Retrieved June 1, 2008 from http://www.helpguide.org/mental/burnout_signs_symptoms.htm

Smither, J. W., London, M., Flautt, R., Vargas, Y., & Kucine, I. (2002). Can executive coaches enhance the impact of multisource feedback on behavior change? A quasi-experimental field study. *Personnel Psychology, 56,* 23–44.

Smither, J. W., London, M., & Reilly, R. R. (2005). Does performance improve following multisource feedback? A theoretical model, meta-analysis, and review of empirical findings. *Personnel Psychology, 58*(1), 33–66.

Snyder, M. (1974). Self-monitoring of expressive behavior. *Journal of Personality and Social Psychology, 30,* 526–537.

Vroom, V. (1964). *Work and motivation.* New York: Wiley.

Walker, A. G., & Smither, J. W. (1999). A five-year study of upward feedback: What managers do with their results matters. *Personnel Psychology, 52,* 393–423.

Weber, J. M., Kopelman, S., & Messick, D. M. (2004). A conceptual review of decision making in social dilemmas: Applying a logic of appropriateness. *Personality and Social Psychology Review, 8,* 281–307.

Weinberger, J. (1995). Common factors aren't so common: The common factors dilemma. *Clinical Psychology: Science and Practice, 2*(1), 45–69.

Welch, J., & Welch, S. (2005). *Winning.* New York: HarperCollins.

Werner, J. M., & DeSimone, R. L. (2006). *Human resource management.* Mason, OH: Thompson South-Western.

Author Index

Subject Index